Authors & Artists for Young Adults

ISSN 1040-5682

Authors & Artists for Young Adults

VOLUME 38

GALE GROUP

Detroit
New York
San Francisco
London
Boston
Woodbridge, CT

Scot Peacock, *Managing Editor, Literature Product*
Mark Scott, *Publisher, Literature Product*

Alan Hedblad, *Managing Editor*
Susan Trosky, *Literature Content Coordinator*

Kristen Dorsch, Lisa Kumar, Thomas McMahon, Colleen M. Tavor, *Editors;*
Shayla Hawkins, Arlene M. Johnson, Thomas Wiloch, *Associate Editors;*
Alana Foster, Jennifer Kilian, *Assistant Editor;*
Joshua Kondek, *Technical Training Specialist*

Victoria B. Cariappa, *Research Manager*
Tracie A. Richardson, *Project Coordinator*
Andrew Guy Malonis, Gary J. Oudersluys, Cheryl L. Warnock, *Research Specialists*
Tamara C. Nott, *Research Associate,*
Tim Lehnerer, *Research Assistant*
Maria Franklin, *Permissions Manager*
Edna Hedblad, *Permissions Specialist*
Shalice Shah, *Permissions Associate*

Mary Beth Trimper, *Manager, Composition and Prepress*
Carolyn A. Roney, *Composition Specialist*

Dorothy Maki, *Manager, Manufacturing*
Stacy L. Melson, *Buyer*

Randy Bassett, *Image Database Supervisor*
Michael Logusz, *Graphic Artist*
Robert Duncan, *Imaging Specialist*
Pamela A. Reed, *Imaging Coordinator*
Dean Dauphinais, Robyn V. Young, *Senior Image Editors*
Kelly A. Quin, *Image Editor*

Library of Congress Catalog Card Number 89-641100
ISBN 0-7876-4671-7
ISSN 1040-5682

10 9 8 7 6 5 4 3 2 1

Printed in the United States of America

Contents

Introduction

Authors and Artists for Young Adults is a reference series designed to serve the needs of middle school, junior high, and high school students interested in creative artists. Originally inspired by the need to bridge the gap between Gale's *Something about the Author,* created for children, and *Contemporary Authors,* intended for older students and adults, *Authors and Artists for Young Adults* has been expanded to cover not only an international scope of authors, but also a wide variety of other artists.

Although the emphasis of the series remains on the writer for young adults, we recognize that these readers have diverse interests covering a wide range of reading levels. The series therefore contains not only those creative artists who are of high interest to young adults, including cartoonists, photographers, music composers, bestselling authors of adult novels, media directors, producers, and performers, but also literary and artistic figures studied in academic curricula, such as influential novelists, playwrights, poets, and painters. The goal of *Authors and Artists for Young Adults* is to present this great diversity of creative artists in a format that is entertaining, informative, and understandable to the young adult reader.

Entry Format

Each volume of *Authors and Artists for Young Adults* will furnish in-depth coverage of twenty to twenty-five authors and artists. The typical entry consists of:

—A detailed biographical section that includes date of birth, marriage, children, education, and addresses.

—A comprehensive bibliography or filmography including publishers, producers, and years.

—Adaptations into other media forms.

—Works in progress.

—A distinctive essay featuring comments on an artist's life, career, artistic intentions, world views, and controversies.

—References for further reading.

—Extensive illustrations, photographs, movie stills, cartoons, book covers, and other relevant visual material.

A cumulative index to featured authors and artists appears in each volume.

Compilation Methods

The editors of *Authors and Artists for Young Adults* make every effort to secure information directly from the authors and artists through personal correspondence and interviews. Sketches on living authors and artists are sent to the biographee for review prior to publication. Any sketches not personally reviewed by biographees or their representatives are marked with an asterisk (*).

Highlights of Forthcoming Volumes

Among the authors and artists planned for future volumes are:

Berenice Abbott	Donald R. Gallo	Mark Mathabane
Laurie Halse Anderson	Jack Gantos	Peter Matthiessen
Amelia Atwater-Rhodes	James Cross Giblin	Ed McBain
Gary L. Blackwood	Nadine Gordimer	Gloria Naylor
Lewis Carroll	Edward Gorey	I. M. Pei
Francis Ford Coppola	Duane Hanson	Marsha Qualey
Chris Crutcher	Will Hobbs	Rick Reilly
Leonardo da Vinci	Nalo Hopkinson	Charles M. Schulz
Sarah Dessen	Jerry Jenkins	William Sleator
Fedor Dostoevsky	Tim LaHaye	Orson Welles
W. E. B. Du Bois	C. S. Lewis	June Rae Wood
Shelby Foote	Jan Marino	Lois-Ann Yamanaka

Contact the Editor

We encourage our readers to examine the entire *AAYA* series. Please write and tell us if we can make *AAYA* even more helpful to you. Give your comments and suggestions to the editor:

BY MAIL: The Editor, *Authors and Artists for Young Adults,* 27500 Drake Rd., Farmington Hills, MI 48331-3535.

BY TELEPHONE: (800) 347-GALE

Acknowledgments

Grateful acknowledgment is made to the following publishers, authors, and artists for their kind permission to reproduce copyrighted material.

DAVID ALMOND. Vojnar, Kamil, illustrator. From a dust jacket from *Skellig*, by David Almond. Delacorte Press, 1999. Jacket illustration copyright 1999 by Kamil Vojnar. Reproduced by permission of Dell Books, a division of Random House, Inc. / Vojnar, Kamil, illustrator. From a jacket of *Kit's Wilderness*, by David Almond. Delacorte Press, 2000. Jacket illustration 2000 by Kamil Vojnar. Reproduced by permission of Delacorte Press, an imprint of Random House Children's Books, a division of Random House, Inc.

MIRIAM BAT-AMI. Andreasen, Dan, illustrator. From a cover of *Dear Elija*, by Miriam Bat-Ami. Jewish Publication Society, 1997. Originally published by Farrar Straus Giroux. Cover illustration 1995 by Dan Andreasen. Reproduced by permission of Farrar, Straus and Giroux, LLC. / Mosberg, Hilary, illustrator. From a jacket of *Two Suns in the Sky*, by Miriam Bat-Ami. Front Street / Cricket Books, 1999. Jacket 1999 by Hilary Mosberg. / Bat-Ami, Miriam, photograph. Reproduced by permission.

SOOK NYUL CHOI. From a cover of *Gathering of Pearls*, by Sook Nyul Choi. Houghton Mifflin Company, 1994. Copyright 1994 by Sook Nyul Choi. Reproduced by permission. / Patrick, Pamela, illustrator. From a cover of *Year of Impossible Goodbyes*, by Sook Nyul Choi. Yearling Books, 1991. Reproduced by permission of Random House Children's Books, a division of Random House, Inc. / Patrick, Pamela, illustrator. From a cover of *Echoes of the White Giraffe*, by Sook Nyul Choi. Yearling Books, 1993. Reproduced by permission of Random House Children's Books, a division of Random House, Inc. / Choi, Sook Nyul, photograph. Reproduced by permission.

DAVID DRAKE. Keegan, Charles, illustrator. From a cover of *The Dragon Lord*, by David Drake. Baen Publishing Enterprises, 1979. Reproduced by permission of the publisher. / Berkey, John, illustrator. From a cover of *Cross the Stars*, by David Drake. Baen Publishing Enterprises, 1984. Reproduced by permission of the publisher. / Elmore, Larry, illustrator. From a cover of *The Sharp End*, by David Drake. Baen Publishing Enterprises, 1993. Reproduced by permission of the publisher. / Elmore, Larry, illustrator. From a cover of *Caught in the Crossfire*, by David Drake. Baen Publishing Enterprises, 1998. Reproduced by permission of the publisher. / Keegan, Charles, illustrator. From a cover of *The Butcher's Bill*, by David Drake. Baen Publishing Enterprises, 1998. Reproduced by permission of the publisher. / Donato, illustrator. From a cover of *Servant of the Dragon*, by David Drake. Tor Books, 1999. Reproduced by permission of St. Martin's Press. / Drake, David, photograph. Copyright 1987 by John Caker. Used by permission.

JEAN FERRIS. Mosberg, Hilary, illustrator. From a cover of *Invincible Summer*, by Jean Ferris. Farrar, Straus & Giroux, Inc., 1987. Cover art 1994 by Hilary Mosberg. Reproduced by permission of Farrar, Straus & Giroux, LLC. / Hays, Michael, illustrator. From a jacket of *All That Glitters*, by Jean Ferris. Farrar, Straus & Giroux, Inc., 1996. Jacket art 1996 by Michael Hays. Reproduced by permission of Farrar, Straus & Giroux, LLC. / Lee, Paul, illustrator. From a jacket of *Bad*, by Paul Lee. Farrar, 1998. Jacket art 1998 by Paul Lee. Reproduced by permission of Farrar, Straus and Giroux, LLC. / Guerguerian, Claudine, photographer. From a jacket of *Love among the Walnuts*, by Jean Ferris. Harcourt, 1998. Reproduced by permission of Harcourt, Inc. / Ferris, Jean, photograph. Reproduced by permission.

VICKI GROVE. Grove, Vicki, photograph. Mike Grove. Used by permission of Vicki Grove.

JOE HALDEMAN. Montealegre, Toni Luna, illustrator. From a cover of *Saul's Death & Other Poems*, by Joe Haldeman. Anamnesis Press, 1997. Cover illustration copyright 1997 by Toni Luna Montealegre. Reproduced by permission of the publisher. / Haldeman, Joe, in Vietnam, 1968, photograph. Reproduced by permission. / Haldeman, Joe, photograph by Gay Haldeman. Reproduced by permission.

KIMBERLY WILLIS HOLT. Archambault, Matt, illustrator. From a cover of *My Louisiana Sky*, by Kimberly Willis Holt. Yearling Books, 1998. Reproduced by permission of Dell Publishing, a division of Random House, Inc. / Holt, Kimberly Willis, photograph by Diane Bondareff. AP/Wide World Photos. Reproduced by permission.

TANYA HUFF. Morrissey, Dean, illustrator. From a cover of *Gate of Darkness, Circle of Light*, by Tanya Huff. DAW Books, Inc., 1989. Reproduced by permission of the publisher. / Lee, Jody, illustrator. From a cover of *Sing the Four Quarters*, by Tanya Huff. DAW Books, Inc., 1994. Reproduced by permission of the publisher. / Palencar, John Jude, illustrator. From a cover of *Blood Debt*, by Tanya Huff. DAW Books, Inc., 1997. Reproduced by permission of the publisher. / Hess, Mark, illustrator. From a cover of *Summon the Keeper*, by Tanya Huff. DAW Books, Inc., 1998. Reproduced by permission of the publisher. / Royo, Luis, illustrator. From a cover of *Valor's Choice*, by Tanya Huff. DAW Books, Inc., 2000. Reproduced by permission of the publisher.

IRIS JOHANSEN. Schneider, Wendi, illustrator. From a cover of *Last Bridge Home*, by Iris Johansen. Bantam Books, 1987. Cover art copyright 1992 by Wendi Schneider. Reproduced by permission by Bantam Books, a division of Random House, Inc. / Hallman, Tom, illustrators. From a cover of *The Ugly Duckling*, by Iris Johansen. Bantam Books, 1996. Cover art copyright 1996 by Tom Hallman. Reproduced by permission from Bantam Books, a division of Random House, Inc. / Ayers, Alan, illustrator. From a cover of *Long After Midnight*, by Iris Johansen. Bantam Books, 1997. Cover art copyright 1997 by Alan Ayers. Reproduced by permission from Bantam Books, a division of Random House, Inc. / Ayers, Alan, illustrator. From a cover of *And Then You Die*, by Iris Johansen. Bantam Books, 1998. Cover art copyright by Alan Ayers. Reproduced by permission from Bantam Books, a division of Random House, Inc. / Ayers, Alan, illustrator. From a cover of *The Face of Deception*, by Iris Johansen. Bantam Books, 1998. Cover art copyright 1999 by Alan Ayers. Reproduced by permission from Bantam Books, a division of Random House, Inc.

WILLIAM JOYCE. From *Humphrey's Bear*, by Jan Wahl, illustrated by William Joyce. Illustrations copyright, 1987 by William Joyce. Reprinted by permission of Henry Holt and Company, LLC. / Joyce, William, photograph by Philip Gould. Reproduced by permission. / Joyce, William, photograph by Philip Gould. Philip Gould/Corbis. Reproduced by permission.

JOAN LINGARD. Lingard, Joan, photograph by Gunnie Moberg. Reproduced by permission of Joan Lingard.

ANDREW LLOYD WEBBER. Crawford, Michael, in the title role of *The Phantom of the Opera*, photograph. AP Wide World Photos. Reproduced by permission. / Elliman, Yvonne, as Mary Magdalene in *Jesus Christ Superstar* by Andrew Lloyd Webber and Tim Rice, July 13, 1971, photograph. AP/Wide World Photos. Reproduced by permission. / Madonna, in the film *Evita*, 1996, photograph. The Kobal Collection. Reproduced by permission. / Cast members of *Cats*, written by Andrew Lloyd Webber, Winter Garden Theater in New York, June 19, 1997, photograph. Reuters/Mike Segar/Archive Photos, Inc. Reproduced by permission. / Webber, Andrew Lloyd, 1990, photograph. AP/Wide World Photos. Reproduced by permission.

JANET LUNN. Deines, Brian, illustrator. From a cover of *Charlotte*, by Janet Lunn. 1998 by Janet Lunn--text and 1998 by Brian Deines--illustration, published by Tundra Books. Reproduced by permission of Tundra Books. / Lunn, Janet, photograph by Anthea Weese. Reproduced by permission of Janet Lunn.

LURLENE MCDANIEL. McDaniel, Lurlene, photograph. Reproduced by permission.

PATRICIA C. MCKISSACK. Pinkney, Brian, illustrator. From a cover of *The Dark-Thirty: Southern Tales of the Supernatural*, by Patricia C. McKissack. Knopf Paperbacks, 1992. Reproduced by permission of Alfred A. Knopf, Inc. / Ransome, James E., illustrator. From a cover of *Let My People Go* by Patricia and Fredrick McKissack. Jacket illustration 1998 James E. Ransome. Reprinted with the permission of Atheneum Books for Young Readers, an imprint of Simon & Schuster Children's Publishing Division. / McKissack, Patricia C., photograph. Reproduced by permission.

MIKE RESNICK. Giancola, Donato, illustrator. From a cover of *Widowmaker*, by Michael Diamond Resnick. Bantam Spectra Books, 1996. Reproduced by permission of Bantam Books, a division of Random House, Inc. / Harris, John, illustrator. From a cover of *Kirinyaga*, by Mike Resnick. Del Rey Books, 1998. / Ranson,

Peggy, illustrator. From a cover of *Birthright: The Book of Man*, by Mike Resnick. Farthest Star, 1982. Cover Art: Copyright 1997 Peggy Ranson. Reproduced by permission of Creativity, Inc. / Whelan, Michael, illustrator. From a cover of *Santiago: A Myth of the Far Future*, by Mike Resnick. Tor Books, 1986. Reproduced by permission of St. Martin's Press, Inc. / Cover of *A Hunger in the Soul*, by Mike Resnick. Tor Books, 1998. Reproduced by permission of St. Martin's Press, Inc. / Resnick, Mike, photograph. Reproduced by permission.

DIEGO RIVERA. Rivera, Diego, photograph by Kipp Ross. AP/Wide World Photos. Reproduced by permission. / Rivera, Diego, photograph. AP/Wide World Photos. Reproduced by permission. / Rivera, Diego, photograph. Archive Photos, Inc. Reproduced by permission. / Rivera, Diego, Kahlo, Frida, photograph. Archive Photos, Inc. Reproduced by permission.

MARTIN SCORSESE. Jodie Foster and Robert De Niro in film *Taxi Driver,* photograph. Columbia Pictures/Archive Photos, Inc. Reproduced by permission. / De Niro, Robert, in the film *Raging Bull*, 1980, photograph. The Kobal Collection. Reproduced by permission. / The cast of *Goodfellas* (l-r) Ray Liotta as Henry Hill, Robert De Niro as Jimmy Conway, Paul Sorvino as Paul Cicero and Joe Pesci as Tommy DeVito, 1990, photograph. Archive Photos, Inc. Reproduced by permission. / Pfeiffer, Michelle, and Daniel Day-Lewis, in the film *The Age of Innocence,* 1993, photograph by Phillip Caruso. The Kobal Collection. Reproduced by permission. / Scorsese, Martin, directing the film *Kundun,* photograph. The Kobal Collection. Reproduced by permission.

CHARLES SHEFFIELD. Blair, Drew, illustrator. From a cover of *Transvergence*, by Charles Sheffield. Baen Publishing Enterprises, 1992. Reproduced by permission of the publisher. / Ruddell, Gary, illustrator. From a cover of *Proteus in the Underworld*, by Charles Sheffield. Baen Publishing Enterprises, 1995. Reproduced by permission of the publisher. / Mills, Cliff, illustrator. From a cover of *Starfire*, by Charles Sheffield. Bantam Spectra Books, 1999. Cover art copyright 1999 by Cliff Mills. Reproduced by permission from Bantam Books, a division of Random House, Inc. / di Fate, Vincent, illustrator. From a jacket of *Putting Up Roots*, by Charles Sheffield. Tor Books, 1997. Jacket illustration copyright 1997 by Vincent di Fate. Reproduced by permission of St. Martin's Press. / di Fate, Vincent, artist. From a cover of *Higher Education*, by Charles Sheffield and Jerry Pournelle. Tor, A Tom Doherty Associates Book, 1996. Copyright 1996 by Kirkwood Research, Inc., and Jerry Pournelle. Reproduced by permission of St. Martin's Press, Inc. / From a cover of *The Billion Dollar Boy: A Jupiter Novel*, by Charles Sheffield. Tor, A Tom Doherty Associates Book, 1997. Copyright 1997 by Charles Sheffield. Reproduced by permission. / Sheffield, Charles, photograph. Reproduced by permission.

GLORIA SKURZYNSKI. Crehore, Amy, illustrator. From a jacket of *Spider's Voice*, by Gloria Skurzynski. Atheneum Books for Young Readers, 1999. Jacket illustration copyright 1999 by Amy Crehore. Reproduced by permission of Atheneum Books for Young Readers, an imprint of Simon & Schuster Macmillan. / Harlin, Greg, illustrator. From a jacket of *Wolf Stalker*, by Gloria Skurzynski and Alane Ferguson. National Geographic Society, 1997. Jacket illustration copyright 1997 Greg Harlin. Reproduced by permission of the publisher. / Skurzynski, Gloria, photograph. Reproduced by permission.

JEFF SMITH. Smith, Jeff, illustrator. From *Bone, Volume One: Out From Boneville*, by Jeff Smith. Cartoon Books, 1995. Reproduced by permission. / Smith, Jeff, illustrator. From a jacket of *Bone, Volume Two: The Great Cow Race*, by Jeff Smith. Cartoon Books, 1996. Reproduced by permission. / Smith, Jeff, illustrator. From a jacket of *Bone, Volume Three: Eyes of the Storm*, by Jeff Smith. Cartoon Books, 1996. Reproduced by permission. / Smith, Jeff, illustrator. From *Bone, Volume Four: The Dragonslayer*, by Jeff Smith. Cartoon Books, 1997. Reproduced by permission. / Smith, Jeff, photograph. Reproduced by permission.

NEAL STEPHENSON. Jensen, Bruce, illustrator. From a cover of *Snow Crash*, by Neal Stephenson. Bantam Spectra Books, 1992. Cover art copyright 2000 by Bruce Jensen. Reproduced by permission of Bantam Books, a division of Random House, Inc. / Jensen, Bruce, illustrator. From a cover of *The Diamond Age, or, a Young Lady's Illustrated Primer*, by Neal Stephenson. Bantam Spectra Books, 1995. Cover art copyright 2000 by Bruce Jensen. Reproduced by permission of Bantam Books, a division of Random House, Inc. / Jensen, Bruce, illustrator. From a cover of *Zodiac*, by Neal Stephenson. Bantam Books, 1995. Cover art copyright 1995 by Bruce Jensen. Reproduced by permission of Bantam Books, a division of Random House, Inc.

RICHARD WORMSER. From a jacket of *Hoboes: Wandering in America, 1870-1940*, by Richard Wormser. Walker and Company, 1994. Jacket photograph courtesy of The Library of Congress. Reproduced by

Mitch Albom

■ Personal

Born May 23, 1958, in Passaic, NJ; son of Ira and Rhoda Albom. *Education:* Brandeis University, B.A., 1979; Columbia University, M.J., 1981, M.B.A., 1982.

■ Addresses

Home—Franklin, MI. *Office*—*Detroit Free Press*, 321 West Lafayette, Detroit, MI 48231.

■ Career

Queens Tribune, Flushing, NY, editor, 1981–82; contributing writer for *Sport, Philadelphia Inquirer,* and *Geo*, 1982–83; *Fort Lauderdale News and Sun Sentinel*, Fort Lauderdale, FL, sports columnist, 1983–85; *Detroit Free Press*, Detroit, MI, sports columnist, 1985—; WLLZ–radio, Farmington Hills, MI, sports director, 1985–96, cohost of sports talk show, "The Sunday Sports Albom" (renamed "The Monday Sports Albom"), 1988—; WDIV–TV, Detroit, broadcaster and commentator, 1987–96; host of radio show, "The Mitch Albom Show," WJR–radio, Detroit, 1996—. Appears on ESPN–TV's "The Sports Reporters" and "Prime Monday" shows. Piano player; composer of a song for the television movie *Christmas in Connecticut*, 1992.

■ Member

Baseball Writers of America, Football Writers of America, Tennis Writers of America.

■ Awards, Honors

Award for best sports news story in the United States, 1985; named number one sports columnist in Michigan, Associated Press (AP) and United Press International (UPI), 1985, 1986, 1987, and 1988; named number one sports columnist in the United States by AP Sports Editors, 1987, 1988, 1989, 1990, 1991, 1992, and 1993; named number one sports columnist in Michigan, National Association of Sportswriters and Broadcasters, 1988 and 1989, and national sportswriter of the year, 1998; number two outstanding writer, National Headliners Award, 1989; award for best feature writing, AP Sports Editors, 1993, for article on University of Michigan basketball player Juwan Howard.

■ Writings

The Live Albom: The Best of Mitch Albom, Detroit Free Press, 1988.
(With Bo Schembechler) *Bo*, Warner Books, 1989.
Live Albom II, foreword by Ernie Harwell, Detroit Free Press, 1990.

Live Albom III: Gone to the Dogs, Detroit Free Press, 1992.

Fab Five: Basketball, Trash Talk, the American Dream, Warner Books, 1993.

Live Albom IV, Detroit Free Press, 1996.

Tuesdays with Morrie: An Old Man, a Young Man and Life's Greatest Lesson, Doubleday (New York City), 1997.

Also author of foreword to *Making Loss Matter: Creating Meaning in Difficult Times,* by David J. Wolpe, Riverhead, 1999. Contributor to newspapers and periodicals, including the *New York Times, Gentlemen's Quarterly, Sports Illustrated,* and *Sport.*

■ Adaptations

Tuesdays with Morrie was made into a 1999 television movie starring Hank Azaria and Jack Lemmon.

■ Sidelights

Mitch Albom, a Michigan journalist, has earned national attention and awards for his sports columns distinguished by insight, humor, and empathy. Disdaining the questionable ethical conduct, drug problems, and over–inflated egos often found in the sports world, Albom highlights instances of athletic courage and determination while providing honest commentary on a team's performance. Collections of his columns have appeared every few years since 1988 and include *The Live Albom: The Best of Mitch Albom* and *Live Albom IV.* He has also co–authored a biography of legendary University of Michigan football coach Bo Schembechler, and written about another sport at the school in *Fab Five: Basketball, Trash Talk, the American Dream,* published in 1993. But Albom scored a surprise hit in 1997 that had little to do with athletics: *Tuesdays with Morrie,* his poignant chronicle of several insightful dialogues conducted with a former college professor during the onetime mentor's final months of a terminal illness, spent over two years on the *New York Times* bestseller lists. It was also made into a television film in 1999, starring Jack Lemmon and Hank Azaria.

Motor City Sportswriter

Albom attended Brandeis University, where he first met Morrie Schwartz, a professor of sociology, but lost touch with him after moving on to earn two graduate degrees from Columbia University. After stints in New York and Florida, Albom arrived in Detroit, Michigan, in 1985 as a staff member of the *Detroit Free Press.* Introducing himself to his new audience in his first column, he explained that readers could expect "some opinion, some heart, some frankness. Some laughs. Some out of the ordinary." Albom also made a good first impression with area sports fans by rejecting the negative stereotype—a crime–ridden and dying city—that Detroit held for the nation. He added, "Some people apparently look at a new job in Detroit as something to be endured or tolerated. . . . I, for one, am thrilled to be here. For sports, they don't make towns any better than this one."

"I try to be honest. . . . This is not always a pretty job. Sometimes you have to write that the good guys lost, or that somebody's favorite baseball hero in the whole world just checked into the rehab clinic. Still, sports are the only show in town where no matter how many times you go back, you never know the ending. That's special."

—Mitch Albom

One of Albom's most distinguished traits as a columnist is his sympathy with disappointed fans when local professional teams struggle unsuccessfully for championships. He commiserated with area readers in 1988 when Detroit's basketball team, the Pistons, battled to the National Basketball Association (NBA) finals and pushed Los Angeles to a full seven–game series, only to lose the last game by three points. He reasoned, "They went further than any Pistons team before them. They came onto the stage as brutes and left with an entire nation's respect—for their courage, for their determination, for their talent. . . . They took on all comers. . . . They could beat any team in the league. They just couldn't beat them all." A year earlier, when the underdog Red Wings reached the National Hockey League (NHL) semifinals but lost, Albom reported how, on the long flight home, the players dealt with this defeat. Upon learning that a devoted fan—who was riding the team's charter plane home—had flown to Edmonton to watch the game, Detroit players chipped in to reimburse him for his ticket. They also joined in on a chorus of that fan's favorite cheer. Witnessing this, Albom wrote, "Amazing. Here were these bruising, scarred, often toothless men, on the night of a season–ending loss, singing a high school cheer. Simply because it made an old guy happy. Many people will remember goals and saves and slap shots from this season. I hope I never forget that cheer."

Becomes Popular Radio Host

With columns such as these, Albom earned a loyal following and a reputation as a blue–collar sports fan. His success in print carried over to other media, including radio and television. He joined the staff of rock station WLLZ in 1985, initially serving as sports director. In 1988 he and cohost Mike Stone began a weekly program, "The Sunday Sports Albom." Guests included both local and national sports figures and the program's format allowed calls by listeners. His stellar guest list was evidence of the comfortable rapport Albom shared with many area athletes and coaches. This accord extended beyond interviews; in 1987 he was even a good luck charm for Detroit's NHL team, the Red Wings. As he explained in a column reprinted in *The Live Albom*, "I am not sure when my car and the fortunes of the Red Wings actually became intertwined. I do know [coach] Jacques Demers and I have now driven to five playoff games together and Detroit has won all five, and now even Demers, who is not superstitious, is asking me what time we're leaving."

Albom's relationship with another state sports figure, former University of Michigan football coach Bo Schembechler, led to a collaboration on Schembechler's autobiography, *Bo*. Respected as a top college coach for his Big Ten championships and frequent bowl appearances, Schembechler reputedly had a quick temper and churlish personality. In *Bo*, Albom presents Schembechler as a sincere family man whose demeanor was a deliberate act and who inspired love and respect from his football players. Albom credits Schembechler with turning the Michigan football program around. When he began as coach, Michigan was a perennial runner–up to Ohio State. Bo promised championships, and he delivered without ever suffering through a losing season. Albom notes a greater accomplishment, however, is that Schembechler ran a program free from rules violations and saw his athletes graduate. A reviewer for the *New York Times Book Review* concluded that while *Bo* did not offer much new information about Schembechler, the work strengthened Schembechler's position as a role model for college athletes.

Chronicled Downside of Professional Sports

While Albom has reigned as the darling of the Detroit sports scene, he has also been involved with his share of controversy. He raised the ire of a Detroit Tigers' pitcher with a column and, eleven months later, had a bucket of ice water dumped over his head in the Tigers' clubhouse (the pitcher blamed his disintegrating effectiveness on Albom's commentary). Albom also broke the 1988 story of the after–curfew bar visits of several Red Wings players. He reported that, when confronted with the news, the coach "looked as if he was going to cry." Albom added that this black mark on the team's accomplishments was "not the story I wanted to write. Not the one you wanted to read."

In these instances, a prediction Albom made in his first column came true: "I try to be honest. . . . This is not always a pretty job. Sometimes you have to write that the good guys lost, or that somebody's favorite baseball hero in the whole world just checked into the rehab clinic. Still, sports are the only show in town where no matter how many times you go back, you never know the ending. That's special."

"The last class of my old professor's life took place once a week in his house, by a window in the study where he could watch a small hibiscus plant shed its pink leaves. The class met on Tuesdays. It began after breakfast. The subject was The Meaning of Life. It was taught from experience."

—from *Tuesdays with Morrie*

In 1996, Albom signed on with one of the Detroit area's top AM radio outlets, WJR 760AM, as host of "The Mitch Albom Show." Airing Monday through Friday during the crucial afternoon drive–time period, the new show focused on current events, local issues, the popular arts, and celebrity interviews, but he still hosted the occasional athlete or coach as a guest. Other interviewees included the Reverend Jesse Jackson, conservative politician Pat Buchanan, horror writer Stephen King, and actress Sally Field. The show was a great ratings success, and furthered Albom's status as a Motor City celebrity. A weekend version is syndicated and airs in several major markets on the ABC Radio network, including New York and Los Angeles; he still hosts "The Monday Sports Albom," which has moved to the WJR station as well.

Albom continued to write for the *Free Press* sports section, but was also offered a Sunday slot with a column called "Voices," which focuses on human–interest topics or current events. The Elian Gonzalez controversy and the slaying of a first–grader in Flint, Michigan by a classmate have provided fodder for his pen. In the latter case, Albom urged increased gun control laws. "You live in a country where . . . our lawmakers still will not budge on even register-ing a gun the way you register a car," he wrote in March of 2000, shortly after the death of six–year–old Kayla Holland. "Guns are protected. As for your children? The good news is, this time it was not yours who was shot."

Reaps Unexpected Reward from Tragedy

Albom's popular *Free Press* columns are still regu-larly collected into volumes and published by the paper every few years. In addition to the Schem-bechler biography, Albom has also written *Fab Five: Basketball, Trash Talk, the American Dream*, which chronicles the arrival and phenomenal college ca-reers of a quintet of young hoops stars at the Uni-versity of Michigan. But it was his 1997 book, *Tues-days with Morrie: An Old Man, a Young Man and Life's Greatest Lesson*, that bestowed upon Albom a more national literary celebrity. The work became a sur-prise bestseller, was featured on *Oprah,* inspired a made–for–television film, and was translated into several different languages.

Schwartz was Albom's sociology professor at Bran-deis in the late 1970s. Albom came to love the chal-lenge presented by Schwartz's innovative teaching methods, which encouraged students to think and discuss philosophical issues, and the teacher came to be a friend to him as well. Schwartz even sug-gested Albom's senior thesis topic, and presented him with a briefcase upon Albom's 1979 graduation. But the pair lost touch with one another, and when Albom saw his former mentor one 1995 evening as a guest on the ABC news program *Nightline,* he was shocked. Schwartz was there to discuss his struggle with Lou Gehrig's disease (amyotrophic lateral sclerosis), a terminal condition, but to Albom seemed every bit his former self—cheerful, prag-matic, and in the process of writing a book about the final stages of life. "I thought, 'I'm 37 years old and perfectly healthy. He's 78 and dying, and he seems eminently more happy and satisfied,'" ex-plained Albom to *People* reporter William Plummer.

A Timely Life Lesson

Albom was ashamed that he had not kept in touch with Schwartz, and telephoned him immediately.

That summer, a contentious newspaper strike in Detroit kept Albom away from his desk for a time, and soon he was flying to Boston weekly for visits with Schwartz. From these conversations Albom wrote *Tuesdays with Morrie.* Over the course of five months and fourteen chapters, or "classes," Schwartz attempts to impart some final lessons to his cynical, overworked former student. The two discuss family, work, community, forgiveness, and the meaning of life. "We slid quickly into the famil-iar waters of our old college dialogue," wrote Al-bom in the book, "Morrie asking questions, listen-ing to my replies, stopping like a chef to sprinkle in something I'd forgotten or hadn't realized."

The visits had a great impact upon Albom, and the book is an attempt to share some of the insights gained with a wider audience; he also hoped to de-fray some of the medical expenses that Schwartz and his wife faced by giving them the profits from the book's sales. In the end, Albom writes that the volume is "not a book about death and dying at all. It's a book about how to live well and be fulfilled." In a narrative voice that *Kliatt* reviewer Cindy Lom-bardo called "by turns intense, afraid, funny, and poignant, Albom ensures that his favorite professor will indeed continue to teach, albeit posthumously."

If you enjoy the works of Mitch Albom, you might want to check out the following books and films:

Frank Deford, *The World's Tallest Midget,* 1987.
John Feinstein, *A Season on the Brink,* 1986.
Will Weaver, *Hard Ball,* 1998.
Bang the Drum Slowly, a film starring Rob-ert De Niro, 1973.

Tuesdays with Morrie was the best–selling nonfiction book in the United States in 1998, stayed on the bestseller lists through much of 1999, and reached an impressively wide readership with sales in the three million copies range. "This book, small and easily digested, stopping just short of the maudlin and the mawkish, is on the whole sincere, senti-mental, and skillful," opined a *Kirkus Reviews* writer. A review by Faith McLellan in *Lancet* acknowledged that "some of Schwartz's aphorisms . . . may irritate some readers, who will find them bordering on the trite." Yet the critic noted that other readers "will take something meaningful away from this little book, a last gift from a generous teacher and the student who was fortunate enough to receive it before it was too late."

■ Biographical and Critical Sources

BOOKS

Albom, Mitch, *The Live Albom,* Detroit Free Press, 1988.
Albom, Mitch, *Live Albom II,* Detroit Free Press, 1990.

PERIODICALS

Detroit Free Press, March 30, 1993, p. 1C; March 5, 2000, Mitch Albom, "Another Firearm, Another Tragedy."
Kirkus Reviews, July 1, 1997, review of *Tuesdays with Morrie,* p. 993.
Kliatt, May, 1998, Cindy Lombardo, review of *Tuesdays with Morrie,* p. 56.
Lancet, October 17, 1998, Faith McLellan, "A Teacher to the Last," p. 1318.
New York Times Book Review, November 19, 1989, p. 44.
People, January 12, 1998, William Plummer, "Memento Morrie," p. 141.
Publishers Weekly, June 30, 1997, review of *Tuesdays with Morrie,* p. 60.
Sports Illustrated, December 20, 1999, "Morrie Glory," p. 28.*

—*Sketch by Mary K. Ruby; updated by Carol Brennan*

David Almond

■ Personal

Born May 15, 1951, in Newcastle upon Tyne, England; son of James Arthur and Catherine (Barber) Almond; married Sara Jane Palmer; children: Freya Grace Almond–Palmer. *Education:* University of East Anglia, B.A. (honors).

■ Addresses

Home—15 Westwood Ave., Heaton, Newcastle NE6 5QT, England. *E–mail*—dalmond@lineone.net.

■ Career

Teacher in primary, adult, and special education in England; creative writing tutor for the Arvon Foundation, beginning 1987, and the Open College of the Arts, 1995–99; Huntington School, York, visiting writer, 1996–98; Hartlepool Schools, writer–in–residence, spring, 1999; visiting speaker and course leader.

■ Awards, Honors

Hawthornden Fellowship, 1997; Junior Literary Guild Selection, Children's Book of the Year, Whitbread Award, and Carnegie Medal, American Library Association, all 1998, Michael L. Printz Honor Book, American Library Association, 2000, and Silver Pencil Award, all for *Skellig;* Arts Council Award for outstanding literature for young people, 1998, and Smarties Silver Award, 1999, and highly commended citation, Carnegie Medal, all for *Kit's Wilderness; Heaven Eyes* was shortlisted for the Whitbread Award.

■ Writings

JUVENILE

Skellig, Hodder Children's Books (London, England), 1998, Delacorte Press (New York, NY), 1999.

Kit's Wilderness, Hodder Children's Books, 1999, Delacorte Press, 2000.

Heaven Eyes, Hodder Children's Books, 2000, Delacorte Press, 2001.

OTHER

Sleepless Nights (short stories), Iron Press, 1985.

A Kind of Heaven (short stories), Iron Press, 1997.

Counting Stars (short stories), Hodder Children's Books, 2000.

Skellig (radio play), BBC Radio 4, 2000.

Wild Girl, Wild Boy (children's play), first produced in London at Lyric Theatre, 2001.

Contributor to *London* and *Critical Quarterly*. *Panurge* (fiction magazine), editor, 1987–93. *Kit's Wilderness* and *Skellig* have been translated and published in several other languages.

■ Work in Progress

An untitled novel for children.

■ Sidelights

British writer David Almond wrote for adults for a number of years before he achieved what amounted to overnight success with his first novel for young adults, *Skellig*. This 1998 tale of a young boy's discovery of a possibly supernatural creature in his own backyard was unanimously praised by reviewers, sold out its first printing in four days, and went on to win Britain's prestigious Whitbread Children's Book of the Year Award and the Carnegie Medal.

Like the hero in *Skellig*, Almond grew up on the fringes of a Northern English city, a landscape that offered great imaginative possibilities for him as a youth. As Almond, who was born in 1951, once commented: "Maybe ink was always in my blood. I don't remember it, of course, but as a baby in my mother's arms I used to visit my uncle's printing works on the narrow high street of our town. I used to point and grin and gurgle as the pages of the local newspaper rolled off the machines. It was a small steep town with wild heather hills at the crest and the River Tyne flowing far below. From our windows, we looked out towards the city that packed the opposite bank, towards the distant sea, and even on clear days toward the hazy Cheviots an eternity away. It was a place that had everything necessary for the imagination.

"I grew up in a big extended Catholic family. I listened to the stories and songs at family parties. I listened to the gossip that filled Dragone's coffee shop. I ran with my friends through the open spaces and the narrow lanes. We scared each other with ghost stories told in fragile tents on dark nights. We promised never–ending friendship and whispered of the amazing journeys we'd take together. I sat with my grandfather in his allotment, held tiny Easter chicks in my hands while he smoked his pipe and the factory sirens wailed and larks yelled high above. I trembled at the images presented to us in church, at the awful threats and glorious promises

It takes a move to a new home, a new best friend, and an encounter with the supernatural to convince ten–year–old Michael of the power of love in Almond's multi–award–winning 1998 novel.

made by black–clad priests with Irish voices. I scribbled stories and stitched them into little books. I disliked school and loved the library, a little square building in which I dreamed that books with my name on them would stand one day on the shelves. I loved Arthurian legends, Hemingway, John Wyndham, the tales of the fake Tibetan monk, Lobsang Rampa."

After earning a degree from the University of East Anglia, Almond became a teacher. In 1982, he quit a full–time job, sold his house, and moved to a commune in order to devote himself to writing. The result was a collection of stories, *Sleepless Nights*, published by a small press in 1985. As Almond once stated, "I began to write properly after university, after five years of teaching. Short stories appeared in little magazines. A couple were broadcast on Radio 4. A small press collection, *Sleepless Nights,* appeared to a tiny amount of acclaim and a vast amount of silence. I ran a fiction magazine, *Panurge,* that excited and exhausted me for six years. I wrote The Great English Novel that took five years, went to 33 publishers and was rejected by them all. I went on writing. More stories, more publications, a few small prizes. Another novel, never finished. Another story collection was published, *A Kind of Heaven,* twelve years after the first. Then at last I started writing about growing up in our small steep town: a whole sequence of stories, half–real, half–imaginary, that I called *Stories from the Middle of the World.* They took a year to write."

Writes *Skellig* with Sudden Fervor

It was the act of finishing the Newcastle stories that inexplicably led Almond to the opening lines of *Skellig:* "I found him in the garage on Sunday afternoon," recalls the book's narrator, ten–year–old Michael—an opening line that, Almond said, simply came to him as he was walking down the street. As he explained in an interview with *Publishers Weekly,* "When I wrote the last of these stories, I stuck them into an envelope, and as soon as I'd posted away the book to my agent, the story of *Skellig* just flew into my head, as if it had just been waiting there." On the Sunday in question on which *Skellig* begins, Michael and his family have just taken possession of an old, run–down house; also new to them is a newborn infant sister for Michael, who initially arrives home from the hospital but soon must return for heart surgery.

In the garage, behind a great deal of clutter, Michael discovers a man covered in dust and insects. At first he believes it is an old homeless man, but he finds that Skellig, who communicates with Michael but does not reveal much by way of explanation, has odd wing–like appendages. It seems Skellig has come there to die. As he begins his new school, while his mother is away with his sister at the hospital and his father is understandably preoccupied, Michael begins to bring Skellig food and medicine. He also befriends his new neighbor, a girl named Mina, who is an intelligent, independent thinker. Mina explains to Michael a few of her interests, such as ornithology and the poetry of early nineteenth century Romantic writer William Blake. She also shows him a nest of rare owls, which may have something to do with Skellig's presence.

But as Perri Klass noted, writing about *Skellig* in the *New York Times Book Review,* the book's charm lies in its author's courage for allowing some things to re-

main a mystery. "[I]n its simple but poetic language, its tender refusal to package its mysteries neatly or offer explanations for what happens in either world, it goes beyond adventure story or family–with–a–problem story to become a story about worlds enlarging and the hope of scattering death." As the story progresses, Michael shares the secret of Skellig with Mina, and as they both tend to him in the garage, his health improves considerably. As a result, however, the mysterious occupant becomes even more secretive and mystical before he vanishes.

Michael feels his baby sister's heart beating one day, and realizes that love can achieve miracles that science cannot. Her survival is all the more poignant given the fact that Almond based this subplot of the book on an incident that occurred when he was eight, when his own infant sister died. Klass, in her *New York Times Book Review* critique, praised Almond's talent for weaving in the more prosaic details of life, such as soccer practice and the daily school–bus ride, with larger questions involving the metaphysical world. "Its strength as novel is in its subtlety, its sideways angles," observed Klass. "It is a book about the business of everyday life proceeding on a canvas suddenly widened to include mystery and tragedy, although not everyone has eyes to see."

Earned Laudatory Reviews, Professional Honors

Other reviews were similarly positive. Cathryn M. Mercier, writing in *Five Owls,* called *Skellig* a "novel of faith and hope," and "a book of rare spirituality for young adults." *Reading Time* reviewer Howard George described it as "a haunting story" whose impact lies in "the deep emotions evoked by the family crisis and the love given out to Skellig."

Almond had already completed his second young–adult novel, *Kit's Wilderness,* before *Skellig* took several literary prizes in Britain for 1998, including the Whitbread Award and the Carnegie Medal. The focus of this second book, published the following year, is a game of pretend death that its characters play, and it takes place in a small town not unlike the community of Almond's youth. "In my primary school—a spooky turreted place down by the river where the ancient coal mines had been—a bunch of kids used to play a fainting game in the long grass beyond the school yard wall," wrote Almond in *Carousel* about the source of the plot for his second book.

Set in History–Rich Mining Community

Though he only witnessed the game once, the sight unnerved him and its memory continued to haunt him later. From this he created the story of Christo-

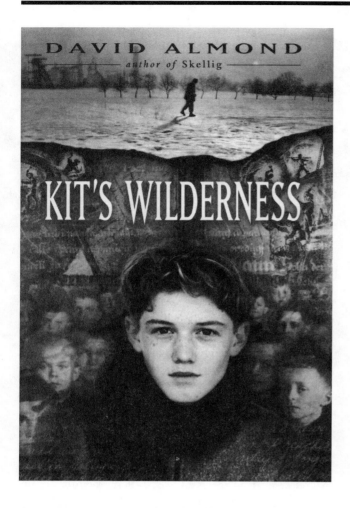

DAVID ALMOND
author of Skellig

KIT'S WILDERNESS

Almond's childhood in a British mining town was the inspiration for his 1999 novel, in which a young boy learns to appreciate both his close–knit family and the history that binds him to his new community.

troubled home, is also leader of the Death game, which is tied to his preoccupation with an 1821 Stoneygate mining disaster in which a hundred child laborers died. In a memorial plaque commemorating them, Kit finds the name of a 13–year–old with the same name as his own. In Askew's macabre game, the youths must venture into the abandoned mine to communicate with ghosts there. Kit takes part in it, but begins to suffer nightmares. His grandfather, from whom he has inherited his storytelling gifts, recounts to him vivid tales about his life as a miner, which only add a realistic strain to Kit's bad dreams. "It was very deep, Kit," his grandfather recollects. "Very dark. And every one of us was scared of it. As a lad I'd wake up trembling, knowing that as a Watson born in Stoneygate I'd soon be following my ancestors into the pit."

The "Seam of Goodness"

Though the others consider it just a game, Kit realizes that Death, as they play it, possesses a deeper significance in their lives. "One of the really exciting things to me in writing for children is the ability to tap into the fluidity of the imagination, mine and the reader's," he told Cooper in the *Booklist* interview. "Children are capable of accepting all sorts of possibilities as long as the parameters of reality are in place." As *Kit's Wilderness* progresses, Askew's game is discovered by school authorities, and he is expelled. Problems at home—his father is an alcoholic—compel him to flee. Kit, meanwhile, is writing a story about a boy in prehistoric times who lives without his family, a version of Askew's own woes, but his friend eventually surfaces. "Unlike others, Kit never loses hope or faith in the 'seam of goodness' that his grandfather insists exists in Askew and everyone," noted Bette Ammon in a *Voice of Youth Advocates* review.

"This is a highly satisfying literary experience, showing readers that some of life's events are beyond explanation," wrote Ellen Fader in a *School Library Journal* review. A *Publishers Weekly* assessment was equally laudatory. "Almond offers another tantalizing blend of human drama, surrealism, and allegory," it noted, and concluded that its "structure is as awe–inspiring as the ancient mining tunnels that run beneath Stoneygate."

Publishes Third Novel

Almond has said that as a work of fiction, *Kit's Wilderness* took him far longer to develop coherently than *Skellig*, but once he became involved in the

pher "Kit" Watson, who has recently moved with his family to their former hometown, Stoneygate, which was once a thriving coal–mining hub. Stoneygate has fallen on hard times, and they have come there to care for Kit's ailing grandfather. Much of the period detail came from the author's own memories. "As I was growing up, all the mines were closing down, but I do have a strong memory of when I was very young seeing the men coming out of the pit, tromping by my grandmother's house," Almond said in an interview with *Booklist's* Ilene Cooper.

Kit, a budding writer, soon befriends a tough youth his own age, who possesses surprising artistic ambitions. But John Askew, who comes from a

writing process, the book seemed to take on a life of its own. He admitted that, "at times I was scared stiff by what was happening in the tale," he wrote in *Carousel.* "Scared that it might all end dreadfully, scared that the darkness would gain the upper hand." As with *Skellig,* it was slated for publication in several foreign translations as well. Almond's third novel for teens, *Heaven Eyes,* appeared in the United Kingdom in early 2000. As with his other books, its plot blends everyday adventure with a dalliance in the netherworld; its characters are escapees of a juvenile home who flee on a raft to an old printing plant on the River Tyne. "These books are suffused with the landscape and spirit of my own childhood," Almond once remarked. "By looking back into the past, by re–imagining it and blending it with what I see around me now, I found a way to move forward and to become something that I am intensely happy to be: a writer for children."

If you enjoy the works of David Almond, you might want to check out the following books:

Graham Joyce, *The Tooth Fairy,* 1998.
Margaret Mahy, *The Tricksters,* 1986.
Jess Mowry, *Ghost Train,* 1996.

With the Whitbread Award for *Skellig,* Almond received a generous prize purse, enabling him to quit his job as a creative writing tutor, which he had been doing since 1987. Instead, he planned to concentrate full–time on writing for the young adult market from his home in Newcastle, which he shares with his wife and daughter. After working so tenaciously for years with very little reward, this turn of events is an unexpected surprise in his life. He admitted to having very little experience with

the children's literature genre before he wrote *Skellig*—a blessing in disguise, as he admitted to Cooper in the *Booklist* interview. "If I had gone to a publisher and said, 'I have an idea for a book, and it's got William Blake imagery and a character somewhere between man and angel, and it's going to sell lots and lots of copies,' I'm sure they would have said, 'No thanks, go away.'"

Though his fiction possesses a dark side to it, both literally and figuratively, it remains a favorite with readers, reviewers, and educational professionals. "One of the great things about writing for children is that you must have a sense of optimism, no matter how troubling things are," Almond told *Booklist*'s Cooper. "You have to believe that the world is going forward, that life is improving."

■ Biographical and Critical Sources

PERIODICALS

Booklist, January 1, 2000, Ilene Cooper, interview with David Almond, p. 898; March 15, 2000, Michael Cart, "Carte Blanche," p. 1370.

Carousel, summer, 1999, David Almond, "Writing for Boys?," p. 29.

Five Owls, May–June, 1999, Cathryn M. Mercier, review of *Skellig,* p. 110.

Horn Book, May, 1999, review of *Skellig,* p. 326.

New York Times Book Review, June 6, 1999, Perri Klass, review of *Skellig,* p. 49.

Publishers Weekly, May 10, 1999, p. 34; June 28, 1999, Elizabeth Devereaux, "Flying Starts," p. 25; January 3, 2000, review of *Kit's Wilderness,* p. 77; November 6, 2000, "Best Children's Books 2000," p. 43.

Reading Time, May, 1999, Howard George, review of *Skellig,* p. 25.

School Library Journal, March, 2000, Ellen Fader, review of *Kit's Wilderness,* p. 233.

Voice of Youth Advocates, April, 2000, Bette Ammon, review of *Kit's Wilderness,* p. 42.*

Miriam Bat–Ami

■ Personal

Surname pronounced "Bott a–*me*"; born June 26, 1950, in Scranton, PA; daughter of Simon H. (a rabbi) and Huddie (a violinist; maiden name, Weinstein) Shoop; married Ronald Rubens (a builder), April 11, 1976; children: Aaron Rubens, Daniel Rubens. *Education:* Hebrew University, Jerusalem, B.A., 1974; California State University, Los Angeles, M.A., 1980; University of Pittsburgh, Ph.D., 1989. *Religion:* Jewish. *Hobbies and other interests:* Research on multiple perspectives in American historical fiction and nonfiction for children, gardening, caring for the families many pets, horseback riding, acting, reading.

■ Addresses

Home—23750 64th Ave., Mattawan, MI 49071. *Office*—Dept. of English, Western Michigan University, Kalamazoo, MI 49008. *Agent*—Barbara Kouts, P.O. Box 558, Bellport, NY 11713.

■ Career

University of Pittsburgh, Pittsburgh, PA, teaching fellow in English, 1980–84; Southwest Missouri State University, Springfield, instructor in English, 1984– 89; Western Michigan University, Kalamazoo, assistant professor, 1989–94, associate professor of English, 1994—. Has also worked as a tutor for Special Services at California State University, team taught English as a Second Language at Los Angeles City College, worked as an executive assistant at the Israeli Consulate in Los Angeles, and consulted on college texts and multicultural literature for Harcourt Brace Jovanovich and Simon & Schuster publishers.

■ Member

Modern Language Association, Children's Literature Association, National Council of Teachers of English, Society of Children's Book Writers and Illustrators, Michigan Council of Teachers of English.

■ Awards, Honors

First prize, CELERY Short Story Award, Western Michigan University, 1982, for "Nielah"; John Gilmore Emerging Artists' Grant, 1991, for completion of *When the Frost Is Gone*; Faculty Research and Creative Arts Support Grant (FRACAS), Western Michigan University, 1993, for completion of *Punctuation Porpoises and Other Space People*; Highlights Awards Foundation Scholarship, 1993; Scott O'Dell Award, 2000, for *Two Suns in the Sky*.

■ Writings

Sea, Salt, and Air, illustrated by Mary O'Keefe Young, Macmillan, 1993.

When the Frost Is Gone, illustrated by Marcy Dunn Ramsey, Macmillan, 1994.

Dear Elijah, Farrar, Straus, 1995, Jewish Publications Society, 1997.

Two Suns in the Sky, Front Street/Cricket Books, 1999.

Contributor of short stories, including "My Beautiful Feet" and "All Because of the Pines," to *Cicada*. Contributor of critical essays to journals, including *Beacham's Guide to Literature for Young Adults*, *Children's Literature in Education*, *Children's Literature Association Quarterly*, and *Language Arts Journal of Michigan*, among others. Contributor of short stories and poetry to periodicals, including *Voices: A Magazine for English Poetry in Israel*, *Response*, *Davka*, *Tree*, *Gargoyle*, and *Statement: California State University Journal*.

■ Work in Progress

Horse's Right Eye, a young adult novel.

■ Sidelights

Miriam Bat–Ami is the author of books for children and adolescents that examine topics such as friendship, prejudice, and religion. Her works *When the Frost is Gone*, *Dear Elijah*, and *Two Suns in the Sky* feature teenage protagonists who struggle to establish their own identities under confusing and often painful circumstances.

Bat–Ami once said: "I have always wanted to move people. I love to hear children laugh. I love to see them laugh when I'm reading to them. I suppose I get this from my father, who would stand on the pulpit and move us all to laughter and tears. I love the tears, too, that come after the laughter when suddenly the world opens, and we see something new, something perhaps that's always been there.

"I think I've always had a gift for voice, for remembering how people say things. Dialogue is very important to me, even when I write picture books. I find that, in speech, I reach down into what my characters are about. I also have a flair for the dramatic, and my years working in the theatre have influenced the way I write."

"I Often Felt Somehow Different"

Bat–Ami continued, "In many respects teaching is very important to me. I don't want to tell people what to think, but I love posing questions and guiding my students into new thoughts.

"As a child, I often felt somehow different. Given my background, I was different, and so I find my characters to be sensitive to difference—slightly outside looking in on many worlds. I've also thought it very important to have an empathetic imagination. I want children to feel worlds that aren't necessarily their own and yet, also, to delight in worlds they have.

"My second book grew out of my experiences on what one might call a 'marginal' block. On that block, though, I found deep community, and so I wanted to tell children how what is outside (poverty) sometimes masks a real richness of people pulling together. This book, *When the Frost Is Gone*, was written because I needed to believe in harmony. I still do. I also want my literature to sometimes address action. Children will read it and feel optimistic about what they can do in the world."

Childhood Experiences Stirred Creativity

Bat–Ami once remarked, "My first and third books came from personal feelings about my own past. *Sea, Salt, and Air*, my first picture book, deals with the yearly summer trips my family took to the beach: how we packed for the trip, the long ride, our feelings of freedom when we swam in the ocean, and the whole sense of timelessness one feels at the beach. It also deals with my love for my grandparents, who welcomed us into their summer cottage. Mary O'Keefe Young, working in vibrant pastels, wonderfully captured that sense of freedom and love."

Bat–Ami's 1994 book, *When the Frost Is Gone*, marked the start of her venturing into fiction for older children. In this story, twelve–year–old Natalie recounts an eventful, if difficult summer. Natalie lives with her father, and carries with her a certain degree of anger toward her mother, a substance abuser who has left them. She resents entering her teen years without a sympathetic female figure to discuss things, but when her mother returns for a time that summer and tries to build a new relationship, Natalie cannot see past her own anger at her mother's former behavior. Tasha, Natalie's close friend, lives nearby in the rough urban neighborhood, and Natalie recounts her friend's own woes that summer, which culminate in a fire that destroys the house for which Tasha's grandmother has just finished paying. Natalie forges an unlikely but positive friendship with her neighbor, a stonemason named Mr. Pettinato, who offers to rebuild Tasha's grandmother's house and "helps Natalie achieve equilibrium," noted a *Publishers Weekly* review, which commended *When the Frost Is Gone* as "a portrait of urban life in all its colors." Connie Tyrrell Burns, writing for the *School Library Journal*, described it as "a deceptively simple, richly written depiction of a young girl's coming of age."

A Young Girl's Struggle

Bat–Ami once described the substance of her next book, *Dear Elijah*, as "a middle grade novel [that] explores a young Jewish girl's feelings about God. Rebecca's father has had a heart attack; Passover is coming; and no one in her house is doing anything to get ready. She writes to the prophet Elijah, and, in the writing, begins to understand herself. She needs to find her own route to prayer: it isn't her father's. She also needs to find her own place in the world. In this sense, she is not only a Jewish girl coming to terms with faith, she is every girl exploring female identity." Bat–Ami also stated, "Her questions are closely tied to ones I had at her age, ones which have no easy answers and which, sometimes, I still ask. In this sense, *Dear Elijah* was a particularly painful book for me to write. Painful, too, was the fact that my own father died of a heart attack. Rebecca's father does not die, though the reader doesn't know what will ultimately happen. I don't think I could have made him die. It would have been too painful."

Dear Elijah earned its author mixed reviews. A *Publishers Weekly* review faulted Bat–Ami's portrayal of the confused Rebecca, asserting that the girl "never becomes a flesh–and–blood character," while her letters to the biblical prophet "sometimes seem like the effort of an ambitious religious school teacher." Sharon Glover, writing for *School Library Journal*, concurred, remarking that "while the premise is interesting, the choice of Elijah as a pen pal for an adolescent girl seems strange." Yet Becky Korman, writing in *Voice of Youth Advocates*, felt the work had a more positive message. "The issue of whether to adopt your parents' faith is one that most young people will face," Korman noted. A *Booklist* critique from Ilene Cooper commended Bat–Ami for delv-

Disappointed when her father is forced to spend Passover in the hospital recovering from a heart attack, eleven–year–old Rebecca struggles to understand her relationship with God by writing a series of letters to the prophet Elijah in Bat–Ami's 1995 novel.

ing into some weighty topics about life, Jewish heritage, and general spiritual issues. "There are certainly too few books that deal with that topic," Cooper remarked.

Interfaith Romance

Bat–Ami won rave reviews for another work for adolescent readers, *Two Suns in the Sky*, which appeared in 1999. The story is set in 1944 in Oswego, New York, a time when the United States was in the midst of World War II. A teenage girl, Chris Cook, is bored by life in upstate New York, and duly fascinated when the federal government establishes a refugee shelter for European Jews at nearby historic Fort Ontario. It was the only such shelter in the United States for Jewish refugees, though at the time, the presence of Nazi Germany's concentration camps in Eastern Europe, where Jews were systematically murdered, was not known to the general public.

There are a nearly thousand Jews living at Fort Ontario, and Chris establishes a friendship with Adam, one of the teenagers from the camp who attends her high school. Both she and Adam recount their stories in alternating first–person narrative chapters. Adam was fortunate enough to leave Rome with his mother and sister when that part of Italy was liberated from Nazi occupation by the Allied forces but, as with the others, is dismayed to find himself fenced inside in what he believed was the land of freedom. As *Two Suns in the Sky* progresses, the friendship between the two quickly turns to romance. Chris's xenophobic father vehemently expresses his disapproval, and even her Roman Catholic priest warns her to stay away. Their prejudicial attitudes reflect the conflicts that other residents of Oswego have about the refugee camp in their midst. Bat–Ami includes actual recollections of the camp from surviving residents and refugees as epigraphs that precede each chapter. However, the attitudes of Adam's teachers also reflect how many people in the community came to the aid of the refugees.

Some reviewers compared Bat–Ami's against–all–odds teen romance to Shakespeare's *Romeo and Juliet*. "Bat–Ami captures the startled awareness of young adolescents in love for the first time, the awareness of two individuals who, briefly, exist only in relation to one another," noted a *Bulletin of the Center for Children's Books* review. Though the townspeoples' suspicion toward foreigners and Jews is a strong undercurrent in the work, Martha Walke, writing in *Horn Book,* commended the way the issue was handled: "Never didactic, Bat–Ami uses her story to probe this issue with sensitivity and depth." *Booklist* critic Hazel Rochman offered a similarly positive assessment. "The relationships are complex," she noted, and commended the author's creation of "a docunovel that gives a strong sense of the times." A *Publishers Weekly* review described the epigraphs as "convincing observations," and asserted that readers "will be challenged by the questions Bat–Ami realistically frames about tolerance and its absence."

Bat–Ami recalled her own youth as a Jewish girl growing up in America in the postwar years in an interview with *Authors and Artists for Young Adults* (*AAYA*). "I was both an active kid and a quiet kid. I

had a lot of 'block' friends," she told *AAYA*. "Back in the fifties, kids often made these kinds of friends in the neighborhood and activities centered around the block. We had a big back yard and so did our neighbor who had children my age. We played outdoor games, many of them quite imaginative in nature and full of ancient rituals. One was 'pies,' a form of tag wherein the 'devil with the dirty hands and face' had to guess the name of pies. When he did, he chased them, and, if they were caught, they got put in the pickle jar. There was TV tag. You shouted out a TV show before you got tagged. If you repeated a show, you were 'frozen' and we played 'statues,' another tag game wherein we actually role played parts that came to the twirlers mind by the way we were twirled. We also played 'king of the mountain' on the hill behind our house and some fairly standard games like 'kick the can,' 'red Rover,' and 'dodge ball.'"

Difficult Experiences as Early Reader

Bat–Ami stated, "I liked to bike ride to the candy store near our house with friends and I liked to roller skate down hills. I came from Scranton, Pennsylvania, and lived in what was referred to as the hill section, and so we had wonderful skating hills and bumpy slate sidewalks. These were neighborhood things I did. On an organized level, I was in Girl Scouts and took ballet lessons. I also rode a horse (generally once a week) with a friend. Stories were always part of my life. My parents liked to tell stories about their childhood. In our synagogue I belonged to the storytelling group, and we learned Jewish tales that we told during the service.

"I actually had a very difficult first reading experience," Bat–Ami continued in the *AAYA* interview. "I think part of this has to do with my eyes. I had an operation when I was five and wore glasses (or contacts) from then on. At first I didn't read well and was tutored by a wonderful teacher. I loved learning from her. After school, I'd sit on her porch—her name was Mrs. Farber and we'd read together. I liked the shared experience of reading. At school I wasn't a 'blue bird.' Those were the best readers. I think I was in the second group. I always felt compelled to do better. But at school we read aloud in circles and it didn't feel as communal as it did on Mrs. Farber's porch. When I was a pre–teen I caught the reading bug. I guess I'm a lot like my second son: a late reading bloomer who now delights in the whole venture of moving into imaginary worlds. I loved to lie in bed with the covers over me, eat chips or ice cream, and read and read and read. Later I loved reading to my mother, particularly plays. After the initial fear of reading in groups, I loved reading aloud to people. I liked to dramatize events.

"I read just about everything. I wasn't a discriminating reader. My parents got *Reader's Digest Books of Stories.* I'm not quite sure that's the right title, but the *Reader's Digest* people put out books of short stories. I read those. I read any horse book I could get my hands on. I read Golden Books. My favorite was an abridged version of *Heidi.* Summers, I'd join the Reading Clubs and I read Nancy Drew Mysteries and The Bobbsey Twins' series, and I loved Hans Christian Andersen. His sad stories always touched me. I remember sitting in a big stuffed chair in our attic and wishing that the little mermaid would be able to marry the prince. I remember wondering how she could endure suffering so much. I read books about girls who suffered and survived: biographies about people like Helen Keller. I was particularly attracted to Madame Curie. If only I could be an inventor like her. And I imagined myself a 'National Velvet' racing my horse. My parents always encouraged me to read."

College Years in Israel

Bat–Ami recalled, "In school I was a good student, not a genius but good. I was persistent and worked hard. I liked algebra and had a good deal of trouble with geometry. I love English and hated art. I had no faith in my abilities to draw and very little patience. I also asked many questions. Some teachers liked this. Some didn't.

"As a teenager I wanted to be a ballet dancer with some dance company. I had famous dancers on my wall (alongside pictures of running horses), and I always saw myself in movement, but I wasn't cut out to be a dancer. I came to writing slowly. My freshman year, I had a teacher who really encouraged me and put me on the writing staff of our high school newspaper. I began by writing poetry. Poetry cleanses the soul, and I continue to return to it when I want to suck on the seeds of life.

"I went to Boston University my first year of college and then transferred to Hebrew University in Jerusalem," Bat–Ami stated in the *AAYA* interview. "I finished my B.A. in Israel. . . . I loved college. [At] Hebrew University I got to travel quite a bit. I remember swimming in oases, in the Mediterranean, picking dates, hiking, seeing Greece and Paris. I lived in Jerusalem and felt it to be the most spiritual place on the earth. After graduation, I went back to the States as I always thought of myself as American. Perhaps, though, this sense of myself as Jewish and American influenced a great deal of my writing, for in this duality there was that sense that I was neither fully one thing or another, or rather I was two things. I belonged to a people whose roots were not in the States. My grandparents were immi-

Bat–Ami's award–winning 1999 novel is a romance with a twist as two teens from different faiths find their friendship blooming into love against an historic backdrop: the only refugee camp for European Jews to be established on U.S. soil.

grants from Poland and Russia. And yet, I have always felt very American. After graduation I held many insignificant jobs, worked part–time and wrote, traveled around the United States until, at the age of 28, I went back to school. I did my master's at California State University, Los Angeles, and my doctorate at the University of Pittsburgh."

Own Children Inspired Work

Discussing her entry into the world of children's book publishing, Bat–Ami stated, "I was amazed when my first book was published. I was very fortunate to work with Harold Underdown, children's book editor. In 1989 he was an assistant editor at

Macmillan and working his way up. I was new. He was looking for fresh voices. I sent him *Sea, Salt, and Air* and he literally showed me how to make a picture book from it. It is scary to be a picture book writer when you are not the illustrator. You have to trust that the illustrator will carry the vision you had—and even extend that. I still love looking at *Sea, Salt, and Air,* although I was saddened that Macmillan Children's books folded.

"Where do I get my ideas? Listening to kids, and being with my children. My books have tended to follow my children, in that I've written for an older and older audience. My last book was for teens and some of what my older son said was in it. My children keep me in touch with how kids are thinking because one can forget. Just recently my eldest got his permit and I experienced that whole feeling of being behind the wheel, taking your mom's keys and hanging onto them, asking your mom to move over into the passenger's side. An event that occurred to me or my kids will trigger ideas. My youngest grew the biggest sunflower the summer before kindergarten, and he measured his growth through that sunflower. This became the basis of a picture book manuscript, 'The Practicing Sunflower.'

"For historical fiction, I read history books and become intrigued by certain events in history. When I researched *Two Suns in the Sky,* I depended quite a bit on interviews and newspaper articles. The newspaper can give you so much: tell you of fashions, prices, current events (of that time), movies that are popular, hair styles. I use the newspaper like freezer paper. It gives me grounding."

"When the Child in Us Dies, We Die"

Asked about her writing practices, Bat–Ami told *AAYA,* "When I write, I need quiet. I write in my office on the second floor of our house. I face a window because I need to look out at the trees from time to time. How do I balance my time? I'm fortunate in that I teach at a university and so don't have a 9 to 5 job. I write mornings, teach afternoons and prepare classes/grade papers in the evenings.

"I write children's books because they tell us the truth about ourselves," Bat–Ami continued. "They sustain us. Because when the child in us dies, we die. The unique thing about young readers is that they so willingly enter into a fictional world and are engaged with characters in that world. A friend of mine told me about how her daughter read my book. She took it out to the back yard, sat against a tree trunk and read all afternoon. Fourteen–year–old girls need that escape, and, in escaping, they handle their own worlds so much better. They are refreshed. I think I love adolescent readers because they read like they eat—hungrily. I also am intrigued that young readers possess a willingness to enter into other worlds, to engage with characters inside a fictional context and to be moved by it. I myself want my readers to discover new worlds and see things they hadn't before—consider questions which they hadn't thought about."

Works Forge a Sense of Community

"I try to give a reader something which tastes good but isn't pablum. I want my readers to use their teeth and their tongues and feel the swallowing. Regarding goals, the majority of my work addresses community. 'No man is an island' has become a cliche, but there is truth in this statement. We are all connected, and I ask my reader to consider connections. I ask my reader to think about what we can do for each other, and I want them to have faith in themselves. My characters feel the immensity of life, often they are close to getting lost in the bigness of it all, but they find support. Often support comes from an older person, Mrs. Dubchek in *Two Suns in the Sky,* and Mr. Pettinato in *When the Frost Is Gone.* That older person is close to nature or to God [and] feels comfortable with life. My main characters find best friends who move them to see differently and they are willing to take chances. Living for them is taking a chance and exploring the other.

"I hope that my readers feel good about themselves, that they believe they can do something for others, can work with others to affect some change for the better in this world. Chris says this in *Two Suns in the Sky.* She says, 'Roosevelt had been the president of the United States almost as long as I'd lived on the earth. He said that we were citizens of the world. We couldn't be ostriches or dogs in the manger. We had to be responsible. We had to act responsibly. So I had to figure out what to do for myself.'

"When I think of all my books, I realize that I speak of family and community, of being inside a group and of feeling left out or outside, of wanting to become part of a larger circle. My characters are in the midst of change, sometimes bored with their lives, feeling that they need to connect to something bigger than themselves."

If you enjoy the works of Miriam Bat–Ami, you might want to check out the following books:

Christa Laird, *But Can the Phoenix Sing?*, 1995.
Carol Matas, *Greater than Angels*, 1998.
Uri Orlev, *The Lady with the Hat*, 1995.

■ Biographical and Critical Sources

PERIODICALS

Booklist, May 15, 1993, p. 1695; April 1, 1995, Ilene Cooper, review of *Dear Elijah*, p. 1391; April 15, 1999, Hazel Rochman, review of *Two Suns in the Sky.*

Bulletin of the Center for Children's Books, April, 1994, Betsy Hearne, review of *When the Frost Is Gone*, p. 251; July, 1999, review of *Two Suns in the Sky*, pp. 379–380.

Horn Book, July, 1999, Martha Walke, review of *Two Suns in the Sky*, p. 460.

Kirkus Reviews, April 15, 1994, review of *When the Frost Is Gone*, p. 552.

Publishers Weekly, March 7, 1994, review of *When the Frost Is Gone*, p. 72; January 16, 1995, review of *Dear Elijah*, p. 455; May 17, 1999, review of *Two Suns in the Sky*, p. 80.

School Library Journal, June, 1993, p. 70; April, 1994, Connie Tyrrell Burns, review of *When the Frost Is Gone*, p. 124; May, 1995, Sharon Grover, review of *Dear Elijah*, p. 104; July, 1999, Shirley Wilton, review of *Two Suns in the Sky*, p. 92.

Voice of Youth Advocates, August, 1994, Kitty Krahnke, review of *When the Frost Is Gone*, p. 142; August, 1995, Becky Korman, review of *Dear Elijah*, p. 154.

Sook Nyul Choi

■ Personal

Born in 1937, in Pyongyang, Korea; came to the United States; married; husband deceased; children: two daughters. *Education:* Received B.A. from Manhattanville College.

■ Addresses

Home—Cambridge, MA.

■ Career

Writer; teacher of creative writing to high school students. Boston Public Library, selected author for creative writing workshop, 1992. Former teacher of elementary school students in New York City.

■ Member

Authors Guild, Authors League of America, Society of Children's Book Writers and Illustrators, National Writers Union, Women's National Book Association.

■ Awards, Honors

Bulletin Blue Ribbon citation, *Bulletin of the Center for Children's Books,* and Judy Lopez Book Award, both 1991, Young Adults Library Services Association best book for young adults citation, New York Public Library best book for the teen age citation, and American Library Association notable book citation, all for *Year of Impossible Goodbyes;* Cambridge YWCA Women of Achievement Award, 1992.

■ Writings

Year of Impossible Goodbyes (novel for young adults), Houghton, 1991.
Echoes of the White Giraffe (sequel to *Year of Impossible Goodbyes*), Houghton, 1993.
Halmoni and the Picnic (picture book), illustrated by Karen Milone–Dugan, Houghton, 1993.
Gathering of Pearls (sequel to *Echoes of the White Giraffe*), Houghton, 1994.
Yunmi and Halmoni's Trip, Houghton, 1997.
The Best Older Sister, illustrated by Cornelius Van Wright and Ying–Hwa Hu, Delacorte Press, 1997.

■ Sidelights

Sook Nyul Choi is the author of a highly commended series of books for young teens that poignantly describe the hardships faced by a young

Korean girl during a time of war and strife in her country. Reviewers of children's literature have written admirably of Choi's talent in creating an indomitable heroine, Sookan, and a first–person narrative voice that is both empathetic and survival–minded. But portraying life in Korea during a time of war and occupation, as well as Sookan's later experiences as a college student abroad, came easily to Choi, for Sookan's fictional life simply mirrored her own. Interwoven throughout this trio of novels—and the two picture books for younger readers that Choi has also penned—are vivid and educational descriptions of Korean heritage, culture, and family life.

"I now have two countries, my native country of Korea, and my adopted country, the United States," Choi once observed. "Through my writing, I want to bring to life the history and culture of Korea to share with all my American friends. I hope that through my books, Americans can gain insight into this very different and interesting culture." For this Choi has earned a reputation as an exceptional multicultural writer, but critics also term her writing so skillful in evoking the human spirit that her books are universal in appeal. "At the center of her stories radiates an ardent optimism and unchained belief in the goodness of humanity," noted an essay on the writer in *Children's Literature Review*.

A Born Writer

Choi was born in Pyongyang, North Korea, in 1937. She once commented, "I have always loved books. As a young girl growing up in Korea, I loved collecting books. I loved the feel and the smell of books; I liked the sound of pages turning; and I liked arranging them on my bookshelf. Sitting under the trellis of grapevines in our backyard, I would sit and read for hours as I snacked on the bitter green grapes. Through books, I could travel to the far corners of the world and meet people from distant lands and cultures. Through books, I could even travel through time. As a grammar school student in Korea, I began writing short stories and poetry. I loved to write, for through writing, I could express my thoughts, ideas, and feelings, and could even express my dreams and visions of the fantastic."

But Choi's childhood was anything but idyllic. She had grown up during a time of great strife in her country; it was occupied by Imperial Japan during World War II, and the Koreans suffered under the oppressive regime. After the war, the country was partitioned into two—a Communist north and a

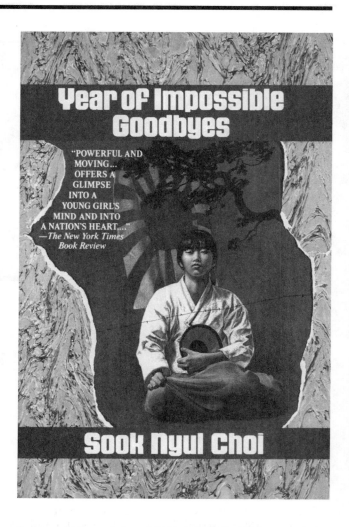

In her widely acclaimed 1991 novel Choi first introduces readers to an indomitable ten–year–old named Sookan as she survives the harsh treatment of Japanese troops during their occupation of Sookan's native Korea during the 1940s.

democratic South—and this situation brought its own hardships. In 1950, war broke out between the two sides, with China assisting North Korea and American military forces allied with its southern counterpart. When the war ended in 1953, the division remained and became even more severe. All of these events would be well chronicled in a trilogy of books, autobiographical in nature, that began with her debut novel, *Year of Impossible Goodbyes*.

Took Her Own Advice

As a young woman, Choi journeyed to the United States to attend college. She studied French, art, and European history at Manhattanville College, outside of New York City, and eventually became a school-teacher in New York City for two decades. She also taught creative writing to high school students and urged them to draw upon their own life experiences; this allowed her to reveal to them some of the privations she herself had undergone. Her students, as well as her friends, were keenly interested in her life story, and encouraged her to write about it herself. It was only in the early 1980s, after her husband died, that Choi took a trip to Korea and considered writing something autobiographical in nature. A few relatives in Korea, however, considered this an unworthy goal. "When I asked my father to tell me about some of his experiences in jail, he said, 'Why do you want to bring back the devils long gone? Why do you want to make people cry?,'" Choi recalled in an interview with Lynda Brill Comerford in *Publishers Weekly*.

Back in the United States, Choi eventually wrote four hundred pages of a story. Her adult daughters and an editor at Houghton helped edit it, and the result was the first of her three tales about the life of young Sookan. *Year of Impossible Goodbyes*, published in 1991, opens in 1945 when Sookan is ten years old; the country is under Japanese occupation, and Korean language and culture are suppressed. Sookan lives in what would become North Korea, and her father, a member of the resistance movement against the detested Japanese, is in hiding. Her older brothers have been sent to labor camps, while her mother runs a sock factory.

Sadness, Loss Permeate Work

Sookan looks after her little brother, Inchun, and secretly studies Korean with her aged grandfather. In the voice of the ten–year–old girl, the family's hardships under occupation are matter–of–factly detailed. Abuse from Japanese soldiers is common, and anything valuable or aesthetically pleasing in the country is wantonly destroyed. Her grandfather, for instance, is discovered with a brush painting he made that contains a few forbidden Chinese characters; he is harshly treated by the Japanese soldiers, and then his favorite pine tree is cut down. "And when Choi ends this particular tale by describing her grandfather's eventual death, one feels a myriad of emotions ranging from anger to futility and helplessness," noted Laura L. Lent in a *Voice of Youth Advocates* review.

The enforced prostitution of young Korean women is also mentioned: if the sock–factory workers fail to meet the difficult production quotas, they risk being sent away for such purposes. "Choi describes the Japanese persecution in an even tone that makes it even more chilling," noted a *Kirkus Reviews* assessment of *Year of Impossible Goodbyes*. Sookan then details the brief period of respite, after Japan is defeated in World War II, that ends abruptly with the division of Korea. The North becomes a Communist nation, and its new leaders forge close ties with the Soviet Union. Russian soldiers then arrive to enforce the new regime, and an equal degree of repression follows. Meanwhile, Sookan's father has made it to South Korea and arranges an escape for his family. The guide hired for Sookan, Inchun, and their mother emerges as a double agent, however, and their lives are endangered. Her mother is detained at a Russian checkpoint as a result of this treachery, and Sookan and Inchun are left alone to make their way south through rain and mud with no food. Some kind adults help them past the searchlights and guard dogs at the border, and they crawl under a stopped train to make it to the other side in Choi's suspenseful conclusion. "We feel their dazed terror, their exhaustion and weakness, as well as the astonishing determination that somehow gets them across," wrote Hazel Rochman in a review for *Booklist*.

Reviews of *Year of Impossible Goodbyes* were unanimously positive. A *Publishers Weekly* critique called it "a sensitive and honest portrayal of amazing courage," while Betsy Hearne, writing for *Bulletin of the Center for Children's Books*, described it as a work that is "both artless and artful, both revealing of a complex culture and moving in its statement of human rights." Lent, in her *Voice of Youth Advocates* review, called Choi "a tremendous author. Her memoirs evoke one emotion after another."

Alter Ego Faces New Hardships

Choi was left with enough material from the editing process to write two more works based on her life. The sequel to *Year of Impossible Goodbyes* appeared in 1993 with the title, *Echoes of the White Giraffe*. Here, readers become engaged in the story of Sookan's new life in South Korea, but the setting also coincides with a new era of adversity: the Korean War, fought between 1950 and 1953. The South Korean capital of Seoul, where Sookan and her family now live, comes under enemy bombardment, and the family must once again flee. They arrive at a rural mountain village near Pusan, and are separated from their father and older brothers once more. The work tracks this difficult two–year period, and Sookan emerges as older, wiser, and as equally indomitable as before. Now a young teenager, she and her best friend build a school for refugees like themselves, so that they might continue

The Korean war provides an historical backdrop to the 1993 installment in Choi's trilogy, as Sookan experiences both romance and tragedy while her family avoids communist domination by living in a refugee camp in the mountains.

their studies. To get to her ramshackle home every day, she must climb a muddy mountainside that is barely passable, and there is little food. The Pusan residents shun the refugees, for they have lost nearly everything. Alleviating some of this hardship is a chaste romance that develops between Sookan and Junho, a fellow teen she has met in a church choir. Both are slated to religious orders, but find common ground through their love of traditional Korean poetry and music. They defy the dictates of that culture, however, by speaking to one another without a chaperone present, and are eventually found out.

Echoes of the White Giraffe takes its title from a poet in the story, Baik Rin, whose name means "white giraffe." Fatally afflicted with tuberculosis, he nevertheless wakes daily, near Sookan's shack, and shouts poetry from the mountaintop—"a good morning greeting to everyone exhorting the refugees to rise and shine because it is a brand new day," noted Lent in another *Voice of Youth Advocates* review. "His greeting reverberates across the mountains, and is a symbol of hope to many." Though some in Sookan's family are urging her to become a nun, she wants to study abroad. She battles to take a qualifying exam for a foreign study visa that is customarily only open to males, and succeeds. The family returns to Seoul after the war, but more tragedy befalls them with the death of their father.

The work concludes with Sookan's departure for college in America, a watershed moment in her already–eventful life. Rochman, reviewing the sequel for *Booklist,* faulted *Echoes of the White Giraffe* for being less compelling than its predecessor, but praised Choi for her skill in depicting "Sookan's struggle for independence within the restrictions of her society." Comparing it to the harsh political traumas depicted in *Year of Impossible Goodbyes,* a *Kirkus Reviews* critique called it a work that instead "examines war's sorrows and the courage and compromises of those growing up in its shadow." A *Publishers Weekly* review remarked that "Choi's graceful writing sews the disparate catastrophes into a satisfying, almost cathartic whole."

A New Beginning

Choi continued her autobiographical saga with her 1994 book, *Gathering of Pearls.* Sookan's life as a scholarship student and sole Korean resident of a Roman Catholic college for women outside of New York City in the 1950s is vividly depicted, as are her feelings of culture shock, homesickness, and excitement about her new life. Many reviewers found this a more introspective book, with far less political or wartime trauma plaguing its heroine, whose intelligence and strong sense of self emerge through her letters home. In the replies, however, Choi incorporates certain aspects of Korean culture—especially those regarding familial obligations—through the chiding tone of letters that she receives from her older sister, Theresa. It is expected that Sookan will return home and enter a religious order.

Meanwhile, Sookan's new American friends urge her to become more individualistic. A conflict emerges between the freewheeling American culture and her own ingrained sense of propriety. Her mother's letters are far more supportive than There-

In the final volume of Choi's semi–autobiographical trilogy, readers follow Sookan to New York as the young Korean woman enrolls in college and works hard to create a new life for herself and escape the poverty of her native land.

The Halmoni Books

Choi has also written three picture books for younger readers that also focus on Korean heritage and customs. For this they have earned a place in multicultural literature for children, and have been well received by educational and library professionals. The first of these, *Halmoni and the Picnic,* appeared in 1993 with Korean–themed illustrations by Karen Milone–Dugan. Halmoni, which means "grandmother" in Korean, is the focus of the work, which begins with her arrival in New York City to live with her family. Granddaughter Yunmi, who was born in America, is at first embarrassed by her very foreign elder. Halmoni is uneasy about learning a new language, and finds the adjustment to a new way of life—so far from home, and so late in her life—also difficult.

But Yunmi's friends feel bad for Halmoni, and they urge Yunmi to ask her to chaperone their class picnic in Central Park. Yunmi worries that others will laugh at her traditional–bound grandparent and the *kimbap* rolls, a Korean delicacy, that she brings to share, but instead Halmoni is a hit with the other children and even summons up the courage to test out her English. "Choi's text, sentimental but never saccharine, captures a jumble of emotions, both Halmoni's and Yunmi's," noted a *Publishers Weekly* review. Their saga was continued in 1997 with the publication of a second picture book, *Yunmi and Halmoni's Trip.* Here, the two journey to Seoul for a visit, and Yunmi experiences her own culture shock and uneasiness. Her travails in Korea, visiting family there, mirror Halmoni's earlier struggle in New York City. Moreover, Halmoni suddenly appears much happier, and now Yunmi worries she will decide to stay. "This book transcends Korean or English, speaking the universal language of the heart," declared Carolyn Phelan in her *Booklist* review.

In another book for younger readers issued in 1997, Choi chronicled a more universal dilemma with *The Best Older Sister.* Illustrated by Cornelius Van Wright and Ying–Hwa Hu, the simple plot follows the difficulty that another Korean child experiences with the arrival of a new baby brother. Sunhi is upset that their household has been so upended, but eventually comes to terms with her new role as Kiju's elder sibling and his important guide in life.

Choi still remembers her own place in her family, and the values they instilled in her. Her mother, she said in the interview with *Publishers Weekly* writer Comerford, passed along that strong sense of optimism and faith in the goodness of humankind. Even during the toughest moments of Korea's recent history, Choi said, "she made me feel that this was not the way things were all over the world."

sa's and provide Sookan with the courage to find a middle ground. "Admirers of the earlier works may find this pristine, cheery world rather dull," opined a *Publishers Weekly* review about the setting of Sookan's new life in America, but Roger Sutton, reviewing the title for *Bulletin of the Center for Children's Books,* described it as "an innocent picture of a 1950s college campus that younger teens will find engrossing." As the work nears a conclusion, another tragic event occurs: Sookan's mother dies, and she is not told until long after the funeral. Other reviewers found the same qualities here that had helped make the author's earlier works so engaging on a personal level. "The soul–searching quality of Choi's prose is at least as important to this beautiful novel as the plot line," opined Margaret Cole in a *School Library Journal* review.

If you enjoy the works of Sook Nyul Choi, you might want to check out the following books:

Margaret Chang, *In the Eye of War,* 1990.
Helie Lee, *Still Life with Rice,* 1996.
Marie G. Lee, *Saying Goodbye,* 1994.

■ Biographical and Critical Sources

BOOKS

Children's Literature Review, Volume 53, Gale, 1999, pp. 40–50.

PERIODICALS

Booklist, September 15, 1991, Hazel Rochman, review of *Year of Impossible Goodbyes,* pp. 140–141; April 1, 1993, Hazel Rochman, review of *Echoes of the White Giraffe,* p. 1424; August, 1993, Ilene Cooper, review of *Halmoni and the Picnic,* p. 2069; September 1, 1994, Hazel Rochman, review of *Gathering of Pearls,* pp. 33–34; May 1, 1997, April Judge, review of *The Best Older Sister,* p. 1504; September 15, 1997, Carolyn Phelan, review of *Yunmi and Halmoni's Trip,* p. 240.

Bulletin of the Center for Children's Books, October, 1991, Betsy Hearne, review of *Year of Impossible Goodbyes,* p. 34; June, 1993, Betsy Hearne, review of *Echoes of the White Giraffe,* p. 311; November, 1994, Roger Sutton, review of *Gathering of Pearls,* p. 83.

Horn Book, January/February, 1992, Martha V. Parravano, review of *Year of Impossible Goodbyes,* p. 69.

Kirkus Reviews, August 15, 1991, review of *Year of Impossible Goodbyes,* p. 1087; April 1, 1993, review of *Echoes of the White Giraffe,* p. 453; August 1, 1993, review of *Halmoni and the Picnic,* p. 999; August 15, 1994, review of *Gathering of Pearls,* p. 1123.

MultiCultural Review, December, 1993, Lyn Miller-Lachmann, review of *Echoes of the White Giraffe,* pp. 86, 88.

New York Times Book Review, Michael Shapiro, review of *Year of Impossible Goodbyes,* November 10, 1991, p. 42.

Publishers Weekly, June 28, 1991, review of *Year of Impossible Goodbyes,* p. 102; December 20, 1991, Lynda Brill Comerford, "Flying Starts: Sook Nyul Choi," pp. 22–23; March 22, 1993, review of *Echoes of the White Giraffe,* p. 80; July 5, 1993, review of *Halmoni and the Picnic,* pp. 71–72; August 8, 1994, review of *Gathering of Pearls,* p. 440; February 3, 1997, review of *The Best Older Sister,* p. 107.

Reading Teacher, September, 1994, "Finding Ourselves as People and as Learners," p. 64.

School Library Journal, October, 1991, Lydia Champlin, review of *Year of Impossible Goodbyes,* pp. 120, 122; May, 1993, Susan Middleton, review of *Echoes of the White Giraffe,* p. 104; November, 1993, Diane S. Marton, review of *Halmoni and the Picnic,* p. 78; October, 1994, Margaret Cole, review of *Gathering of Pearls,* p. 142; June, 1997, Gale W. Sherman, review of *The Best Older Sister,* p. 85; October, 1997, Margaret A. Chang, review of *Yunmi and Halmoni's Trip,* p. 89.

Voice of Youth Advocates, December, 1991, Laura L. Lent, review of *Year of Impossible Goodbyes,* pp. 307–308; August, 1993, Laura L. Lent, review of *Echoes of the White Giraffe,* p. 149; October, 1994, Sue Krumbein, review of *Gathering of Pearls,* p. 206.*

David Drake

■ Personal

Born September 24, 1945, in Dubuque, IA; son of Earle Charles (a maintenance foreman) and Maxine Dorothy (a homemaker; maiden name, Schneider) Drake; married Joanne Mary Kammiller (an office manager), June 5, 1967; children: Jonathan. *Education:* University of Iowa, B.A., 1967; Duke University Law School, J.D., 1972. *Politics:* "I vote."

■ Addresses

Home—P.O. Box 904, Chapel Hill, NC 27514. *Agent*—Pimlico Agency, P.O. Box 20447, Cherokee Station, New York, NY 10021.

■ Career

Town of Chapel Hill, NC, assistant town attorney, 1972–80; part–time bus driver, 1981; full–time freelance writer, 1981—. Partner of Carcosa

(publisher), 1972–94. *Military service:* U.S. Army, 1969–71; served in Vietnam and Cambodia (interrogator, 1970); became specialist 5.

■ Member

International Fortean Organization, Science Fiction Writers of America, Phi Beta Kappa.

■ Writings

The Dragon Lord, Putnam, 1979, revised edition, Tor Books, 1982.

Time Safari, Tor Books, 1982.

Birds of Prey, Baen, 1984.

From the Heart of Darkness (short horror stories, including "The Dancer in the Flames," "Dragons' Teeth," "Firefight," and "The Red Leer"), Tor Books, 1984.

The Forlorn Hope, Tor Books, 1984.

(With Karl Edward Wagner), *Killer,* Baen, 1984.

Bridgehead, Tor Books, 1986.

Ranks of Bronze, Baen, 1986.

Lacey and His Friends, Baen, 1986.

Dagger ("Thieves World" adventure series), Ace Books, 1988.

The Sea Hag, Baen, 1988.

Vettius and His Friends, Baen, 1989.

(Editor) *The Eternal City* (science fiction stories), Baen, 1990.

Surface Action, Berkley/Ace Books, 1990.

(With Jim Kjelgaard) *The Hunter Returns,* Baen, 1991.

The Jungle (sequel to Henry Kuttner's story, "Clash by Night," which is reprinted in this volume), Tor Books, 1991.

The Military Dimension (short stories), Baen, 1991.

Old Nathan, Baen, 1991.

Starliner, Baen, 1992.

The Square Deal, Tor Books, 1993.

The Voyage, Tor Books, 1993, Doherty Associates, 1994.

Igniting the Reaches, Ace Books, 1994.

Tyrannosaur, Tor Books, 1994.

Through the Breach, Ace Books, 1995.

All the Way to the Gallows, Baen, 1996.

Patriots, Tor Books, 1997.

Redliners, Baen Books, 1997.

Fireships, Ace Books, 1997.

With the Lightnings, Simon & Schuster, 1998.

(Editor, with Billie Sue Mosiman) *Armageddon,* Baen Books, 1998.

Lt. Leary, Commanding, Baen Books, 2000.

"LORD OF THE ISLES" SERIES

Lord of the Isles, Tor Books, 1997.

Queen of the Demons, Tor Books, 1999.

Servant of the Dragon, Tor Books, 1999.

"HAMMER'S SLAMMERS" SERIES

Hammer's Slammers (science fiction short stories), Ace Books, 1979.

Cross the Stars, Tor Books, 1984.

At Any Price (contains a novel and two short stories, "The Interrogation Team" and "Code–Name Feirefitz"), Baen, 1985.

Counting the Cost, Baen, 1987.

Rolling Hot, Baen, 1989.

The Warrior (contains a novel and a novella, "Liberty Port"), Baen, 1991.

The Sharp End, Baen, 1993.

"KELLY" SERIES

Skyripper, Tor Books, 1983.

Fortress, Tor Books, 1986.

"NORTHWORLD" SERIES

Northworld, Ace Books, 1990.

Vengeance, Ace Books, 1991.

Justice, Ace Books, 1992.

Northworld Trilogy, Baen Books, 1999.

WITH JANET MORRIS

Active Measures, Baen, 1985.

Kill Ratio, Ace Books, 1987.

Explorers in Hell, Baen, 1989.

Target, Ace Books, 1989.

ARC Riders, Warner Books, 1995.

ARC Riders: The Fourth Rome, Warner Books, 1996.

EDITOR WITH BILL FAWCETT

The Fleet (short stories), Ace, 1988.

The Fleet #2: Counter Attack (short stories), Ace, 1988.

The Fleet #3: Breakthrough (short stories), Ace, 1989.

The Fleet #4: Sworn Allies (short stories), Ace, 1990.

The Fleet #5: Total War (short stories), Ace, 1990.

The Fleet #6: Crisis (short stories), Ace, 1991.

Battlestation (short stories), Ace Books, 1992.

Battle Station—Book Two: Vanguard (short stories), Ace Books, 1993.

OTHER

Tank Lords (compilation), Baen Books, 1997.

The Butcher's Bill (compilation), Baen Books, 1998.

Caught in the Crossfire (compilation), Baen Books, 1998.

Author of "The Noble Savages," in *Blood and War,* created by Gordon R. Dickson, Baen, 1993. The "General Series," published by Baen and including *The Forge,* 1991, *The Hammer,* 1992, *The Anvil,* 1993, *The Steel,* 1993, *The Sword,* 1995, *The Chosen,* 1996, and *The Reformer,* 1999, were written by Steve Stirling based on Drake's outlines; *Cluster Command, An Honorable Defense,* and *The War Machine* were also written by other authors using Drake's outlines. *Team Yankee,* a graphic novel adapted by Drake, is based on a novel by Harold Coyle.

Eric Flint penned five novels in the "Belisarius" series, also outlined by Drake and published by Baen. They include: *In the Heart of Darkness,* 1998, *Oblique Approach,* 1998, *Destiny's Shield,* 1999, and *Fortune's Stroke,* 2000.

Drake is also the editor, with Sandra Miesel, of *A Separate Star* and *Heads to the Storm*, and of *Bluebloods, Men Hunting Things, Space Dreadnoughts, Space Gladiators*, and *Starhunters*. Contributor of more than one hundred stories to periodicals. Assistant editor of *Whispers*.

■ Sidelights

David Drake is perhaps best known for his "Hammer's Slammers" series, which, according to *Booklist* critic Roland Green in a review of *The Warrior*, offers "some of the best in military science fiction." In addition to this sub–genre, Drake has written fantasy novels and other types of science fiction. His experience in Vietnam, his penchant for fantasy and the supernatural, and his extensive knowledge of history, literature, and folklore generate science fiction, fantasies, thrillers, and militaristic stories and novels.

One ever–present element in Drake's works, no matter the sub–genre, is graphic, and often gruesome, violence. "Drake can write. There's no doubt about that," wrote *Analog Science Fiction/Science Fact* critic Tom Easton in a review of *The Forlorn Hope*. "But Oh! He loves the gore." While some critics have lamented this "gore," a critic for *Science Fiction Review* explained in a review of *At Any Price* that it has a purpose: Drake "does not like 'easy' TV deaths . . . which he suspects teach kids that killing is easy and sanitary." Drake himself once expounded about the message he would like to send his readers. "If I were good enough, I would be able to explain to people who haven't been there why wars are so horrible. I'm afraid that the only people who really understand are the veterans, though."

Unforgettable Stint in Vietnam

Born in 1945, Drake grew up in Iowa, and majored in history and Latin in college. A fan of science fiction literature from his early years, he sold his first short story in 1966. A year later, he graduated from the University of Iowa and married, but after enrolling in law school at Duke University in North Carolina, he was drafted into the U.S. Army during the Vietnam War. He was then trained for military intelligence and in the Vietnamese language, and sent to the war–torn southeast Asian country to interrogate prisoners of war. Though Drake had been a military history buff from an early age, his experiences in Vietnam forever humanized the concept of warfare for him, which he would later seek to impart through his fiction.

Arthur of Britain vows to destroy his Saxon foes through the power of a fiery dragon, and two mercenaries aid his efforts by seeking the key to harnessing the dragon's fury in Drake's first novel, published in 1979.

Drake returned to civilian life, began a family, and became an attorney for the city of Chapel Hill, North Carolina. He began writing in earnest in 1980, after finding success with two books the previous year—*The Dragon Lord* and *Hammer's Slammers*. As Drake once recalled: "I started writing in high school because I liked to read and one of my teachers was himself a published writer of mystery stories and articles. I sold my first stories as an undergraduate and continued to write as a hobby for many years thereafter. When I finally came to the conclusion that lawyering was going to kill me, I quit and drove a city bus while I got more serious about writing. To my amazement, my career took off immediately."

Timeless Good vs. Evil Conflict

Hammer's Slammers, the first novel in Drake's popular series, introduces Colonel Alois Hammer and his army of mercenaries, and established Drake as a writer in the military science fiction sub–genre. In *Cross the Stars*, the captain of the group, Don Slade,

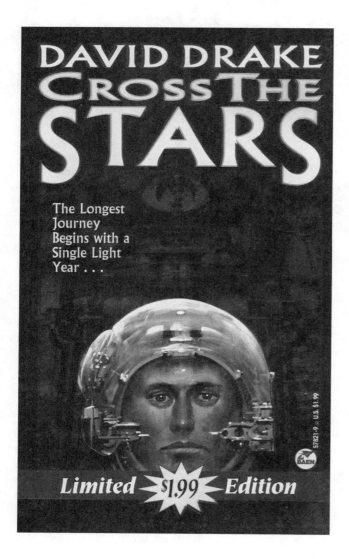

Colonel Alois Hammer and his mercenary band help Captain Don Slade return to his home planet in this 1984 sci–fi work modeled on the ancient quest of Ulysses.

attempts to return to his home planet. As Sally A. Lodge observed in *Publishers Weekly, Cross the Stars* is "patterned after" *The Odyssey*; Slade faces a series of obstacles, including a "future Circe" and Lotus–eaters, as he returns home. In *At Any Price*, Hammer's force is hired by humans to fight the indigenous sentient species living on a planet they are colonizing. *Rolling Hot* follows the group's efforts to rescue a city under siege through the perspective of a news reporter. *The Warrior* features Sergeant "Slick" Des Grieux, who won't follow orders he finds irrational. In the sixth "Hammer's Slammers" novel, *The Sharp End*, some of Hammer's mercenaries are hired out to fight on the violent, chaotic planet Cantilucca in the "sharp end" of the galaxy. *Publishers Weekly* critic Sybil S. Steinberg described *The Sharp End* as "a fast–paced space opera" with a "typically bloody climax."

The Dragon Lord, published in the same year as *Hammer's Slammers*, provides an example of Drake's work in the fantasy sub–genre. *The Dragon Lord* is a sword and sorcery story embedded in what a *Kirkus Reviews* critic called a "quasi–historical Arthurian setting." The barbarian protagonists, Mael and Starkad, join King Arthur's men and help Merlin conjure up a dragon to defeat the Saxons. According to Barbara A. Bannon, a reviewer for *Publishers Weekly*, Drake poses "a debunked view of Arthur and his men" and presents them as "unpleasant." When the dragon gets out of control and threatens to devour the world, it is up to Mael, Starkad, and a witch named Veleda, instead of Arthur and his men, to kill it. While *Booklist* critic Roland Green questioned Drake's decision to use the Arthurian background, he concluded that *The Dragon Lord* is "well–researched" and "fast–moving."

Echoes of Cold War

Skyripper, set in a fictional world of the 1960s, creates a situation in which Soviet physicist Emil Vlasov has designed an anti–missile particle beam that can only be powered with technology the United States possesses. When Vlasov hears voices warning of an impending alien invasion, he realizes that he must get his weapon to U.S. physicists to make it an effective defense against the aliens. While the U.S. government is not worried about alien invasions, it wants the weapon anyway, and reactivates a bitter ex–NSA agent, Tom Kelly, to help Vlasov defect. As he does, Kelly develops a relationship with the ambassador's intelligent and cunning wife. Although, as Algis Budrys noted in *Fantasy & Science Fiction*, the story "goes along nicely with the premise" that Vlasov's preoccupation with the idea of an alien invasion is mere paranoia, the contents

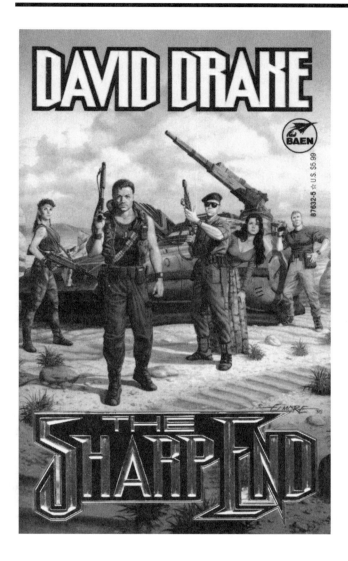

In the 1993 installment of Drake's "Hammer's Slammers" series, a coed team of specialized mercenaries from the Frisian Defense Force is sent to battle warring gangs on the planet Cantilucca ... with typically gruesome results.

of the last page testify otherwise. *Armchair Detective* contributor Ira Hale Blackman asserted that "*Skyripper* is a military espionage thriller masquerading as science fiction," but he found "this hybrid an entertaining change."

Fortress continues Kelly's story in another 1965 in which President John F. Kennedy was not assassinated. In this 1965, the president has plans for the construction of Fortress, a space station defended by lasers. When the body of Kelly's friend, a Kurdish rebel, is found with the corpse of an alien

in Turkey, Kelly is sent to investigate. Through a belly–dancing woman, Kelly learns that some Nazis, who crafted a flying saucer, have been hiding in Antarctica since the end of World War II and are planning to gain control of the Earth. Before Kelly can stop them, the Nazis capture Fortress with the fleet of saucers they have assembled. With the help of the aliens, Kelly recaptures Fortress. Along with "plenty of tough talk" and "detailed descriptions of gore," wrote Steinberg in *Publishers Weekly*, Drake provides readers with "a bloody climax on Fortress." According to Randy Brough in *Voice of Youth Advocates*, *Fortress* is a "brutally effective . . . blunt, visceral novel."

Lawyer–turned–master of military sci–fi Drake collects five shorter works of fiction spanning 1978 through 1998 in a compilation that features non–stop firepower.

A Militaristic Novel with Pacifist Overtones

The planet Northworld, secured by Colonel North for colonization, is a gateway to nine very different worlds in *Northworld,* the first story in a series with the same name that began in 1990. When Commissioner Nils Hansen suspects North in the theft of the planet, he travels to Northworld to investigate. Once on Northworld, Hansen inadvertently enters a peace–loving world, and his weapons disintegrate. Later, after he finds himself in a land of war and violence, he survives and continues his quest for the missing officer North. As *Publishers Weekly* reviewer Penny Kaganoff pointed out, "literary allusions" from "Norse saga, Greek myth, and Arthu-rian legend" appear throughout *Northworld;* the inclusion of these allusions, in Green's opinion in *Booklist,* justify the use of the term "Mythic military SF" to describe the novel.

As a critic for *Kirkus Reviews* noted, Drake draws on the tale of "Jason and the Argonauts' expedition to recover the Golden Fleece" in *The Voyage.* Living in the same universe found in the "Hammer's Slammers" series, a young mercenary, Ned Slade, joins Captain Lissea Doorman in an effort to regain her leadership on Telaria. As they rush to recover a stolen space capsule and battle an assortment of enemies, Slade, Doorman, and the rest of the crew of the *Swift* sadly watch the destruction of various planets. While some critics appreciated the fast action and realism of *The Voyage,* Sybil Steinberg asserted in *Publishers Weekly* that Drake has created something more with this novel—"that most elusive of hybrids"—"an SF adventure with a conscience."

Fascination with Another Drake

Drake embarked upon another epic science–fiction, space–based saga, with echoes of historical reality, beginning with the 1994 title *Igniting the Reaches.* The plot begins at a future date in which the Earth, part of an imperialist–minded "Federation," battles Venus for control of the galaxy. A collapse has brought on a dire economic depression, and billions have died. Both Venus and Earth need resources that include alien slaves and rare microchips factories; they battle one another in the series to control trade routes. From Venus, space explorers Stephen Gregg and Piet Ricimer search for economic opportunity much in the same fashion that Sir Francis Drake circumnavigated the globe on behalf of Elizabeth I of England. "The story," opined a *Publishers Weekly* review, "evokes both the uncertainty of exploration and its questionable morality." *Through the Breach* continued this saga, with Venus battling the Federation Empire. Daringly, Piet takes his ship to the Breach of the title, from which no vessel has ever returned. "Typical militaristic SF from an author who knows how to write it," remarked John O. Christensen in *Voice of Youth Advocates.* In *Fireships,* published in 1996, a fresh character, Sal Blythe, commands her own space vessel, and romance ensues between her and Stephen Gregg. An historic battle, much like the 1588 naval conflict between the Spanish Armada and the English fleet that was victoriously commanded by the adventurer Drake, brings the series to a close.

Colonel Hammer marshals his hand–picked team of crack mercenaries through four short stories and several longer works in Drake's 1998 science fiction collection.

Drake has written several books with co–author Janet Morris, beginning with 1985's *Active Measures* and *Explorers in Hell*, published in 1989. For *Target,* a 1995 collaboration, they created a time–travel story involving an "Anti–Revisionist Command" run by a group of soldiers in the twenty–sixth century. Their century–traversing device, however, can only be used to reconstruct good deeds. Judith H. Silverman, reviewing *ARC Riders,* the next book in the series, in *Kliatt,* termed it "fast–moving and exciting, if difficult."

A sequel, *ARC Riders: The Fourth Rome,* appeared in 1996. The plot is a complex one, again involving time–travel and attempts to alter the course of history. Someone has used the time machine to send subjects back to 9 CE with a mission to establish a Fourth Roman Empire centered in Russia. One half of the ARC team is sent to Rome to do battle with the German threat, but must use ancient weapons, and the others arrive in Moscow in 1992 to solve the crisis. There they come to realize that another group of revisionists, working far past their own twenty–sixth century present, is involved in the situation. "The concept in this series is fascinating— that futuristic time travel technology can be used to revise history," observed Linda Roberts, reviewing it for *Voice of Youth Advocates.* Though she found some of the descriptions of technology hard to follow, Roberts noted that "halfway through the book, the pace picks up and provides lots of suspense and fighting action."

More Time Travel

Drake returned to the enduring Arthurian saga with his 1997 book *Lord of the Isles.* This was the first title in a series involving the fall of the Isles, which sends the sorceress Tenoctris a thousand years into the future. There she meets a peasant scholar, Garric, who is haunted by the ghost of the last king of Isles. "The cast is large and well drawn, the pacing brisk, the world building outstanding," assessed the critic Green in *Booklist.* The story continues in *Queen of the Demons,* with Garric and friends traveling to fulfill their destiny—the revival of the kingdom—but waylaid by four subplots. Among his allies is Zahag, a talking ape, and opposing the plan is King Valence, whose involvement in sorcery is causing him to lose his grip on power. Green, reviewing it for *Booklist,* termed this entry "eminently worth reading."

Servant of the Dragon finds Garric developing a romantic interest in a woman named Liane and finding guidance from an ancestor on his mission to destroy a dangerous bridge that connects dimensions.

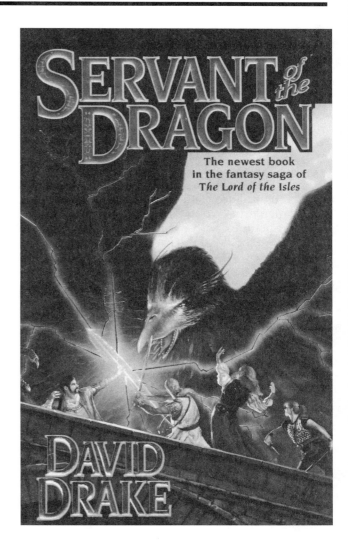

In the 1999 sequel to *Lord of the Isles* and *Queen of Demons,* Drake returns readers to his fantasy world of warring kingdoms and follows one group in their quest for the one true overlord capable of bringing peace to the Isles.

A warrior bird also keeps watch over Garric's allies as well. "As usual with Drake, the nonhuman characters are outstanding," asserted a *Publishers Weekly* review.

In the late 1990s, Drake wrote outlines for the "Belisarius" series that was then penned by Eric Flint. These titles are *In the Heart of Darkness, Oblique Approach,* and *Destiny's Shield.* Their story revolves around an invasion, in 531 CE, of Persia by an army from India. Aide is the name of a special crystal used by a Roman general, Belisarius, that allows him to see into the future. His wife, Antonina, also plays an integral role, as does the child emperor, Photius. Land and sea battles are fought with advanced technology thanks to Aide. "The battle scenes and strategies are as expert as expected in a book with Drake's name on it," stated a *Publishers Weekly* review.

A Prolific Writer

Some of Drake's short stories, previously published in various science fiction and fantasy magazines, are available in two collections. *From the Heart of Darkness* features horror stories set in America, ancient Rome, colonial Africa, and Vietnam. In this collection, as Green noted, Drake proves himself a "master of grisly detail," using his knowledge of military history and Vietnam experiences "effectively." Yet, as *Science Fiction & Fantasy Review* contributor Michael E. Stamm warned, these stories are not "for the squeamish."

Eleven of Drake's military stories are collected in *The Military Dimension*. Drake notes in the foreword to this volume that all of these stories, including those not set in Vietnam, recall his war–time experience in that country. Most of the stories also involve the supernatural. At essence, according to Tom Pearson in a *Voice of Youth Advocates* review, the stories are about "soldiers making the best of a bad situation." In Pearson's opinion, these stories provide "well–done examples of the militaristic science fiction currently so popular."

If you enjoy the works of David Drake, you might want to check out the following books:

Lois McMaster Bujold, *The Vor Game*, 1990.
C. J. Cherryh, *The Pride of Chanur*, 1982.
George R. R. Martin, *A Game of Thrones*, 1996.
Michael Moorcock, *The Runestaff*, 1977.
Jerry Pournelle, *A Spaceship for the King*, 1973.

Drake once revealed his method for continuously producing high quality works: "I get up in the morning, read the paper, and start writing. Every day until the current project is done. When I worked for [Chapel Hill] as an attorney, nobody asked me if I felt inspired to rewrite the dog ordinance or whatever. They expected the work to be done, and done right, and done in time for the Council meeting. Now that I'm working for myself, my standards are the same."

■ Biographical and Critical Sources

BOOKS

Encyclopedia of Science Fiction, edited by John Clute and Peter Nicholls, St. Martin's Press, 1993, pp. 223–224.
Twentieth–Century Science Fiction Writers, third edition, edited by Noelle Watson and Paul E. Schellinger, St. James Press, 1991.

PERIODICALS

Analog: Science Fiction/Science Fact, December, 1983, Tom Easton, review of *Skyripper*, pp. 163–64; 1984, Tom Easton, review of *The Forlorn Hope*, p. 148; October, 1989, p. 177.
Armchair Detective, fall, 1986, Ira Hale Blackman, review of *Skyripper*, p. 430.
Booklist, November 1, 1979, Roland Green, review of *The Dragon Lord*, p. 430; January 1, 1984, Roland Green, review of *From the Heart of Darkness*, p. 666; August, 1988, p. 1894; April 1, 1990, Roland Green, review of *Northworld*, p. 1532; April 15, 1991, Roland Green, review of *The Warrior*, p. 1627; February 15, 1993, Roland Green, review of *Vanguard: Battlestation II*, p. 1041; January 1, 1994, Roland Green, review of *The Voyage*, pp. 810–811; August, 1997, Roland Green, review of *Lord of the Isles*, p. 1886; May 15, 1998, Roland Green, review of *With the Lightnings*, pp. 1600–1601; July, 1998, Roland Green, review of *Caught in the Crossfire*, p. 1867; August, 1998, Roland Green, review of *Queen of the Demons*, p. 1978.
Fantasy & Science Fiction, October, 1983, Algis Budrys, review of *Skyripper*, p. 27.
Fantasy Review, January, 1985, p. 12.
Kirkus Reviews, July 15, 1979, review of *The Dragon Lord*, p. 824; November 15, 1986, p. 1687; November 15, 1993, review of *The Voyage*, p. 1425; February 1, 1994, p. 102; April 15, 1996, review of *Fireships*, p. 568.
Kliatt, May, 1994, Jody K. Hanson, review of *Tyrannosaur*, pp. 14–15; November, 1995, Judith H. Silverman, review of *ARC Riders*, pp. 14–15; January, 1998, Susan Cromby, review of *Redliners*, p. 14;

July, 1998, Katherine E. Gillen, review of *An Oblique Approach,* p. 19; January, 1999, Bette D. Ammon, review of *Lord of the Isles* and *Queen of Demons,* p. 46.

Library Journal, April 15, 1994, Jackie Cassada, review of *Igniting the Reaches,* p. 117; June 15, 1998, Jackie Cassada, review of *With the Lightnings,* p. 111; July, 1999, Jackie Cassada, review of *Destiny's Shield,* p. 143.

Locus, October, 1989, p. 48; December, 1992, p. 52.

Publishers Weekly, July 9, 1979, Barbara A. Bannon, review of *The Dragon Lord,* p. 102; November 2, 1984, Sally A. Lodge, review of *Cross the Stars,* p. 75; November 14, 1986, Sybil S. Steinberg, review of *Fortress,* p. 54; March 16, 1990, Penny Kaganoff, review of *Northworld,* p. 66; September 13, 1993, Sybil S. Steinberg, review of *The Sharp End,* p. 98; November 29, 1993, Sybil S. Steinberg, review of *The Voyage,* p. 57; February 28, 1994, review of *Igniting the Reaches,* p. 76; May 27, 1996, review of *Fireships,* p. 70; March 29, 1999, review of *The Reformer,* p. 97; June 21, 1999, review of *Destiny's Shield,* p. 61; August 30, 1999, review of *Servant of the Dragon,* p. 59.

Science Fiction & Fantasy Review, April, 1984, Michael E. Stamm, review of *From the Heart of Darkness,* p. 26.

Science Fiction Chronicle, May, 1993, p. 34.

Science Fiction Review, summer, 1986, review of *At Any Price,* pp. 47–48.

Voice of Youth Advocates, June, 1987, Randy Brough, review of *Fortress,* p. 89; August, 1989, p. 164; February, 1992, Tom Pearson, review of *The Military Dimension,* p. 381; December, 1992, Suzi Smith, review of *Battlestation,* p. 290; February, 1993, John Callahan, review of *Starliner,* p. 348; June, 1993, Paula Lewis, review of *Vanguard: Battlestation II,* p. 98; October, 1995, John O. Christensen, review of *Through the Breach,* p. 231; December, 1996, Linda Roberts, review of *ARC Riders: The Fourth Rome,* p. 278; April, 1997, William J. White, review of *Fireships,* p. 41; February, 1998, Rebecca Barnhouse, review of *Lord of the Isles,* p. 392.

ON—LINE

David Drake's Official Home Page, located at http://www.david–drake.com (May 7, 2000).

Jean Ferris

ern California Council on Literature for Children and Young People, San Diego Zoological Society.

■ Personal

Born January 24, 1939, in Fort Leavenworth, KS; daughter of Jack W. (an army officer/surgeon) and Jessie (Wickham) Schwartz; married Alfred G. Ferris (an attorney), September 8, 1962; children: Kerry Ordway, Gillian Anne. *Education:* Stanford University, B.A., 1961, M.A., 1962. *Hobbies and other interests:* Travel, reading, movies, and theatre.

■ Addresses

Home—2278 San Juan Rd., San Diego, CA 92103.

■ Career

Writer, 1977—. Veterans Administration Hospital, San Francisco, CA, clinical audiologist, 1962–63; San Diego Speech and Hearing Association, San Diego, CA, clinical audiologist, 1963–64; clinical audiologist in a doctor's office in San Diego, 1975–76; secretary and office assistant in San Diego, 1979–84.

■ Member

Society of Children's Book Writers and Illustrators, Authors Guild, Author's League of America, South-

■ Awards, Honors

Grants from the Society of Children's Book Writers, 1984, for *Invincible Summer,* and 1987, for *Across the Grain;* Outstanding Work of Fiction for Young Adults, Southern California Council on Literature for Children and Young People, Best Books for Young Adults, American Library Association (ALA), Best Books, *School Library Journal,* and Editor's Choice, *Booklist,* all 1987, all for *Invincible Summer;* Young Adults Choice, International Reading Association, 1991, Virginia Young Reader's Award nomination, 1992–93, and Iowa Teen Award nomination, 1992–93, all for *Looking for Home;* Best Books for Young Adults, ALA, 1992, and California Young Reader's Medal nomination, 1992–93, both for *Across the Grain;* Utah Children's Book Award nomination and South Carolina Young Adult Book Award nomination, both 1994–95, both for *Relative Strangers;* Junior Literary Guild selection, 1995, for *Signs of Life;* Oklahoma Sequoyah Book Award nomination, Junior Literary Guild selection, 1996, Young Adult Reading List selection, Texas Library Association, 1997–98, and Virginia Young Reader's Award nomination, 1998–99, all for *All That Glitters;* National Book Award nomination, National Book Foundation, 1998, Best Books for Young Adults, ALA, 1999, and Quick Pick for Young Adults, ALA, 1999, all for *Love among the Walnuts;* Notable Children's Trade

Book in the Field of Social Studies, National Council for the Social Studies–Children's Book Council, and Quick Pick for Young Adults, ALA, both 1999, both for *Bad*.

■ Writings

NOVELS; FOR YOUNG ADULTS

Amen, Moses Gardenia, Farrar, Straus, 1983.
The Stainless Steel Rule, Farrar, Straus, 1986.
Invincible Summer, Farrar, Straus, 1987.
Looking for Home, Farrar, Straus, 1988.
Across the Grain, Farrar, Straus, 1990.
Relative Strangers, Farrar, Straus, 1993.
Signs of Life, Farrar, Straus, 1995.
All That Glitters, Farrar, Straus, 1996.
Bad, Farrar, Straus, 1998.
Love among the Walnuts, Harcourt, 1998.
Eight Seconds, Harcourt, 2000.

NOVELS; "AMERICAN DREAMS" SERIES

Into the Wind, Avon, 1996.
Song of the Sea, Avon, 1996.
Weather the Storm, Avon, 1996.

■ Sidelights

The author of several popular novels for young adult readers, Jean Ferris combines likeable characters, realistic teen problems, and her optimistic outlook to create fiction that has been praised as well–written and engaging. In novels that include *Invincible Summer, Across the Grain,* and *Signs of Life,* Ferris portrays teen feelings "convincingly and movingly," "without providing pat resolutions to problems," according to a *Publishers Weekly* commentator. In addition to her novels featuring modern teens, Ferris has also written several installments in Avon's "American Dreams" series, featuring American privateer Raider Lyons and the beautiful Rosie, and their budding nineteenth–century romance set against a series of adventures, including a voyage to the Yucatan.

Ferris's first novel, *Amen, Moses Gardenia,* was inspired by the attempted suicides of two teens who were schoolmates of her own children. "I began to wonder how many other kids were feeling this

During their tragically short romance, Robin and Rick learn the value of each and every day as they help each other battle leukemia, in Ferris's multi–award–winning 1987 novel.

way," the author recalled, "and why a young person would decide that there would never be anything worth living for in the long future. I became—and remain—deeply concerned about teenage depression, and wrote *Amen, Moses Gardenia* to give some hope and humor to kids who feel depressed and frightened enough to contemplate ending their lives. There is so much time ahead for situations to change; there is so much reason for hope. And *Amen, Moses Gardenia* has a happy ending."

In the novel, the stresses of living with an alcoholic mom and a workaholic dad combine to make tenth–

grader Farrell feel like an outsider. The one confidante Farrell has is her housekeeper, the upbeat Earl Mae. Encouraged to join a high school hiking club, Farrell meets and falls for Ted Kittredge, one of the most popular boys in school. Unsure of both herself and her relationship with Ted, Farrell plans to attempt suicide by taking sleeping pills before she is stopped by a school guidance counselor. While some reviewers noted that the plot and characters were of average YA novel standards, *Booklist* contributor Sally Estes commented in her review of *Amen, Moses Gardenia*, that Farrell "has vitality and credibility, and the relationship between Farrell and Earl Mae is satisfyingly affecting."

"I Try to Be That Sympathetic Grown–Up"

Ferris believes that every young person needs at least one other person who loves them unconditionally, "who is absolutely bonkers about him or her." Such a person isn't always a parent, or even a family member. In *Amen, Moses Gardenia,* for example, Earl Mae is cast as that special person. "My own adolescent years haven't dimmed a bit in my memory," the novelist once explained. "I remember all the things that gave me pain and pleasure, all the things that worried and confused me—and how much I wished I had a sympathetic grown–up I could talk to. Through my books I try to be that sympathetic grown–up for today's teenagers who have things to be concerned about that could never even have occurred to my own teenage mind. Times of change can be the most difficult times—yet, in retrospect, often times of great growth and learning, too. And adolescence is nothing if not a time of change. I'm interested in these changes—in the choices we make, the reasons for these choices, and what we can do to recover from the results of bad choices. This is where I find the ideas for my books."

In her second novel, *The Stainless Steel Rule*, Ferris again focuses on teen friendships during the high school years. Mary, Fran, and Kitty are best friends whose relationship is tested after Mary falls for handsome but controlling Nick. Nick's personality and Mary's increasing willingness to give in to him cause Mary to withdraw from Fran and Kitty after she senses her friends' discomfort with her boyfriend. Meanwhile, the couple's romantic relationship ultimately results in tragedy after Nick convinces Mary—an insulin–dependent diabetic—that she does not need to take insulin to control her condition. Only after Mary sinks into a diabetic coma and then recovers does she realize that her friends had good intentions in trying to break her relationship with Nick. Calling the novel "several cuts above" Ferris's first effort, Audrey B. Eaglen noted in *School Library Journal* that "the plot [of *The Stainless Steel Rule*] is strong, the characters well portrayed, and the denouement is completely believable." A *Publishers Weekly* contributor agreed, calling the novel "taut" and "compelling . . . with moments of high humor." *Booklist* reviewer Hazel Rochman maintained that the story, narrated by Kitty, is "told . . . with warmth and humor."

A life–threatening illness also figures in *Invincible Summer,* published in 1987. Living in a Midwest farming community, Rick and his seventeen–year–old girlfriend, Robin, both have leukemia, and Rick is facing his second series of chemotherapy treatments. Together, the two teens attempt to gain as much life experience as they can, and provide comfort and support as they confront the fact that

In Ferris's 1996 novel, sixteen–year–old Brian rebuilds his fractured relationship with his dad during a summer scuba–diving adventure in the Florida Keys.

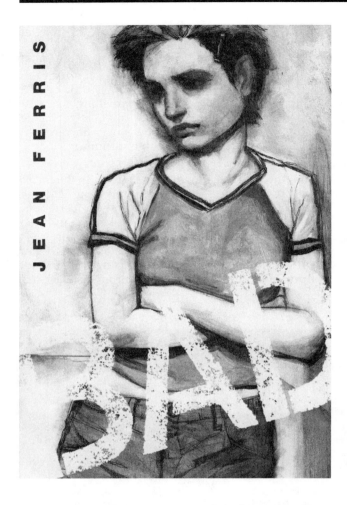

JEAN FERRIS

A crime spree puts sixteen–year–old Dallas in a correctional facility, where she rethinks her "bad girl" attitude and eventually decides to deal with her problems in the author's 1998 work.

from her father, whom she has rarely seen: a two–week trip to Europe, where she meets his new wife and stepdaughter. The process by which Berkeley copes with her mixed emotions about her father and learns to get along with her new family is woven into "an unusually likable and thought–provoking novel," according to a *Kirkus Reviews* critic. In *Signs of Life,* high school senior Hannah and her parents travel to France in the hopes that fresh surroundings will help the family recover from the tragic death of Hannah's twin sister. In France, Hannah meets a gypsy juggler who steals her heart and helps her to tap her inner strength. While some reviewers noted that portions of the novel bordered on melodrama, a *Publishers Weekly* contributor maintained that *Signs of Life* "celebrates the regenerating power of love and the resiliency of the spirit."

Across the Grain is Ferris's first novel to feature a male protagonist. In the wake of his father's disappearance and his mother's death, seventeen–year–old Will is forced to move with his older sister, Paige, to California to find work. Obtaining employment as the manager of a small restaurant in the California desert, Paige puts her brother to work, and the two become friendly with a host of regular customers, including an anthropologist and her daughter, and Sam, a retired man who becomes Will's surrogate father. Praising Ferris for her well–drawn settings and for developing main characters in a way that is "strong, perceptive yet subtle," *School Library Journal* contributor Libby K. White concluded that "the author makes readers care about likable, earnest Will and his friends." Reviewer Gale Ashe also offered a favorable assessment of *Across the Grain*, noting in *Voice of Youth Advocates* that Ferris's novel "is not just another coming–of–age story, but a story of love and friendship."

Rick has little time left to live. Praising Ferris's dialogue, Zena Sutherland of the *Bulletin of the Center for Children's Books* noted that *Invincible Summer* is "not just a compassionate case history, but a good story." Sutherland's enthusiasm was shared by *School Library Journal* contributor Merilyn S. Burrington, who commented that the novel's ending "affirms life with such intensity that it will leave readers appreciating the present moment more fully."

European Adventures

Several of Ferris's novels feature protagonists travelling overseas. In *Relative Strangers,* seventeen–year–old Berkeley receives a special graduation gift

Coming–of–Age Adventure

All That Glitters is another Ferris novel centering on a young man's emotional growth. In this work, Brian braces himself for a summer with his dad, who lives in the Florida Keys. Now sixteen, Brian has a tense relationship with his father, but when some neighbors invite the pair to join them on a scuba diving expedition to explore the wreckage of a Spanish treasure ship, father and son begin to mend their relationship. Although some reviewers felt that the novel fell below Ferris's usual high standards, Deborah Stevenson of the *Bulletin of the Center for Children's Books* commended the author's "good, solid writ[ing]," and *Voice of Youth Advocates* contributor Penny Blubaugh called *All That Glitters* "a pleasant read with a few moments of excitement and some thought–provoking comments on race and identity." Commending Ferris for addressing issues of race and the importance of strong male role models, *School Library Journal* contributor Bruce Anne Shook concluded that *All That Glitters* "is a good YA problem novel with a nice mix of suspense and adventure thrown in for good measure."

In order to realistically portray the setting of her next novel for teens, *Bad*, Ferris visited a correctional facility for teens and interviewed the young women who were being confined there. The insight she gained helped her create *Bad*'s protagonist, sixteen–year–old Dallas, who finds herself in a juvenile–detention facility after the petty crimes she and her friends commit escalate one night into the armed robbery of a convenience store. Her friends manage to flee, and Dallas is caught with a weapon by police. A judge offers her six months of probation, but her father tells the court she has become unmanageable and refuses to allow her to return home.

At the Girls' Rehabilitation Center, Dallas is forced to come to terms with several issues, including the loss of her mother, while adjusting to the harsh rules and routine. She finds herself among much tougher girls than she has ever met, including prostitutes and drug dealers. Guards are often vicious, but there are also sympathetic counselors who help teens like Dallas understand that they themselves are not "bad," but may have been unable to make anything but bad decisions in the past. For the first time in her life, Dallas finds encouragement and support, and learns how to build more solid friendships with members of her peer group. Ferris's "willingness to explore the issues these girls face, as well as her refusal to settle for easy answers and sugarcoated endings, makes for a thoughtful novel," asserted a *Publishers Weekly* review. A *Bulletin of the Center for Children's Books* critique predicted that the work will find a readership among "those who enjoy melodramas with a gloss of respectability."

Some Comic Relief

In her 1999 young–adult novel, *Love among the Walnuts,* Ferris entered into a far different genre than in her previous books—comedy. Sandy, whose life has been full of luxury but rather cosseted on the whole, suddenly finds himself in a trying situation when a pair of malicious uncles attempt to poison his parents and several others one day at Sandy's remote country estate. While the victims are in a coma from the drug, the butler works to find an antidote as

Named a 1999 Best Book for Young Adults by the American Library Association, Ferris's first comic novel features spoiled teen Sandy as he discovers trouble brewing on his family's country estate.

they "rest" in a nearby convalescent home, Walnut Manor. A host of other comical, but sympathetic characters in both homes help bring the plot to a satisfying conclusion—including a nurse at Walnut Manor, Sunny, who intrigues Sandy. "Dripping with charm but never cloying," was Elaine McGuire's description of *Love among the Walnuts* in her *Voice of Youth Advocates* review. A *Horn Book* assessment from Anne St. John praised Ferris for creating a likable protagonist in Sandy. "His emotional responses and internal struggles will ring true with teenagers who are coming of age in a time of turmoil," St. John remarked.

Ferris continues to be concerned about the future of her young readers. "I try, in my work, to give them hope of the future and some guideposts for achieving a satisfying life," she once remarked, "even when circumstances seem bleak and/or dismaying!" She is also fascinated by the adolescent years because, as she noted, "There's so much going on then, so many emotional changes, decisions for the future, social problems. I remember my own teenage years vividly and they weren't all beer and skittles."

If you enjoy the works of Jean Ferris, you might want to check out the following books and films:

Lou Kassem, *The Innkeeper's Daughter,* 1996.
Robert Newton Peck, *Arly's Run,* 1991.
Adam Rapp, *The Buffalo Tree,* 1997.
To Kill a Mockingbird, an Academy Award–winning film, 1962.

The mother of two grown daughters, Ferris makes her home in San Diego, California with her husband, an attorney, and a fat orange cat. "I feel certain that I will continue to write for young people because I care so much about them and find them so brave and complex," she asserted. "My first love will always be writing for kids. They're great."

■ Biographical and Critical Sources

PERIODICALS

Booklist, October 1, 1983, Sally Estes, review of *Amen, Moses Gardenia,* p. 233; April 15, 1986, Hazel Rochman, review of *The Stainless Steel Rule,* p. 1202; July, 1995, p. 1874; February 15, 1996, p. 1004; October 1, 1998, p. 324.

Bulletin of the Center for Children's Books, July–August, 1987, Zena Sutherland, review of *Invincible Summer,* p. 206; July–August, 1989, p. 274; February, 1991, p. 140; March, 1996, Deborah Stevenson, review of *All That Glitters,* p. 224; December, 1998, review of *Bad,* p. 129.

Horn Book, January, 1999, Anne St. John, review of *Love among the Walnuts,* p. 60, review of *Bad,* p. 59.

Kirkus Reviews, June 1, 1989, p. 835; July 15, 1993, review of *Relative Strangers,* p. 933; September 1, 1998.

Publishers Weekly, April 25, 1986, review of *The Stainless Steel Rule,* p. 80; October 26, 1990, review of *Across the Grain,* pp. 70–71; July 12, 1993, p. 81; March 27, 1995, review of *Signs of Life,* p. 86; April 1, 1996, p. 77; July 13, 1998, review of *Love among the Walnuts,* pp. 78–79; October 12, 1998, review of *Bad,* p. 78; November 13, 2000, review of *Eight Seconds,,* p. 105.

School Library Journal, May, 1986, Audrey B. Eaglen, review of *The Stainless Steel Rule,* p. 102; August, 1987, Merilyn S. Burrington, review of *Invincible Summer,* p. 93; December, 1990, Libby K. White, review of *Across the Grain,* p. 121; September, 1993, p. 248; April, 1995, p. 150; March, 1996, Bruce Anne Shook, review of *All That Glitters,* p. 218; August, 1998, Connie Tyrrell Burns, review of *Love among the Walnuts,* p. 163; January, 2001, Francisca Goldsmith, review of *Eight Seconds,* p. 130.

Voice of Youth Advocates, February, 1991, Gail Ashe, review of *Across the Grain,* p. 350; June, 1996, Penny Blubaugh, review of *All That Glitters,* p. 95; October, 1996, p. 208; April, 1997, p. 21; February, 1999, Marcia Mann, review of *Bad,* Elaine McGuire, review of *Love among the Walnuts,* p. 132.*

Vicki Grove

■ Personal

Born in Illinois.

■ Addresses

Home—P.O. Box 36, Ionia, MO 65335–9327.

■ Career

Writer.

■ Awards, Honors

Silver Angel Award, for *He Gave Her Roses.*

■ Writings

Goodbye, My Wishing Star, Putnam, 1988.
Junglerama, Putnam, 1989.

Fastest Friend in the West, Putnam, 1990.
Rimwalkers, Putnam, 1993.
The Crystal Garden, Putnam, 1995.
Reaching Dustin, Putnam, 1998.
The Starplace, Putnam, 1999.
Destiny, Putnam, 2000.

Also author of *Circles of Love,* published by Thomas Bouregy in 1988, and *He Gave Her Roses* and *A Time to Belong,* both issued by Group Publishing in 1990.

■ Sidelights

Vicki Grove has written a number of novels for young readers that revolve around life in the American Midwest, often inside rural farming communities, but the themes and conflicts her protagonists encounter strike a resonant note with adolescent readers everywhere. Grove's teens struggle with sibling rivalry, peer pressure and, most often, economic hardship. As their stories progress, they realize that family, school, and the larger community have provided them with a good moral framework to help them through their particular crises. As Grove told *Authors and Artists for Young Adults* *(AAYA),* "I picture my reader as being a young person with an open heart, trying to find the way to live as a decent and compassionate human being in a complicated yet beautiful world."

Grove is a product of the same Midwestern communities in which her novels are set. "My childhood was idyllic," she told *AAYA.* "I grew up on the

Illinois prairie, in a little one–room schoolhouse near the big white houses of my grandparents and great–grandparents. They were all storytellers from the word go, and I heard all about ancestors who took the Oregon Trail, who fought in the Civil War or went to the front to nurse their fallen sons there, uncles who had jumped off the roof with umbrellas, lightning that hit horses in the corral and left four hoof–prints branded in the ground, ghosts in the attics, etc. etc. I imagine they had more respect for the inner truth of a story than for the absolute facts, as I think all first–class storytellers do.

"My family has farmed until our present generation, and from them I also learned a deep respect for the land and the weather. I probably have the most fun writing when I'm using a farm setting. I have a younger sister and a much younger brother. Kathy and I were Peter Pan and Tinkerbell, or Dorothy and the Scarecrow. She's the pretty one, so I was always the boy in our games. Reed was always our baby. We nursed him with nightgowns over our heads to look like "nurses' hats" or we forced him into one of our doll buggies and wheeled him around until he yelled bloody murder. (I think he may still hold that against us a teeny bit—ha!) My mother read to us, usually from the Bible, but also from big, fat books. She never 'read down' to us, always expected us to pick up the meaning of challenging stories. I especially remember Ralph Moody's *Little Britches*.

"I just want my readers to realize what good hearts they have, what amazing creatures they are, how small and intricate the world is, how much love matters. If I had to describe my work to someone, I'd say I hope it's about people who are learning those things."

—Vicki Grove

"I had wonderful elementary teachers," Grove continued, "and from them I learned the excitement of reading. Last summer I saw my second grade teacher again—after over 40 years, she remembered me! 'You were my best reader,' she said. I still glow when I think of that. As a child, once in a while I would think of how wonderful it would be to be a writer, so that your teachers would be proud of you. So seeing Mrs. Peters, having a chance to send her copies of my books, was literally one of my longest-held and deepest-held dreams, come true.

"Confidence Breeds Confidence"

"I have always been self–conscious," Grove stated. "Not exactly quiet, but very easily flustered and not very sure of myself. I get embarrassed easily, and always have. For instance, I knew I couldn't catch balls as a child, so I couldn't. It doesn't take long for that kind of thinking to translate into being chosen last every time for the team. I often write characters who are self–conscious, and whose self–consciousness turns out to be a self–fulfilling prophecy. I can relate to that. Confidence breeds confidence. I see that, but can't really emulate it, and never have been able to. As you can probably guess, I loved school, but hated physical–education class. I think my most impressive achievement, maybe ever, is to have started going regularly to a gym four years ago. In middle age, I've become something of a weight lifter! Finally, I'm a jock (kind of). I can do push–ups now, but couldn't in school, and hated not being able to. Also, I often spent time crying in the rest room because of some real or, more usually, imagined slight from one of the other kids. I was far too easily bruised. Probably I still am. Yikes!

"When I was twelve we moved from Illinois to Oklahoma, and I lived there until I was 18, going through both junior high and high school there. Teens in Oklahoma do the car thing, drag Main, build bonfires on the beaches of the lakes, live a frontier life that is very fun and outdoorsy and cool. I set one of my books, *Starplace*, in Oklahoma and used a lot of those teen memories. Unfortunately, I also remember blatant small–town racism from those years, and that book concerns those not–so–great memories, too. I would never have said I wanted to be a writer when I was a teen, or even in college. I've never had the self–confidence to make that kind of pronouncement. But from about third grade on I always journaled my feelings, and wrote, wrote, wrote to try and understand the world. I wanted to be an English teacher, and went through graduate school thinking I'd eventually do that.

Contest Led to Publishing Contract

"I fell into writing in my early thirties, much by accident. I sent a few magazine pieces out, and when they began to be accepted I was totally shocked, but I kept with it, and it grew into a career that I love with all my heart. When I'd been writing for magazines for about eight years, I wrote a short book about a farm foreclosure, told from the viewpoint of a twelve–year–old girl. I entered that book in a contest G.P. Putnam's Sons was having for a first novel for young people, and to my vast surprise, it won and was published."

That novel was *Goodbye, My Wishing Star,* published in 1988. The premise was a timely one, for during the 1980s many American farmers had fallen into financial quagmires and were forced to give up their land. The story is told from the point of view of twelve–year–old Jens Tucker, whose mother's family has farmed their property for generations. Jens knows the end is near, however; other farms in the area have been sold off, and her parents discuss following suit and moving to the city to find work instead. The title of the book comes from a knothole in the barn where Jens milks cows before sun–up. Through it, she can see a special star, and wishes upon it that her family's finances might improve. Her father works hard to keep the farm viable, but Jens's mother believes that life in the city will be far easier for Jens and her little brother, Roger.

Loss of an Entire Lifestyle

Jens's story is recounted in diary form, and when it appears that their farm will indeed be sold, she is angry at having to give up the acreage, the animals, and the sense of heritage that the farm gives her. Feeling powerless at first, she plans to hide her journal in the barn, so the new owners might find it and learn how her family agonized over their decision to leave their land, and how heartbroken a twelve–year–old was that she would never be part of its future. But Jens also becomes aware that injustice and hardship are not her own to claim. The father of one of her friends has also lost their farm and then dies of a heart attack. The mother of another classmate drinks and forces the younger brother to beg to support them. In contrast, Jens's best friend, Marla, has had a relatively easy life, but helps Jens come to terms with the change with some astute observations.

Jens must say goodbye to her beloved animals before a public auction in which the Tuckers' farm tools and livestock are sold. When she meets Jack Shire, an eccentric who collects old cars and stores them in an old bank building in town, he reminds her that even if the Tucker farm is sold, it will always remain in her heart. As the diary comes to a close, Jens realizes she is looking forward to the adventure of starting over anew—that after so many farewells "something inside me is about ready for some hellos," she admits. *Goodbye, My Wishing Star* earned enthusiastic reviews for Grove. "The country setting is very appealing as are Jens' family relationships and her friendship with Marla," declared Eleanor Klopp in a *Voice of Youth Advocates* review. "Though the story is sad, there is also a strength as Jens recognizes that she must get on with her life," observed *Booklist*'s Denise M. Wilms.

Second Novel Also Sparkles

Grove's next novel for middle–school readers, *Junglerama,* appeared in 1989. In it, a trio of twelve–year–old boys in a small town find an abandoned carnival trailer one summer and creates a traveling exhibition of animals. The boys' particular hardships are the real focus of the story, however. The work is narrated by T. J., whose parents quarrel constantly, and whose mother neglects them. Jack, an orphan, must care for his alcoholic uncle. Mike's father has lost the family farm and now works as a stablehand. Over the course of the summer, a series of incidents incites gossip and then panic through the town, and some come to believe that their community has fallen under a witch's spell. Blame falls upon an eccentric woman, Cora Beeson, and the boys help rescue her from a dangerous situation in a gripping finale. Again, the work won positive reviews for Grove. T. J's narrative, noted *School Library Journal* reviewer Gerry Larson, "conveys both innocence and discovery . . . . Plot twists, well–paced action, and T. J.'s gradual maturing make this summer unforgettable."

"I honestly believe young teens are the most interesting and important of people, balanced with one foot in childhood and a heavier foot in adulthood, making the most important decisions they'll ever make, forming the most intense of friendships, having the most bitter of feuds and misunderstandings."

—Vicki Grove

In her next novel, *The Fastest Friend in the West,* Grove again presents an adolescent heroine who must deal with personal trauma. When Lori's best friend finds a new crowd and rejects her, she suffers as any twelve–year–old might; her situation is made all the more difficult by her weight problem. In response, she becomes obsessed with all things marine, painting her bedroom dark blue and decorating it with shells. She even renames herself Lorelei, after the legendary mermaid. At school, a girl who is somewhat of an outcast strikes up a friendship with her. Other kids shun Vern Hittlinger because of her odd clothes and disheveled appearance, but Lori worries when Vern stops coming to school. A teacher tells her that the Hittlingers live in their car on the outskirts of town.

In the second half of the book, Lori goes to see Vern, and learns about the hardships the Hittlingers have encountered over the past few years. Vern's strategy, when finding herself in a new school, has been to make one friend as quickly as possible. They depart again, and Lori later receives a postcard from Vern, saying that her family has found a real home. Toward the novel's close, Lori comes to terms with her weight problem, and resolves to make some changes in her life. "The specter of homelessness," remarked *Horn Book* writer Nancy Vasilakis, "the strain it puts on a proud family with little in the way of resources and more than its share of bad luck—will be a revelation to young readers."

Another Farm Story

Grove also won laudatory reviews for her 1993 book, *Rimwalkers*. Told in flashback form from twenty years ahead, the work revolves around the summer that fourteen–year–old Victoria, or "Tory," spent on her grandparents' Illinois farm. Both she and her younger sister, Sara, have been relegated here because their parents have decided to take a second honeymoon overseas. Tory is quiet and studious, and looks forward to the science and nature experiments she will be able to carry out in the country. The more vivacious Sara, however, is resentful at being removed from her familiar world of friends, cheerleading, and the usual summer exploits. Also visiting the grandparents that summer are the girls' cousins, Elijah and Rennie. Elijah, the product of a farm family himself, is there to help the grandfather with the chores and summer crop. Rennie, at sixteen, is the oldest of them all and is a high–school dropout from California. At first, the others are put off by his free–spirited, rebellious attitude and daring pranks.

Tory, Elijah, and Rennie soon begin to bond, however, when they believe they see the ghost of a small child at the boarded–up old homestead that sits at the edge of the family property. It had been built by their great–great grandparents, and when Tory asks her grandmother about the family history, she learns that a four–year–old boy died one summer in the 1840s when four cousins were visiting. Meanwhile, Sara begins to feel left out, especially when Rennie shows Tory and Elijah how to "rimwalk," or traverse a narrow ledge or attic beam. They try it successfully over a river bridge; jealous, Sara tries it as well, but falls and is badly hurt. "The true magic" in Grove's tale, noted Margaret Cole in a *School Library Journal* review, revolves around the alliance between the other three, by which "the teens teach one another to believe in themselves and in life's delicate balance between risk and security." Writing

for *Booklist,* Jeanne Triner also offered words of praise for *Rimwalkers.* "The setting is richly drawn, making the farm and its magic real to even the most urban reader," she noted.

Rejection, Redemption

A death in the family brings changes to her heroine's life in Grove's 1995 novel, *The Crystal Garden.* Eliza's father has been killed in an accident, and she and her mother struggle to make ends meet. In time, they decide to move to a small Missouri town with Burl, her mother's friend, who is also a country–music hopeful. There, Eliza tries to fit in at school, and keeps her distance from a neighbor girl around her own age, Dierdre, whose difficult home life has made her somewhat of an outcast at school. A science–fair project brings them together, and Eliza discovers that one of Dierdre's parents has an alcohol problem, and their household is very nearly destitute. Yet Dierdre manages her situation so well that Eliza realizes that her peer is far more balanced than she is. Other revelations help Eliza come to terms with the loss of her father. "A satisfying ending and epilogue leave room for hope, thought, and discussion," observed *School Library Journal* reviewer Susan Oliver.

Grove won unstinting praise for her 1998 book, *Reaching Dustin.* The tale involves Carly, a sixth–grade aspiring writer who comes from a pleasant, supportive family. But Carly is dismayed by a new school assignment to interview a classmate when she is paired with her grade's most reviled member. Dustin is sullen and withdrawn, and rumors abound around Carly's Missouri farm community involving his family, their isolated compound, and their possible ties to white supremacist militia groups. As Carly recounts, Dustin's behavioral problems began in the third grade, not long after his mother committed suicide, and she and her friends have snubbed him ever since.

Dustin's family is suspected of harboring a cache of weapons and running an illegal drug enterprise as well. As Carly begins to learn more about Dustin's situation, she is surprised by some of the revelations. He loves animals, for example, and carries a pet frog with him; he also "plays the recorder allotted to each sixth grader with a grace that belies his dirty and hard exterior," wrote *Horn Book*'s Susan P. Bloom. When the frog creates an incident and the situation escalates into a town uproar, Dustin is removed from school. Carly, worried and feeling guilty about her own role in one incident back in the third grade, tries to help him. "Carly's inner development is convincingly painful as she realizes the part she played in creating Dustin's problems," noted Steven Engelfried in a *School Library Journal* review. The "heartfelt story," noted a *Publishers Weekly* review, "unmasks the vulnerabilities of two preadolescents from very different walks of life." Bloom's *Horn Book* review found that "the emotional tone rings true," and *Kirkus Reviews* also praised Grove's talents. "Among a cast of memorable characters, Dustin is obviously pitiable but also noble," its assessment noted, and described *Reaching Dustin* as "written with grace" and "brimming with compassion."

History's Darker Side

As she noted, Grove drew upon some of her own experiences growing up in Oklahoma for her 1999 novel *The Starplace*. Its story is told through the voice of Frannie, who is thirteen years old in 1961 when an African American family moves into their small town of Quiver. Frannie makes friends with the daughter, Celeste, but soon learns that others in the town, and even at her school, are far less accepting. Celeste is greeted with taunts, and racist incidents occur, but she maintains her poise amidst the ugliness. Her father is a historian writing a book about white–supremacist groups in this part of Oklahoma, and her grandfather was the victim of a lynching in the area. Celeste shows Frannie some old Ku Klux Klan books she found in the attic of their home, which others believe may be haunted, and "Quiver's sunny image is gradually shattered for Frannie," noted a *Publishers Weekly* assessment.

At school, Celeste finds her niche in the school choir because of her talents, but is ejected from the group just before a competition. In a *Kirkus Reviews* critique, the newcomer is described as "beautiful, mature, worldly, and a great singer . . . close to being a type," but asserted that the other adolescents presented in the novel offered a more balanced portrait. Writing in *School Library Journal*, Connie Tyrell Burns commended *The Starplace* as a "powerful coming–of–age tale, written with grace and poignancy," and found Grove's "characterizations, particularly of Frannie and Celeste, are strong and memorable."

Destiny Creates Her Future

The title character of Grove's eighth novel for Putnam, *Destiny,* is another young woman who emerges from hardship to find her own strength. As the work begins, Destiny recounts a home life in which her unskilled mother is addicted to playing the lottery in the hopes of becoming rich. Jack, her mother's deceitful boyfriend, forces Destiny to help him at his job—selling shoddy fruits and vegetables door–to–door in their town, which humiliates her. When a sympathetic adult helps Destiny find better work as a reader to a homebound elderly woman, Mrs. Peck, Destiny starts to see some parallels in her life with the travails of the beleaguered heroes of the Greek myths she reads aloud. When Jack auctions a beloved pet rabbit belonging to Destiny's younger brother, she saves it in her own act of heroism. Mrs. Peck reveals to her some enlightening truths about Destiny's family, and after Jack winds up in jail, Destiny's mother decides to go back to school. The critic Burns, writing for *School Library Journal*, praised "Grove's lyrical writing style" and the "narration, which rings true with Destiny's memorable and poignant voice."

"As for the goals and concerns I bring to my work, I guess . . . I'll have to use that word 'compassion.' As the world gets more various and challenging, I think it's got to be a big goal for everyone, to truly empathize with other people."

—Vicki Grove

Though some of Grove's characters come from supportive family environments, others are forced to find other role models in their immediate community, as Destiny, Dierdre, Vern, and the boys from *Junglerama* must do. Recognizing that her own encouraging home life was not a universal one spurred Grove to write for adolescents. "My parents always gave me the most amazing encouragement and support of all kinds, and still do," she told *AAYA*. "They are my models for compassionate thinking, and I hope I do them honor in my characterizations of people trying to be compassionate in complicated situations. They are always my models for the striving, sacrificing parents in my books—I've been told by readers and teachers that I use a lot of those. They have always put other people before themselves, especially their children.

"I'm very disciplined in my work," Grove continued. "My father built me a wonderful, tiny office in the hayfield behind our house, and I spend most of every day out there (out here!), writing.

Writing is really rewriting, and it takes me most of a year to do a book—slow! I begin a book with a character that intrigues me. Sometimes he or she will be from memory, sometimes from observation, or even, occasionally, purely imaginary. This person could be a girl whose father has just died, or a boy in a white supremacist compound, or someone experiencing prejudice at school. At the moment I'm writing about a girl in a family that experiences tragedy and, as a way of escaping from themselves (ultimately impossible, as they will find out), goes on the migrant circuit. I've done lots of research into the lifestyles and challenges of migrant farmworker families, have talked to kids involved in that life, etc.

"Still, it's a huge responsibility trying to put someone else's life on paper, especially a life so much unlike your own, and probably much harder. I take that responsibility very, very seriously. And, as I mentioned, I'm always thankful my parents taught me to view other people with compassion, first and foremost. I hope I learned that lesson well. I hope I learned how to empathize well enough to actually slip into other hearts. I have to have lots of quiet around me when I work, and lots of peace in my life when I'm in the middle of a book. It's a weird sensation, living your own life and also the life of your main character, simultaneously! My family says I zombie out when I'm immersed in a book, and that's true. I burn dinner, have car wrecks (seriously), the whole ball of wax.

Found Voice of Adolescence

"I didn't decide to write for young adults—I wrote for 'regular old adults' like myself when I started magazine writing. But when I wrote the book I entered in the Putnam contest, *Goodbye, My Wishing Star*, I felt like I'd died and gone to heaven. Once I tried it, I realized I absolutely love to write in the voice of a 13– or 14– or 16–year–old. Maybe because I honestly believe young teens are the most interesting and important of people, balanced with one foot in childhood and a heavier foot in adulthood, making the most important decisions they'll ever make, forming the most intense of friendships, having the most bitter of feuds and misunderstandings. I tapped into something deep inside myself when I first wrote in a teen voice, and I've become addicted to going back to that well of memory, sensation . . . whatever it is.

Grove hopes her readers will take away a lesson from her books through the difficulties that her characters rise above. She realizes that all teens face their own personal challenges. "I want to tell that person that I admire the quest they're on, and think it's worthy of their immense effort," she told *AAYA.* "As for the goals and concerns I bring to my work, I guess one more time I'll have to use that word 'compassion.' As the world gets more various and challenging, I think it's got to be a big goal for everyone, to truly empathize with other people. My characters are flawed and vulnerable, but you've got to say for them that in their stumbling ways, they all attain compassion for others. Two of my recent books, *Reaching Dustin* and *Starplace,* deal with white supremacy and the KKK. These are things that make me livid, so angry I can hardly breathe. For that reason, those books weren't easy to write, but I almost had to write them.

If you enjoy the works of Vicki Grove, you might want to check out the following books:

Judy Blume, *Just as Long as We're Together,* 1987.
Chris Crutcher, *Staying Fat for Sarah Byrnes,* 1993.
Tim Wynne–Jones, *The Maestro,* 1996.
Rachel Vail, *Wonder,* 1991.

"It still staggers me to think that my books might possibly have some effect—what an idea, and what an obligation. It's thrilling to get a letter from a young reader telling me that one of my books influenced how they thought about someone at their school, or how they acted toward someone, or how they felt about themselves. Mind–boggling, and humbling. I just want my readers to realize what good hearts they have, what amazing creatures they are, how small and intricate the world is, how much love matters. If I had to describe my work to someone, I'd say I hope it's about people who are learning those things."

■ Biographical and Critical Sources

PERIODICALS

ALAN Review, fall, 2000, Anne Sherill, review of *Destiny,* p. 35.

Booklist, April 15, 1988, Denise M. Wilms, review of *Goodbye, My Wishing Star,* p. 1431; July, 1990, Deborah Abbott, review of *The Fastest Friend in the West,* p. 2089; October 15, 1993, Jeanne Triner, review of *Rimwalkers,* pp. 430–431; May 1, 1998, Michael Cart, review of *Reaching Dustin,* p. 1518; June 1, 1999, Hazel Rochman, review of *The Starplace,* p. 1813.

Horn Book, July–August, 1990, Nancy Vasilakis, review of *The Fastest Friend in the West,* p. 455; March–April, 1998, Susan P. Bloom, review of *Reaching Dustin,* p. 220.

Kirkus Reviews, May 1, 1988, review of *Goodbye, My Wishing Star,* p. 692; March 1, 1998, review of *Reaching Dustin,* p. 339; May 15, 1999, review of *The Starplace,* p. 800.

Kliatt, January, 1997, Dean E. Lyons, review of *Rimwalkers,* p. 8.

Publishers Weekly, September 29, 1993, review of *Rimwalkers,* p. 64; May 11, 1998, review of *Reaching Dustin,* p. 68; July 5, 1999, review of *The Starplace,* p. 72; July 31, 2000, review of *Destiny,* p 96.

School Library Journal, July, 1989, Gerry Larson, review of *Junglerama,* p. 82; October, 1993, Margaret Cole, review of *Rimwalkers,* p. 151; May, 1995, Susan Oliver, review of *The Crystal Garden,* p. 106; May, 1998, Stephen Engelfried, review of *Reaching Dustin,* p. 142; June, 1999, Connie Tyrell Burns, review of *The Starplace,* p. 129; April, 2000, Connie Tyrell Burns, review of *Destiny,* p. 134.

Voice of Youth Advocates, October, 1988, Eleanor Klopp, review of *Goodbye, My Wishing Star,* p. 181; December, 1993, Deborah A. Feulner, review of *Rimwalkers,* p. 291; June, 2000, Roxy Ekstrom, review of *Destiny,* p. 114.*

—Sketch by Carol Brennan

Joe Haldeman

other schools; Massachusetts Institute of Technology, adjunct professor, 1983—. *Military service:* U.S. Army, 1967–69; became combat engineer; served in Vietnam; wounded in combat; received Purple Heart and other medals.

■ Personal

Born June 9, 1943, in Oklahoma City, OK; son of Jack Carroll (a hospital administrator) and Lorena (Spivey) Haldeman; married Mary Gay Potter (a teacher), August 21, 1965. *Education:* University of Maryland, B.S., 1967; University of Iowa, M.F.A., 1975; also attended American University and University of Oklahoma; participated in the Milford Writer's Workshop. *Politics:* "Skeptic." *Religion:* "Skeptic." *Hobbies and other interests:* Folk guitar, bicycling, woolgathering, strong drink, travel, astronomy, painting.

■ Addresses

Home and office—5412 Northwest 14th Ave., Gainesville, FL 32605. *E–mail*—haldeman@mit.edu. *Agent*—Ralph Vicinanza, 111 Eighth Ave., #1501, New York, NY 10011.

■ Career

Freelance writer, 1970—. University of Iowa, teaching assistant, 1975; former editor of *Astronomy;* has taught writing at University of North Florida and

■ Member

Authors Guild, Authors League of America, Science Fiction Writers of America (treasurer, 1970–72; chair of Grievance Committee, 1979–80; president, 1992–94), National Space Society, Writers Guild, Poets and Writers.

■ Awards, Honors

Hugo Award, World Science Fiction Convention, 1975, Nebula Award, Science Fiction Writers of America, 1975, and Locus Award, *Locus* magazine, 1975, all for *The Forever War;* Hugo Award, World Science Fiction Convention, 1976, and Locus Award, *Locus* magazine, 1976, both for best short story, for "Tricentennial"; Ditmar Award, 1976; Galaxy Award, 1978, for *Mindbridge;* Rhysling Award, Science Fiction Poetry Association, 1984, 1990; Hugo Award, World Science Fiction Convention, 1991, for the novella *The Hemingway Hoax;* Nebula Award, Science Fiction Writers of America, 1993, and World Fantasy Award, World Fantasy Convention, 1993, both for

"Graves"; Hugo Award, World Science Fiction Convention, 1995, Nebula Award, Science Fiction Writers of America, 1995, and Locus Award, *Locus* magazine, 1995, all for "None So Blind"; Homer Award, 1995; Hugo Award, World Science Fiction Convention, 1998, Nebula Award, Science Fiction Writers of America, 1998, and John W. Campbell Memorial Award, University of Kansas, for *Forever Peace.*

■ Writings

SCIENCE FICTION NOVELS

The Forever War, St. Martin's (New York City), 1974.
Mindbridge, St. Martin's, 1976.
Planet of Judgment (a *Star Trek* novel), Bantam (New York City), 1977.
All My Sins Remembered, St. Martin's, 1977.
(Author of introduction) Robert A. Heinlein, *Double Star,* Gregg (Boston, MA), 1978.
World without End: A Star Trek Novel, Bantam, 1979.
(With brother, Jack C. Haldeman) *There Is No Darkness,* Ace (New York City), 1983.
Tool of the Trade, Morrow (New York City), 1987.
Buying Time, introduction by James Gunn, illustrated by Bryn Barnard, Easton Press (Norwalk, CT), 1989, published in Britain as *The Long Habit of Living,* New English Library (London).
The Hemingway Hoax (novella), Morrow, 1990.
Forever Peace, Ace Books, 1997.
Forever Free, Ace Books, 1999.
The Coming, Ace Books, 2000.

"WORLDS" TRILOGY; SCIENCE FICTION NOVELS

Worlds: A Novel of the Near Future, Viking (New York City), 1981.
Worlds Apart, Viking, 1983.
Worlds Enough and Time: The Conclusion of the Worlds Trilogy, Morrow, 1992.

ADVENTURE NOVELS; UNDER PSEUDONYM ROBERT GRAHAM

Attar's Revenge, Pocket Books (New York City), 1975.
War of Nerves, Pocket Books, 1975.

WAR NOVELS

War Year, Holt Reinhart (New York City), 1972, original version, Pocket Books, 1978.

1968: A Novel, Hodder and Stoughton (London, England), 1994, Morrow, 1995.

SHORT STORY COLLECTIONS

Infinite Dreams, St. Martin's, 1978.
Dealing in Futures: Stories, Viking Press, 1985.
More than the Sum of His Parts, Pulphouse (Eugene, WA), 1991.
Vietnam and Other Alien Worlds (with essays and poetry), New England Science Fiction Association Press (Framingham, MA), 1993.
None So Blind, Morrow, 1996.

POETRY

Saul's Death and Other Poems, Anamnesis Press, 1996.

PLAYS

The Devil His Due (produced at the University of Iowa Film Workshop), published in *Fantastic* (New York City), August, 1974.
The Moon and Marcek, published in *Vertex* (Los Angeles), August, 1974.
The Forever War, produced in Chicago, 1983.

SCREENPLAYS

Robot Jox, Empire, 1990.
Mindbridge, Blur Studios, 2001.

EDITOR

Cosmic Laughter: Science Fiction for the Fun of It, Holt Reinhart, 1974.
Study War No More: A Selection of Alternatives, St. Martin's, 1977.
Nebula Award Stories 17, Holt Reinhart, 1983.
(With Martin H. Greenberg and Charles G. Waugh) *Body Armor: 2000,* Ace, 1986.
(With Greenberg and Waugh) *Supertanks,* Ace, 1987.
The Best of John Brunner, Ballantine (New York City), 1988.
(With Greenberg and Waugh) *Spacefighters,* Ace, 1988.

OTHER

Work included in numerous "best of" anthologies, including *The Best from Galaxy,* edited by Ejler Jakobbsen, Universal–Award, 1972; *Best SF: 1972,* edited by Harry Harrison and Brian Aldiss, Putnam, 1973; *The Best Science Fiction of the Year–1972*, edited by Terry Carr, Ballantine, 1973; *Best SF: 1973*, edited by Harrison and Aldiss, Putnam, 1974; *The Best from Galaxy*, Volume 3, Award, 1975; *Nebula Award Stories 11*, Harper, 1975; *Best Science Fiction Stories*, Dutton, 1977; *Nebula Award Stories XII*, Harper, 1977; *Annual World's Best SF*, DAW, 1978; *The Best of Destinies*, Ace, 1981; *Best SF Stories of the Year*, Dutton, 1980; *Best of OMNI Science Fiction*, 1980; *Vicious Circles: The Best Modern Sestinas*, 1994; *The Year's Best Science Fiction, Eleventh Annual,* St. Martin's Press, 1994; and *Year's Best Science Fiction*, edited by David Hartwell, HarperPrism, 1996.

Contributor to major science fiction anthologies, including *Orbit Eleven*, edited by Damon Knight, Putnam, 1971; *Showcase*, edited by Roger Elwood, Harper, 1973; *Analog 9*, edited by Ben Bova, Doubleday, 1973; *Combat SF*, edited by Gordon Dickson, Doubleday, 1975; *Frights*, edited by Kirby McCauley, St. Martin's, 1976; *Close Up: New Worlds*, St. Martin's, 1977; *Time of Passage*, Taplinger, 1978; *The Endless Frontier*, Ace Books, 1979; *The Road to SF 3*, Mentor, 1979; *Thieve's World*, edited by Robert Asprin, Ace Books, 1979; *The Future at War*, Ace Books, 1980; *Dark Forces*, edited by McCauley, Viking, 1980; *Alien Stars*, Baen, 1984; *In the Fields of Fire*, Tor, 1986; *Cutting Edge*, Tor, 1986; *Blood Is Not Enough*, Morrow, 1989; *2040*, Delacorte, 1992; *There Won't Be a War*, Tor, 1992; *Far Futures*, Tor, 1995; *Far Horizons*, Avon, 1999; and *Destination 3001*, Flammarion, 2000.

Contributor of numerous short stories and articles to *Analog, Galaxy, Isaac Asimov's SF Adventures, Magazine of Fantasy and Science Fiction, Omni, Playboy,* and other publications.

"People who talk about 'the writing game' are usually being sarcastic or cynical, but in many ways the activity does resemble a game, with its peculiar rules and rewards, and like most interesting games, success is the result of both skill and luck."

—Joe Haldeman

Haldeman's novels have been translated into numerous languages, including French, Italian, German, Dutch, Japanese, Hebrew, Spanish, Swedish, Russian, Greek, Czech, Bulgarian, Serbo–Croatian, Polish, Finnish, Portuguese, and Korean.

■ Work in Progress

Listen to the Raven, a science fiction novel.

■ Sidelights

In his award–winning science fiction novel *The Forever War*, Joe Haldeman combines his experiences as a soldier during the Vietnam War, in which he was severely wounded, with a realistic, scientifically–accurate presentation. The novel tells of a war that stretches across intergalactic distances and long periods of time, the soldiers involved traveling to remote battlefields via black holes. Because the soldiers travel at faster–than–light speeds, they age far more slowly than the civilians for whom they fight. This difference in relative age—the soldiers a few years older, their society centuries older—results in an alienation between the soldiers and the people they defend.

"Haldeman exercises his literary license," James Scott Hicks wrote in the *Dictionary of Literary Biography*, "to comment on, and ultimately to expunge from his memory, America's last ground war [Vietnam]." Hicks points out that Haldeman's first novel, *War Year*, based on his army diaries, deals with the Vietnam fighting directly. "But the demon of Vietnam," Hicks continued, "was not exorcised from Haldeman's soul by writing [*War Year*], and frontline combat became the subject of . . . *The Forever War*." Haldeman, Hicks believed, is particularly adept at presenting his "theme of quiet resentment felt by those waging war."

Astronautical Ambitions

Born in Oklahoma City in 1943, Haldeman dreamed of being a "spaceman," or astronaut, from his early childhood. He earned a degree in astronomy from the University of Maryland in 1967, but also received a draft notice from the U.S. military around the same time. It was the height of the Vietnam war, when American soldiers often did not return alive. Briefly, Haldeman entertained the idea of eluding his draft notice by fleeing to Canada, Mexico, or Sweden, as many others had done. He knew, however, that it would forever ruin his chance of entering an astronaut–training program.

In Vietnam, Haldeman was assigned to an demolition squad which moved about Vietnam's Central Highlands with small infantry units fighting Viet

Cong and North Vietnamese forces. It was early 1968, just after the Tet Offensive, and a period of fierce fighting in the war. Haldeman and his squad discovered an enemy ordnance pile, but while they were waiting for permission to dispose of it, it exploded. "It was boobytrapped, with a time–delay or a radio–frequency fuse," Haldeman recalled. "After we'd been standing guard for thirty or forty minutes, it suddenly blew." The three others in his squad were killed, and Haldeman suffered hundreds of small puncture wounds as well as several bullet and shrapnel wounds.

The Forever War

The trauma earned him a Purple Heart, and a month off with a stipend when he returned home to his family. In college, Haldeman had taken a creative–writing class and written two science–fiction stories for it. After his homecoming, he spent his time retyping them and sending them out. He sold one to a science–fiction magazine, *Galaxy,* for their September, 1969 issue; the other eventually found a home in *Fantastic* magazine in 1970. Soon, Haldeman had decided to earn a graduate degree in computer science, but before he began his studies, he garnered an invitation to a science–fiction writing workshop to which only a few fledgling writers were accepted. There he met several prominent names in the genre, including Ben Bova, whom Haldeman told about his idea for a Vietnam novel. Bova offered to read it and pass it on. The manuscript won Haldeman a contract from the publisher, Holt, within two weeks, which published *War Year* in 1972. He never went back to school.

His next work, however, would be his first full–length science–fiction novel and earn him both the Hugo and Nebula Awards, among the genre's highest honors. Because of his scientific training in physics and astronomy, Haldeman is particularly careful to present *The Forever War* as realistically and accurately as possible. "The technology involved in this interplanetary campaign," Martin Levin of the *New York Times Book Review* noted in his review of *The Forever War,* "is so sophisticated that the book might well have been accompanied by an operator's manual. But then, all the futuristic mayhem is plugged into human situations that help keep the extraterrestrial activity on a warm and even witty plane."

Among newer novelists in the field, Haldeman, Richard Geis of *Science Fiction Review* believed, "is one of the best realistic science fiction writers going; maybe *the* best." Hicks found that "Haldeman con-

Haldeman, pictured here in 1968, was wounded during combat in Vietnam while a member of the U.S. Army and received the Purple Heart.

fronts his readers with painful questions, but he asks them with no small literary skill and with careful attention to scientific credibility." "It's comforting to know," wrote Algis Budrys of the *Magazine of Fantasy and Science Fiction,* "that the cadre of impressive talent among younger writers is not diminishing, and to think that people like Haldeman will be around for a long time to set high standards."

The "Worlds" Series

Haldeman's "Worlds" trilogy, published over a span of a dozen years, follows the exploits of Marianne O'Hara, who is, summarized Michael Pavese in *Best Sellers,* "an intelligent, promiscuous (in space promiscuity is encouraged) New New York citizen." Born in space, she travels from her orbiting, man-made world to Earth to engage in post–graduate studies at New York University in the first book,

Worlds: A Novel of the Near Future. It details her adventures and misadventures on twenty–second century Earth, a far poorer, more decadent, chaotic, and dangerous extension of contemporary society. It is a society rapidly nearing a total breakdown—which, by the denouement, it indeed has, with Marianne's space ship veritably riding the shockwave of nuclear devastation home to New New York. *Worlds Apart* details Marianne's career as an ambitious politician of the orbital worlds, who, thinking her former lover, Jeff Hawkings, is dead (he isn't) from the nuclear holocaust, takes a pair of husbands.

In addition, the book not only tracks Jeff's career, now peddling medications to devolved Earth tribes, it includes, noted Charles Platt in the *Washington Post Book World*, "a grab–bag of extraneous notions in between: a Manson–worshipping death cult, a starship with an anti–matter drive, a formalized menage–a–trois, a hijacked space shuttle, an expedition into regressed Florida, a new science of behavioral conditioning, and more." In the final book, *Worlds Enough and Time*, Marianne, her two husbands and her cybernetic "twin sister," along with 10,000 other would–be colonists, venture forth in the starship *Newhome* to seek their destinies on an Earth–like planet in the Epsilon Eridani system. A *Publishers Weekly* reviewer lauded: "Haldeman shows his strengths here: the workings of *Newhome* are believably complex, the novel's scientific background is neither strained nor especially complicated, and the reader's attention is focused on O'Hara's character, her inner life and her interpersonal relationships."

Tackles Timeless Issues

In addition to the obvious recurring theme of war—both real and imagined—in many of Haldeman's books, essayist Duncan Lunan noted another theme in the *St. James Guide to Science Fiction Writers*. Referring back to *The Forever War*, where the enemy aliens are controlled by a hive–mind, Lunan said, "*Mindbridge* was another examination of human contact with a hive–mind, while *All My Sins Remembered* was a damning indictment not merely of big government but also of the standard SF attitude toward individuality. SF used to be full of people who find out that they're really someone else (usually someone more powerful), and part of the problem in identifying with central characters is often they lack individuality." Said Lunan, "McGavin in *All My Sins Remembered* is a government agent, repeatedly given new identities through psychological conditioning and plastic surgery." Lunan added, "he is an individual moved and controlled by an organisation which commands his loyalty but

In a stylistic change of pace from his science–fiction novels, Haldeman's 1996 poetry collection posits the effects of violent horrors and futuristic warfare on our tenuous humanity.

is beyond his control." The theme of individuals preyed upon and controlled by ultra–powerful agencies or corporate entities is also central to Haldeman's "Worlds" trilogy, as with the CIA and KGB in *Tool of the Trade*, and by the wealthy in *Buying Time*. A *Publishers Weekly* contributor wrote, "Evoking painful nostalgia, . . . Haldeman uses bold language, powerful images and a graphic style to tell his emotional tale, in which concentrated, diary–like entries intensify the drama and despair."

Sue Martin, writing in the *Los Angeles Times Book Review*, termed *The Hemingway Hoax* "a bright, short science fiction novel, . . . [this] quirky effort offers a unique solution to one of the enduring literary mysteries of our time: Just what DID happen to Ernest Hemingway's missing manuscripts, lost in 1922 at the Gare de Lyon in Paris?" She continued, "For Hemingway fans, Haldeman's answer is a hoot, and as different a theory as you can find."

The Post–*War* Era

Forever Peace is a follow–up novel to the problems raised in Haldeman's acclaimed *Forever War.* In 2043, an American–led alliance has been battling with the third–world Ngumi confederation, primarily, on the alliance's part, with "soldierboys"—killing machines controlled by brain–linked "mechanics," among them the protagonist, physicist Julian Class. Meanwhile, the Jupiter Project, the most ambitious scientific experiment of all time, circles Jupiter. Julian's lover, Amelia, discovers it may endanger not only our solar system but the entire universe, in a new "Big Bang." Among other complications, their attempt to stop the disaster runs afoul of an influential Christian cult, the Hammer of God, dedicated to bringing on the Endtime. A *Publishers Weekly* reviewer concluded: "As always, Haldeman, a Vietnam vet, writes with intelligence and power about the horrors of war, and about humanity's seeming inability to overcome its violent tendencies."

Haldeman has also written a sequel to *The Forever War, Forever Free.* Its plot involves *Forever War* refugees William and Marygay, who are forced to live on a half–frozen planet, Middle Finger. The human race is now highly evolved, but they belong to the older, more archaic type, and have been shunted out of sight. Frustrated, William and some other vets steal a starship, but when its antimatter engines fail, they must return to Middle Finger in an escape craft—and find it deserted. Their attempts to solve this crisis and regain some of their former status carry the plot toward a conclusion. *Publishers Weekly* called it "a well–written and worthy sequel to one of SF's most enduring classics."

"The Result of Both Skill and Luck"

Haldeman admits he has been quite fortunate as a writer. His wife supported them in the early years as a teacher, and he was also talented enough to gain admittance to the Iowa Writers' Workshop at the University of Iowa, perhaps the best–known writers' program in the United States. He earned an M.F.A. from there in 1975, and through the program came to know such outstanding Americana fiction writers as John Cheever and Raymond Carver before their deaths. In addition to his science–fiction

novels, Haldeman has worked with renowned filmmaker George Lucas on a "Tour of the Solar System" theme–park attraction for Disney, which never obtained corporate sponsorship for construction. From this connection, he was hired to write the novel version of the 1982 Steven Spielberg film, *Poltergeist.* He was given the script, and "it was absolutely appalling," Haldeman once said. The project soon found another writer.

If you enjoy the works of Joe Haldeman, you might want to check out the following books:

David Brin, *Earth,* 1990.
Michael Flynn, *In the Country of the Blind,* 1990.
Robert A. Heinlein, *To Sail Beyond the Sunset,* 1987.
Neal Stephenson, *Snow Crash,* 1992.
John Varley, *The Persistence of Vision,* 1978.

Still, Haldeman's impressive credentials landed him a post with the Writing Program at the Massachusetts Institute of Technology in 1983. He continues to teach there, while rising early to write in the pre–dawn hours. He has homes in Cambridge, Massachusetts and Gainesville, Florida, and is an avid cyclist who commutes by bike daily. A planned bike trip across the southern portion of the United States in the late 1990s was stalled by a collarbone fracture, which offered Haldeman a chance to reflect upon his career to date. "People who talk about 'the writing game' are usually being sarcastic or cynical, but in many ways the activity does resemble a game, with its peculiar rules and rewards, and like most interesting games, success is the result of both skill and luck," Haldeman noted. "The usual pattern for a writer is to collect piles of rejection slips, and after some months or years finally to make a sale, and eventually build a reputation and sell most of what he or she writes." But there are few like himself, he continued, who sold their first effort. "That's luck. It's also talent, but after a couple of decades of teaching writing on the side, I know that talent isn't rare. In a class of twenty, there are usually one or two or several who have enough talent to write for a living, eventually. Whether they're willing to play the game, and accept its rewards and penalties, is another matter."

■ Biographical and Critical Sources

BOOKS

Contemporary Literary Criticism, Volume 61, Gale, 1990.

Dictionary of Literary Biography, Volume 7: *Twentieth–Century American Science Fiction Writers,* Gale (Detroit, MI), 1981.

The Encyclopedia of Science Fiction, St. Martin's Press, 1993.

Gordon, Joan, *Joe Haldeman,* Starmont House (Mercer Island, WA), 1980.

Science Fiction and Fantasy Literature, 1975–1991, Gale, 1992.

Science Fiction Writers: Critical Studies of the Major Authors from the Early Nineteenth Century to the Present Day, second edition, Scribner, 1999.

St. James Guide to Science Fiction Writers, St. James Press, 1996.

Twentieth–Century Science–Fiction Writers, third edition, St. James Press, 1991.

PERIODICALS

Algol, summer–fall, 1977; summer–fall, 1978.

Analog, March, 1978; September, 1978; July, 1979; November, 1982, pp. 164–65; September, 1983, p. 164; March, 1984, p. 168; February, 1986, p. 182; December, 1986, p. 182; January, 1990, pp. 308–9.

Best Sellers, June 15, 1972; December, 1976; February, 1978.

Bloomsbury Review, January–February, 1996, pp. 3, 20.

Booklist, June 1, 1975; June 1995; September 15, 1997; May 15, 1999, Sally Estes, review of *Far Horizons,* p. 1676; January 1, 2000, review of *Forever Free,* p. 832.

Book World, July 2, 1995, p. C95.

Chicago Tribune, September 26, 1976; September 2, 1991, p. 10.

Chicago Tribune Book World, June 14, 1981.

Commonweal, October 27, 1972.

Destinies, November–December, 1978.

Foundation, May, 1978.

Futures, June, 1975.

Galaxy, December, 1976; March, 1978.

Library Journal, September 15, 1972; October 15, 1997, p. 97; December, 1999, Jackie Cassada, review of *Forever Free,* p. 192.

Los Angeles Times Book Review, October 30, 1983, p. 4; July 8, 1990, p. 9.

Magazine of Fantasy and Science Fiction, May, 1975; October, 1975; April, 1977; September, 1979; August, 1981, pp. 55–56; March, 1984, pp. 43–45.

New Republic, November 26, 1977.

New York Times Book Review, May 21, 1972; March 23, 1975; February 27, 1977; January 15, 1984, p. 29; February 10, 1985, p. 40; June 7, 1987, p. 18; July 2, 1989, p. 15; June 14, 1992, p. 24.

Observer (London), May 8, 1977.

Publishers Weekly, March 13, 1987, p. 70; December 7, 1990, p. 78; April 6, 1992, p. 54; April 17, 1995, p. 38; April 22, 1996, review of *None So Blind,* p. 64; August 25, 1997, p. 49; November 15, 1999, review of *Forever Free,* p. 59; November 20, 2000, review of *The Coming,* p. 51.

Science Fiction Review, August, 1976; February, 1977; February, 1978.

Science Fiction Studies, Volume 21, 1994, pp. 238–40.

Starlog, Volume 17, 1978.

Thrust, summer, 1979.

Times Literary Supplement, July 8, 1977.

Washington Post Book World, April 26, 1981; May 13, 1990, p. 8; May 31, 1992, p. 6; July 2, 1995, p. 4.

ON–LINE

Joe Haldeman's Home Page, located at http://home.earthlink.net/~haldeman. (January 3, 2001).

Kimberly Willis Holt

lection, American Library Association, 1999, all for *My Louisiana Sky*; National Book Award for Young People's Literature, 1999, for *When Zachary Beaver Came to Town.*

■ Personal

Born September 9, 1960, in Pensacola, FL; daughter of Julian Ray (a data processing manager) and Brenda (a teacher; maiden name, Mitchell) Willis; married Jerry William Holt (director of Amarillo CVC), February 23, 1985; children: Shannon. *Education:* Attended University of New Orleans, 1978–79, and Louisiana State University, 1979–81.

■ Career

Radio news director, 1980–82; worked in advertising and marketing, 1982–87; interior decorator, 1987–93; writer, 1994—.

■ Addresses

Home—Amarillo, TX. *Office*—P.O. Box 20135, Amarillo, TX 79114. *Agent*—Flannery Literary Agency, 114 Wickfield Ct., Naperville, IL 60563.

■ Awards, Honors

Boston Globe–Horn Book Award for Fiction, 1998, Notable Book selection, American Library Association, 1999, and Top Ten Best Books for Young Adults se-

■ Writings

My Louisiana Sky, Holt, 1998.
Mister and Me, Putnam, 1998.
When Zachary Beaver Came to Town, Holt, 1999.

■ Work in Progress

Dancing in Cadillac Light, Putnam, expected 2001.

■ Sidelights

Kimberly Willis Holt writes poignant coming–of–age fiction for young readers, books that hum with the sleepy rhythms of small–town life in her native South and the cadences of its vernacular. Since her 1994 debut novel, *My Louisiana Sky*, Holt has won a number of awards, including two American Library Association citations for that particular work, and a prestigious National Book Award for Young People's Literature for her third, 1999's *When Zachary Beaver Came to Town*. But all of her titles have garnered enthusiastic praise from critics of young–adult fiction for their realistic portrayals of life in the rural South, and for the iconoclastic, but sympathetic characters she creates to lead her stories.

Holt was born in 1960, in Pensacola, Florida, the site of a large U.S. Navy base. Her father worked for many years as a chef for the U.S. Navy, and her mother was a teacher. Julian Willis's job took the family to several far–flung places during Holt's young life, including France and the Pacific Ocean territory of Guam. They also lived in a number of American states, but always made Forest Hill, Louisiana, their spiritual home. Holt's grandmother lived there, and the future author loved spending time in a place where her roots ran so deep. She began to consider writing as a career at the age of twelve, when she read Carson McCullers's *The Heart Is a Lonely Hunter*. This 1940 work, like others by the Georgia native, explored human isolation and life in the South through the vantage point of an eloquent outsider, and the style of fiction moved the young Holt. "It was just life–changing because of the characters," she told *School Library Journal* writer Kathleen T. Horning. "That was the first time I read a book where the characters seemed like real people to me."

"The story ideas that I have are usually coming–of–age stories, I'd say anywhere from ten– to fifteen–year–olds. And I always joke, but I think it's true when I say it, that I don't think I've ever gotten over being twelve. Maybe most of us haven't."

—Kimberly Willis Holt

Holt studied broadcast journalism at the University of New Orleans in the late 1970s and Louisiana State University until 1981, but left school to work as a news director for a radio station. The work was far from challenging, however, and so she took another job at the station selling advertising time. She also worked as an interior decorator for six years before thinking about writing for publication. As a teen and young adult, she had always envisioned a life as an author, but never pursued it in earnest. Part of the reason she abandoned her calling was due to

a tough writing teacher she once had, who refused to provide her with any encouraging feedback. "In all fairness to her, she was a great teacher, but she would praise other people's writing but not mine," Holt told Horning in the *School Library Journal* interview. "I was very shy and insecure and I took it as though I really wasn't meant to be a writer."

Isolation Spurred Creative Juices

Around 1994, Holt—by then married and with a young child—moved to Amarillo, Texas, for her husband's job. She was bereft, as she recalled, but recognized the sudden isolation as a surprise opportunity to begin writing for children. "I didn't know a soul there and I thought, 'If I'm ever going to do it, this is the time,'" she told Horning. The result was *My Louisiana Sky*, published by Holt in 1998. Set in a small town in central Louisiana, the story was inspired by a memorable incident that occurred when Holt was just nine. She had been traveling through rural Louisiana with her parents, and saw a woman carrying groceries walking on the side of the road. "This lady looked strange to me," Holt recalled in the interview with Horning. "She just had a different look about her on her face and I mentioned her to my mom and my mom said, 'That lady's mentally retarded and her husband is mentally retarded and they have a lot of kids.' It haunted me for the rest of my life."

Tiger Ann Parker is the unlikely heroine of *My Louisiana Sky*, which takes place in a town called Saitter in 1957. Tiger is twelve years old. She does well in both school and athletics, but she feels a certain degree of social ostracism because of her parents. Her father, who works in a local plant nursery, cannot even do simple math, but Tiger's mother is even more developmentally challenged. As a young child, it used to delight Tiger that her mother played games with her so enthusiastically, but entering adolescence and yearning for a more "normal" life, Tiger begins to feels embarrassed by her parents' limitations. She knows that some townspeople view the family as odd and are of the opinion that the Parkers should have never been allowed to marry and start a family.

Must Choose Between Worlds

Fortunately, Tiger also lives with her astute, practical grandmother, who helps her face the teasing of others. Her beloved grandmother points out that "people are afraid of what's different. That don't mean different is bad. Just means different is differ-

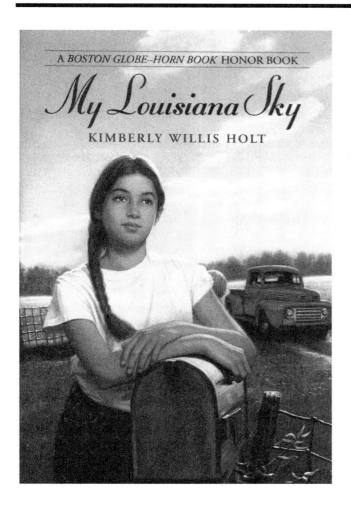

Named an American Library Association Notable Book, Holt's debut novel portray's pre–teen Tiger Ann's struggle between loyalty to her mentally impaired parents and a more glamorous life far from her small Louisiana home town.

marked Lynn Evarts in a *Voice of Youth Advocates* critique of *My Louisiana Sky*. The debut work won a slew of awards for Holt, and sincere words of praise from reviewers. Betsy Hearne, writing in the *Bulletin of the Center for Children's Books,* found that in Tiger, the writer had created a character "with a distinctive voice" as well as "a credible resolution showing Tiger's values to be as strong as her family ties." *School Library Journal* writer Cindy Darling Codell asserted that "Holt has nicely portrayed the rhythms, relationships, and sometimes harsh realities of small–town life." Marilyn Bousquin, writing in *Horn Book,* found that Holt "eases the action along with a low–key, unpretentious plot, never resorting to over–dramatization or sentimentality in developing her uncannily credible characters." *Booklist*'s Hazel Rochman opined that "all the characters, including Tiger's parents, are drawn with warmth but no patronizing reverence," while a *Publishers Weekly* assessment asserted that Holt "presents and handles a sticky dilemma with remarkable grace."

"Mister Leroy"

Holt followed the success of her debut with another work published that same year, *Mister and Me.* Just eighty pages in length, the work is aimed at younger readers, aged seven to eleven, but still won praise for its depiction of a time and place that had long passed. Young Jolene Johnson, however, knows no other world except the sometimes tough realm of life in the segregated South as an African American child in the 1940s. Jolene lives in a logging town in Louisiana—two of Holt's great–grandfathers had worked in the industry—and is the daughter of a widowed seamstress mother, and also lives with her grandfather. Life begins to change a bit too quickly for Jolene when a Mister Leroy Redfield, a logger new to the town, begins wooing her mother. The presence of this rival for her mother's affection makes Jolene miss her deceased father, whom she never knew, even more.

ent," she says in *My Louisiana Sky*. But things begin to change in sleepy Saitter: Tiger's baseball–playing pal surprises her with a kiss one day, and then her grandmother dies suddenly. Tiger's sophisticated aunt comes to Saitter in the midst of the crisis, and offers to take Tiger home with her to the big city of Baton Rouge. Tiger is torn between her parents, who love her dearly, and the glamorous Dorie Kay and a world of new opportunities far from the small–mindedness of Saitter.

When a natural disaster nearly wrecks her father's workplace and another crisis arises, Tiger begins to realize the more positive aspects of life in Saitter. "With the help of Hurricane Audrey, Tiger learns how strong she is and where she truly belongs," re-

During the course of *Mister and Me,* Jolene tries in vain to rid "Mister," as she calls him, from their lives, but her strategies only backfire. On one occasion, Leroy buys her mother some expensive fabric, and Jolene cuts it to small, unusable pieces. Then her mother and grandfather must suddenly travel to New Orleans for a brief time, and Jolene is left with Leroy for caretaking. They come to a truce, and then a new beginning. Lynda Short, writing in *School Library Journal,* called it a "touching short novel" that depicts Jolene's coming to terms with the presence of a "man whose love and patience allow her to expand her notion of family." A *Publishers Weekly* review declared that "the warmth and

love in the Johnson household envelops the novel," and Kay Weisman, critiquing it for *Booklist,* noted that "this heartfelt story is filled with richly developed characters who deal with all–too–real problems."

Based Third Novel on Unusual Encounter

Holt's third novel, *When Zachary Beaver Came to Town,* won the National Book Award for Young People's Literature after its 1999 publication, and it made her a sought–after speaker in schools. On her visits and in her interviews, Holt makes it a point to remind aspiring writers—and all other aspirants—not to become discouraged by perceived negativity from a teacher, as she had once done.

The plot of *Zachary Beaver* originated with another memorable event in Holt's life; when she was thirteen, she went to the Louisiana state fair and paid two dollars to see a youth billed as "the fattest boy in the world." He sat in a small trailer and, in a manner somewhat out of character for the shy Holt, she asked him several questions about himself. He answered them, but he was understandably a bit surly about it.

"I find that a high compliment when people say that they think my characters are eccentric or quirky, because I guess that's what I love about life."

—Kimberly Willis Holt

Later in life, Holt met someone who had met the boy as well when the trailer made a stop near an office. The woman in question paid two dollars every day to see him, but ate her lunch with him. "And I just remember thinking, 'I didn't do that. I didn't come across in a kind way,'" she told Horning in the *School Library Journal* interview. Holt sets her story in Antler, Texas—a composite of two towns she knows in the Texas Panhandle—in the summer of 1971. This time, her protagonist is a boy, Toby Wilson, who is thirteen that summer. Antler is so small that the arrival of a trailer bearing "the world's fattest teenaged boy" is an interesting event, and Toby and his best friend Cal are fascinated by the tragic figure of Zachary.

A Sea of Changes

Toby's life is somewhat difficult for him that summer. His mother has left the family in order to pursue a career in the music industry in Nashville. His father, Otto, is Antler's postmaster, but also runs a worm business for bait–supply shops on the side. Toby and Cal dream of life and its possibilities outside of Antler and, like others, have made Cal's popular older brother, Wayne, a role model. Toby is also suffering from a crush on a girl named Scarlett. When Zachary Beaver arrives in his trailer, Toby and Cal visit the 643–pound boy and ask him innumerable questions. Zachary seems to possess an oddly encyclopedic knowledge of the world, but relies on his legal guardian—who disappears shortly after Zachary's trailer arrives in the parking lot of the local Dairy Maid. Toby and Cal do a bit of sleuthing and wonder why Zachary, who says he's been baptized, possesses a Bible that doesn't register that date in it, as was customary in the rural United States. Zachary finally confesses the truth, and the boys help him fulfill this dream of his. "This rebirth twists the small–town perspective in a way that serves the novel well," noted Bousquin in a *Horn Book* review. "To Zachary, Antler becomes the place on the map that has opened his heart and his life to barely–hoped–for possibilities."

Meanwhile, military officials arrive at Cal's house to tell the family that his brother Wayne has been killed in Vietnam. Toby realizes that his parents' marriage is irreparably damaged, but his quiet, kind father helps him through these difficult times. "Holt tenderly captures small–town life and deftly fills it with decent characters who ring true," wrote Linnea Lannon in the *New York Times Book Review.* Other reviewers gave it equally solid praise. "Picturesque images . . . drive home the point that everyday life is studded with memorable moments," stated *Publishers Weekly.*

Holt lives with her husband and daughter in Amarillo still, and she is working on another book, *Dancing in Cadillac Light,* scheduled to appear in 2001. When Horning asked her, in the *School Library Journal* interview, about the eccentricity of her characters and whether she would concur with this assessment, the author agreed wholeheartedly. "I think I am too," she laughed. "I'm attracted to people like that. I like the flaws in people . . . . And I also love the people that seem normal on the surface and then they're really not. I find that a high compliment when people say that they think my characters are eccentric or quirky, because I guess that's what I love about life."

If you enjoy the works of Kimberly Willis Holt, you might want to check out the following books:

Sue Ellen Bridgers, *Notes for Another Life,* 1981.
Louis Sachar, *Holes,* 1998.
Jean Thesman, *The Rain Catchers,* 1991.

■ Biographical and Critical Sources

PERIODICALS

Booklist, April 15, 1998, Hazel Rochman, review of *My Louisiana Sky,* p. 1438; November 15, 1998, Kay Weisman, review of *Mister and Me,* p. 590; January 1, 2000, review of *When Zachary Beaver Came to Town,* p. 820.

Bulletin of the Center for Children's Books, June, 1998, Betsy Hearne, review of *My Louisiana Sky,* p. 364.

Horn Book, July–August, 1998, Marilyn Bousquin, review of *My Louisiana Sky,* p. 489; November, 1999, Marilyn Bousquin, review of *When Zachary Beaver Came to Town,* p. 741.

New York Times Book Review, December 19, 1999, Linnea Lannon, review of *When Zachary Beaver Came to Town.*

Publishers Weekly, May 4, 1998, review of *My Louisiana Sky,* p. 213; August 31, 1998, review of *Mister and Me,* p. 76; November 1, 1999, review of *When Zachary Beaver Came to Town,* p. 85.

School Library Journal, July, 1998, Cindy Darling Codell, review of *My Louisiana Sky,* pp. 95–96; November, 1998, Lynda Short, review of *Mister and Me,* p. 122; February, 2000, Kathleen T. Horning, "Small Town Girl," pp. 43–45.

Texas Monthly, December, 1999, Mike Shea, review of *When Zachary Beaver Came to Town,* p. 34.

Voice of Youth Advocates, August, 1998, Lynn Evarts, review of *My Louisiana Sky,* p. 202; February, 1999, review of *My Louisiana Sky,* p. 411.*

Tanya Huff

■ Personal

Born September 26, 1957, in Halifax, Nova Scotia, Canada; partner, Fiona Patton (a writer). *Education:* Ryerson Polytechnical Institute, B.A.A.

■ Addresses

Home—Milford, Ontario, Canada. *Agent*—Joshua Bilmes, JABberwocky, P.O. Box 4558, Sunnyside, NY 11104–0558.

■ Career

Bakka (science fiction bookstore), Toronto, Ontario, manager and buyer, 1984–92; writer. *Military service:* Served three years in the Canadian Naval Reserve.

■ Awards, Honors

CASPER nomination, 1987, for "And Who Is Joah?," and 1990, for *Gate of Darkness, Circle of Light.*

■ Writings

Child of the Grove, DAW, 1988.
The Last Wizard, DAW, 1989.
Gate of Darkness, Circle of Light, DAW, 1989.
The Fire's Stone, DAW, 1990.
Blood Price, DAW, 1991.
Blood Trail, DAW, 1992.
Blood Lines, DAW, 1993.
Blood Pact, DAW, 1993.
Sing the Four Quarters, DAW, 1994.
Fifth Quarter, DAW, 1995.
Scholar of Decay, TSR, 1995.
No Quarter, DAW, 1996.
Blood Debt, DAW, 1997.
Summon the Keeper, DAW, 1998.
The Quartered Sea, DAW, 1999.
Wizard of the Grove, DAW, 1999.
What Ho, Magic! (short stories), Meshia Merlin, 1999.
Stealing Magic: The Complete Adventures of Magdelene and Terazin, Tesseract Books, 1999.
Valor's Choice, DAW, 2000.

Contributor of short stories to books, including "What Little Girls Are Made Of," published in *Magic in Ithkar, No. 3,* edited by Andre Norton and Robert Adams, Tor Books, 1986. Also contributor, sometimes under name T. S. Huff, of novellas and short stories to periodicals, including "Third Time Lucky," "And Who is Joah?," "The Last Lesson," and "The Chase Is On" to *Amazing Stories* and *Marion Zimmer Bradley's Fantasy.*

■ Work in Progress

A fifth vampire book set in Vancouver.

■ Sidelights

Wizards, magical evil, goddesses, a good measure of adventure, and other fantasy elements are the basis for several of Canadian author Tanya Huff's young adult novels. In addition to these more traditional fantasy novels, Huff is also the author of a series of books featuring a woman detective who has a vampire for a partner and a full caseload of supernatural crimes.

Huff was born in 1957 in Nova Scotia, but spent her childhood in Kingston, Ontario. She began writing at an early age, but forestalled college for a while to join the Canadian Naval Reserves, hoping to eventually serve as one of her country's first female cadets. She worked as a cook, in part because "they'd just opened [the Reserves] up to women and I figured it would be the first trade that would send women to sea," as she wrote in a biography that appeared on a Web site. "I was right. Unfortunately it happened a year after I left. No tattoos."

Huff earned a radio and television arts degree from Ryerson Polytechnical Institute in Toronto, but found a tough job market when she left school. Canada's largest electronic media outfit in the early 1980s, the Canadian Broadcasting Company, had recently laid off 750 employees. Instead, Huff found work at Bakka in Toronto, the second–oldest science–fiction bookstore in North America at the time. She worked there from 1984 to 1992, serving as both manager and buyer, and began writing fiction during this period as well. One of her first successes came when a short story, "What Little Girls Are Made Of," appeared in a 1986 issue of *Magic in Ithkar.* DAW became the publisher of her first novel, *Child of the Grove,* which appeared in 1988.

Won Steady Following with Fantasy Fiction

Although most fantasy battles between good and evil are adventure stories, Huff's second novel, *The Last Wizard,* is more of an internal battle. The wizard, Crystal, was created when seven goddesses became one to form her in order to win the battle against evil. Now that evil is no longer a threat, the goddesses want their own identities back, and Crystal must struggle to keep herself together. At the same time, she embarks on an adventure with two brothers who are searching for the tower of the ancient and evil wizard Aryalan. Challenges are encountered along the way, but the greatest are faced at the tower itself in the form of traps set by Aryalan several years ago. "The situation is highly original; the characters well developed and unique," maintained Joanne M. Riley in *Voice of Youth Advocates,* adding: "Much of the success of this book is due to the finely crafted writing style."

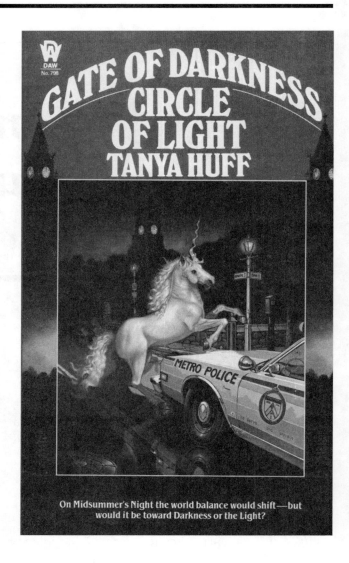

On Midsummer's Night the world balance would shift—but would it be toward Darkness or the Light?

Threatened by immortal evil forces, the future of Toronto is put in the hands of a band of misfits bound together only by their willingness to believe in the magic forces that threaten their city in Huff's 1989 novel.

The modern city of Toronto is the setting for Huff's 1989 fantasy novel *Gate of Darkness, Circle of Light.* The city is threatened by a magical evil because very few of its inhabitants still believe in magic. Among those who join together to fight this approaching darkness are a mentally disadvantaged woman who is able to see things that others cannot, a bag lady, a street musician, and a social worker.

The three heroes of *The Fire's Stone* are also thrown together in order to protect their city: Aaron, a thief; Darvish, the king's third son who has saved Aaron's life; and Chandra, an aspiring Wizard of Nine and Darvish's reluctant fiancée. When the Stone of Is-

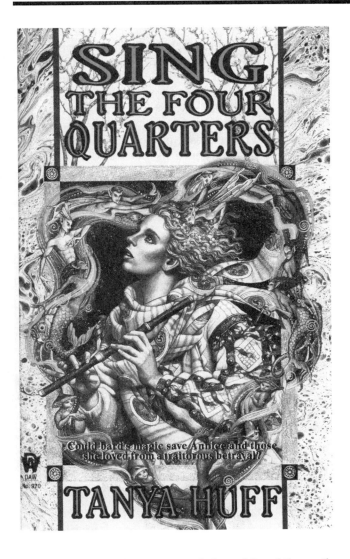

The power of music to command the spirits of the earth is at the heart of Huff's 1994 fantasy novel, as Princess Annice must draw on her natural talent to save both herself and the man she loves.

chia, which guards the city from a volcano, is stolen, Aaron, Darvish, and Chandra each bring special talents and weaknesses to their pursuit of the thief as they try to save the city. A *Publishers Weekly* reviewer observed that *The Fire's Stone* was fun to read because of the "delightful camaraderie of three unlikely heroes and well–controlled fantasy elements that are integral to the plot."

Began "Blood" Series

The character Detective Vicki Nelson is introduced in Huff's 1991 novel, *Blood Price,* and reappears in

Blood Trail, Blood Lines, and *Blood Pact.* Previously a police officer, Vicki Nelson is faced with finding the person who is killing people and draining their blood in *Blood Price.* As the murders accumulate, the media reports that it is the work of a vampire, accusations that vampire Henry Fitzroy does not appreciate. The two eventually meet and work together to solve the case. "The characterization is excellent in this tale," related Karen S. Ellis in *Kliatt.* "Tanya Huff's craft improves with each novel."

Vicki's next case, *Blood Trail,* also involves the supernatural, this time in the form of a family of werewolves—the Heerkens. Someone has killed two members of their family, and their friend, Henry Fitzroy, goes to Vicki for help. The case grows in complexity as attacks on the Heerkens continue and Detective Sergeant Mike Cellucci, Vicki's old partner and sometime–love interest, is assigned to the case. Samantha Hunt, looking forward to another book in the series, wrote in *Voice of Youth Advocates:* "These first two are fun, with entertaining characters, wry humor, crazy plots, glimpses of horror, the occult, romance, and just a dollop of sex."

After facing a mummy that poses a serious threat to the city of Toronto in Huff's third book in the series, *Blood Lines,* Vicki must next contend with her mother's death and then her animated corpse after it disappears from the funeral home in *Blood Pact.* In the meantime, she is romantically involved with both Henry and Mike, and is forced to choose between them. "Tanya Huff takes a wild mix of genres and weaves them into a surprisingly successful fantasy–mystery series featuring ex–cop Vicki Nelson," asserted Carolyn Cushman in her review of *Blood Lines* in *Locus.* Hunt, in her *Voice of Youth Advocates* review of *Blood Pact,* concluded: "Huff has retained her humor along with her horror, her characters have continued to develop, and her plots are quirky and original. All we can hope is that she'll have something new out there soon."

Huff lived in Toronto herself until 1992, when she and her partner, fellow writer Fiona Patton, moved to a more rural area. Though she seemed to have concluded the saga of Vicki Nelson with 1993's *Blood Pact,* Huff revived the popular character for *Blood Debt* in 1997. Henry Fitzroy reappears as well, and the plot of this work revolves around some troubles that begin when ghosts start to terrorize him. He tries to determine who it is that is behind their mission, and through a series of brief clues he manages to elicit from each, realizes that they are all victims who want him to kill their killers. Such vengeful bloodletting would violate the vampire code, how-

In the fifth installment in her "Blood" series, Huff teams detective Vickie Nelson and vampire Henry Fitzroy in an effort to stop a rash of murders whose supernatural perpetrators are terrorizing the city of Toronto.

koder, who extracts a deathbed promise from her father that she will be schooled for leadership. This ambition earns her the enmity of her brother, Theron, who is heir to the throne. He tries to arrange a political marriage for her, which she rejects. He then revokes her royal status, and Annice is forbidden to marry without his permission. She becomes a "bard" instead, one of Shkoder's itinerant singers who also serve as eyes and ears of the kingdom. Bards possess musical gifts as well as total memory recall, and can summon the four "Kigh" spirits of earth, fire, water, and air. Annice begins a

ever, so he enlists Vicki's help in finding justice for the restless spirits. "Huff's writing is a joy to read," wrote *Kliatt*'s Joseph R. DeMarco, who asserted that each novel in the series is so well–developed that it could be read alone.

Returned to Fantasy Fiction

Huff also began a new series in the romantic fantasy genre in 1994 with *Sing the Four Quarters*. The heroine of this novel is Annice, the princess of Sh-

Claire Hansen's job of keeping the Universe in check becomes particularly taxing when she finds herself tricked into overseeing the Elysian Fields Guesthouse and tending to its odd assortment of residents, in Huff's whimsical 1998 fantasy.

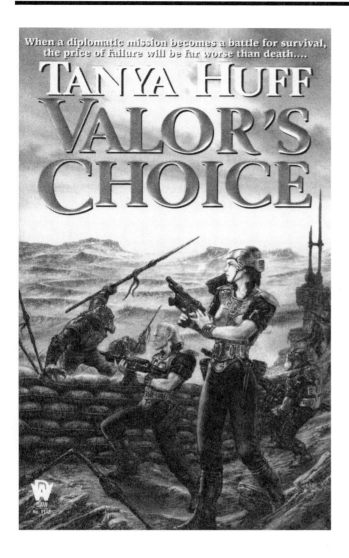

When a diplomatic mission becomes a battle for survival, the price of failure will be far worse than death....

TANYA HUFF
VALOR'S CHOICE

Huff's knack for creating strong female protagonists is central to her 2000 novel about a professional woman staff sergeant whose low-level assignment as part of a diplomatic mission to an alien world escalates into the task of saving the Confederation world from destruction.

relationship with a female bard, and eventually realizes that she is expecting a child. She learns the father is a controversial duke who is suspected of treason. As a result, Annice is drawn into some vicious family discord within the duke's realm. Jane Anne Hannigan, reviewing *Sing the Four Quarters* for *Voice of Youth Advocates*, praised Huff for creating in Annice another "feisty but always intelligent, vocal, and vigorous heroine . . . . the reader recognizes her consistent growth into a woman to be reckoned with, in what may be hoped are future bardic tales."

Other works in Huff's "Quarter" series rely heavily upon elemental magic and those who possess it to create page–turning stories. In *Fifth Quarter*, published in 1995, a pair of brother and sister assassins have been sent to kill Aralt, the aging commander of a city under siege. But Vree and Bannon become involved in several other subplots involving body–snatching, and at one point, Bannon is forced to live inside his sister's body. The kighs and the bards who can summon them again play an important role in the plot. One evil character, Kars, can sing the forgotten fifth kigh, which reanimates the dead. Vree and Bannon battle him and work to save a prince. As with the other works in the series, there is a great deal of violence and sexual content, but *Voice of Youth Advocates* critic Hannigan found that once again, Huff was able to create a sympathetic cast of characters. "As she often does, Huff throws a new perspective on evil," noted Hannigan, asserting that many of the most nefarious characters, like Kars, "seem to be victims of an inevitable fate."

If you enjoy the works of Tanya Huff, you might want to check out the following books:

Steven Brust, *Jhereg*, 1983.
Charles de Lint, *Greenmantle*, 1988.
Diane Duane, *The Door into Fire*, 1979.
P. N. Elrod, "The Vampire Files Series," 1990–92.
Elizabeth Ann Scarborough, *The Godmother*, 1994.

At the onset of *No Quarter*, which appeared in 1996, Vree and the prince, Gyhard, have fallen in love. They share a body, and set out in the end to find a healer who can help them. An army of the dead, commanded by Kars, is still a threat, while Bannon has become bodyguard to Prince Otavas. Vree and Gyhard visit the Shkoder kingdom, and bards there ask them to reveal more about the fifth kigh in exchange for helping Gyhard find a vacant body to inhabit. Such plans worry Bannon's employers, and he is sent on a mission to kidnap his sister. Bonnie Kunzel, writing about *No Quarter* for *Voice of Youth Advocates*, called it "unputdownable," while Susan Cromby, reviewing it for *Kliatt*, asserted that Huff's new series has improved with each entry, "culminating in an exciting and satisfying story of love, hate and madness."

■ Biographical and Critical Sources

BOOKS

Bliss, Laurel, *Northern Dreamers: Interviews with Famous Science Fiction, Fantasy, and Horror Writers,* Quarry, 1998.

St. James Guide to Fantasy Writers, edited by David Pringle, St. James Press, 1996, pp. 296–297.

PERIODICALS

Booklist, November 1, 1989, p. 528.

Library Journal, May 15, 1988, p. 95; November 15, 1989, p. 108; April, 1998, Jackie Cassada, review of *Summon the Keeper,* p. 119.

Locus, November, 1992, Carolyn Cushman, review of *Blood Lines,* p. 29; October, 1993, p. 27; February, 1994, p. 75.

Kliatt, September, 1991, Karen S. Ellis, review of *Blood Price,* p. 24; November, 1995, Susan Cromby, review of *Fifth Quarter,* p. 17; March, 1996, Gail Roberts, review of *Scholar of Decay,* pp. 16–17; July, 1996, Susan Cromby, review of *No Quarter,* p. 20; November, 1997, Joseph R. DeMarco, review of *Blood Debt,* p. 16.

Publishers Weekly, August 24, 1990, review of *The Fire's Stone,* p. 59.

Voice of Youth Advocates, October, 1989, Joanne M. Riley, review of *The Last Wizard,* p. 224; April, 1991, pp. 43–44; June, 1992, Samantha Hunt, review of *Blood Trail,* p. 109; February, 1994, Samantha Hunt, review of *Blood Pact,* p. 382; April, 1995, Jane Anne Hannigan, review of *Sing the Four Quarters;* February, 1996, Jane Anne Hannigan, review of *Fifth Quarter,* pp. 383–384; October, 1996, Bonnie Kunzel, review of *No Quarter,* p. 218.

ON—LINE

A Tribute to Tanya Huff, located at http://www.hickorytech.net/~vireyda/tanyahuff.htm (January 3, 2001).*

Iris Johansen

■ Personal

Children: two.

■ Addresses

Home—Atlanta, GA. *Agent*—c/o Bantam Books, 1540 Broadway, New York, NY 10036.

■ Career

Romance and romantic suspense novelist. Previously worked for a major airline.

■ Writings

NOVELS

Stormy Vows, Bantam Books (New York City), 1983.
Tempest at Sea, Bantam Books, 1983.
The Reluctant Lark, Bantam Books, 1983.
The Bronzed Hawk, Bantam Books, 1983.
The Lady and the Unicorn, Bantam Books, 1984.
The Golden Valkyrie, Bantam Books, 1984.

The Trustworthy Redhead, Bantam Books, 1984.
Return to Santa Flores, Bantam Books, 1984.
No Red Roses, Bantam Books, 1984.
Capture the Rainbow, Bantam Books, 1984.
Touch the Horizon, Bantam Books, 1984.
The Forever Dream, Bantam Books, 1985.
White Satin, Bantam Books, 1985.
Blue Velvet, Bantam Books, 1985.
A Summer Smile, Bantam Books, 1985.
And the Desert Blooms, Bantam Books, 1986.
Always, Bantam Books, 1986.
Everlasting, Bantam Books, 1986.
'Til the End of Time, Bantam Books, 1987.
Last Bridge Home, Bantam Books, 1987.
Across the River of Yesterday, Bantam Books, 1987.
The Spellbinder, Bantam Books, 1987.
Magnificent Folly, Bantam Books, 1987.
One Touch of Topaz, Bantam Books, 1988.
Star Light, Star Bright, Bantam Books, 1988.
This Fierce Splendor, Bantam Books, 1988.
Man from Half Moon Bay, Bantam Books, 1988.
Blue Skies and Shining Promises, Bantam Books, 1988.
Strong, Hot Winds, Bantam Books, 1988.
Notorious, Doubleday Loveswept, 1990.
Wicked Jake Darcy, Bantam Books, 1990.
The Golden Barbarian, Doubleday Loveswept, 1990.
Tender Savage, Bantam Books, 1991.
The Tiger Prince, Bantam Books, 1993.
Star Spangled Bride, Bantam Books, 1993.
The Magnificent Rogue, Bantam Books, 1993.
The Beloved Scoundrel, Bantam Books, 1994.
Midnight Warrior, Bantam Books, 1994.

Dark Rider, Bantam Books, 1995.
Lion's Bride, Bantam Books, 1995.
The Ugly Duckling, Bantam Books, 1996.
Long After Midnight, Bantam Books, 1996.
The Face of Deception, Bantam Books, 1998.
And Then You Die, Bantam Books, 1998.
The Killing Game, Bantam Books, 1998.
The Search, Bantam Books, 2000.

"SHAMROCK" SERIES

York the Renegade, Bantam Books, 1986.

"WILD DANCER" TRILOGY

The Wind Dancer, Bantam Books, 1991.
Storm Winds, Bantam Books, 1991.
Reap the Wind, Bantam Books, 1991.

"DELANEYS OF KILLAROO" SERIES

Matilda the Adventuress, Bantam Books, 1997.
Wild Silver, Bantam Books, 1988.
Satin Ice, Bantam Books, 1988.

OTHER

Also author of the novella "Christmas Past," published in *The Delaney Christmas Carol,* with novellas by Kay Hooper and Fayrene Preston, Doubleday (New York City), 1992.

■ Sidelights

Popular romance and romantic suspense novelist Iris Johansen is a prolific writer, having published seven novels in 1984, eight novels in 1988, and more than one novel in most other years since 1983. Quantity of output, however, has not stopped her from being an innovator, in the view of Barbara E. Kemp in *Twentieth–Century Romance and Historical Writers.* "She has stretched the boundaries of the standard formulas in the category romance field and has written some of the best historical romance novels," declared Kemp.

Johansen writes category romances set in several historical eras and has become known for the conviction with which she describes bygone places and people. Her characterizations are considered among the more complex in the genre. As for sex, Kemp pointed out that the presence of one or more long

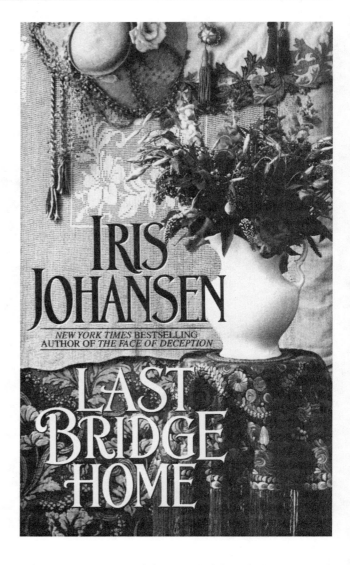

Johansen's 1987 novel features a likeable heroine and an unseen threat, as widowed Elizabeth Ramsey meets and becomes fascinated by a handsome, charismatic, yet somehow unsettling stranger who claims to be a link to the husband she still loves.

seduction scenes is a hallmark of Johansen's work, and that, although the seduction often contains "an element of punishment," it is always made clear that the heroine is not in real physical danger. Commented Kemp, "The uncertainty of remaining safely on the edge of possible pain adds sexual tension to the stories."

Fictional States

Several of Johansen's novels have belonged to Bantam/Doubleday's Loveswept line of romances, beginning with *Stormy Vows*, Johansen's first novel, published in 1983. However, her historical novels have taken her—and her readers—into far corners of the earth. In particular, Johansen has made two imaginary countries, the Middle Eastern kingdom of Sedikhan and the Balkan state of Tamrovia, her own. Characters recur from book to book, and the two nations are linked by marriage; thus, Johansen's loyal readers can follow the fortunes of favorite characters such as recovering drug addict David Bradford (who originally appeared in *The Trustworthy Redhead*), who finds love and contentment in *Touch the Horizon* with a woman, Billie Callahan, herself a star of *Capture the Rainbow*.

Johansen's novels are sometimes included in established series which feature novels written by several authors. For example, in the "Shamrock" Trilogy, a series about the Delaney brothers of Ireland, Johansen wrote *York the Renegade* while the two other novels were written by Kay Hooper and Fayrene Preston. The "Delaneys of Killaroo" series is a spinoff of the Shamrock tales, focusing on three sisters in the Australian branch of the Delaney family. Although not officially part of the Delaney series, the novel *This Fierce Splendor* deals with a male character who is a Delaney. The trio of authors contributing to the trilogy also wrote a Christmas book, *The Delaney Christmas Carol*, in which each writer contributed a novella.

Well–Paced Historical Dramas

Johansen wrote the novels comprising the "Wind Dancer" trilogy of 1991, the first two volumes of which received considerable acclaim from romance reviewers. The novels, spanning much of European history, deal with the Andreas family's quest for a legendary golden statue called the Wind Dancer. The first novel, *The Wind Dancer*, is set in sixteenth–century Italy, and the second, *Storm Winds*, in France during the Reign of Terror near the end of the eighteenth century. *The Wind Dancer*, which had a first printing of 700,000 copies, is "a lively and imaginative blend of romance and adventure," according to *Publishers Weekly*; that magazine's reviewer also applauded the character of Lorenzo Vasaro, the hero's friend, who is "an unlikely but likable character . . .[,] a worldly–wise and intriguing blend of ruthlessness and charm."

Peggy Kaganoff, another *Publishers Weekly* reviewer, called *Storm Winds* "a diverting romance" with "plot twists worthy of a mystery novel." However, Kaganoff felt that the concluding segment of the trilogy, *Reap the Wind*, suffered under the weight of the au-

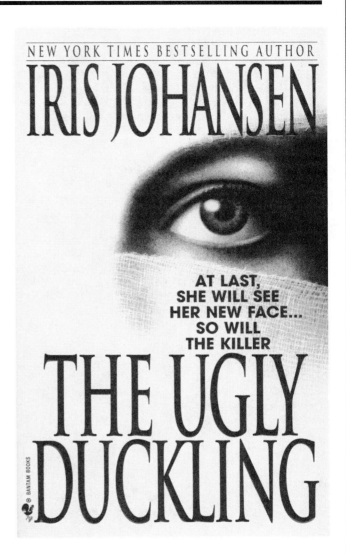

Johansen's first foray into the modern thriller genre was in 1996, with her story of a woman injured in a murder attempt whose reconstructed face proves to be no deterrent to the killer who wants to try again.

thor's apparent aspiration to make it a contemporary spy novel involving the CIA and the KGB. Kemp, while expressing opinions similar to those of *Publishers Weekly* regarding the relative merits of the three volumes in the trilogy, pointed out that "a disappointing novel by Johansen is still far better than the work of many other authors."

A Career Milestone

Johansen went on to produce other well–received romance novels in the 1990s. Of *The Magnificent*

The struggle between career and motherhood are given a sharp twist of fate in Johansen's 1996 novel as successful scientist Kate Denby finds herself and her son the target of a killer determined to stop her research at any cost.

Rogue, published in 1993, *Booklist* commented, "Passion and suspense abound in [this]. . . robust romance. . . . Spellbinding romantic fiction from a master of the genre." *Library Journal*'s Bettie Alston Spivey called the 1994 novel *The Beloved Scoundrel,* a romance of the Napoleonic era, "absorbing" and thought readers would find it a page–turner by an author who "has outdone herself here." The same year, Johansen produced *Midnight Warrior,* a tale of England and Wales set in 1066. Kristin Ramsdell of *Library Journal* commented on the book and wrote:

"Believable, thoughtfully constructed characters, complex plotting, and lively dialog characterize this sensual historical."

Johansen achieved a personal milestone in 1996 with the publication of *The Ugly Duckling.* It was her most prestigious publication to date, although not the "hardcover debut" that a *Kirkus Reviews* critic termed it (at least two of her previous novels had been placed between hardcovers, but in the Loveswept line rather than as solo creations). In *The Ugly Duckling,* commented the *Kirkus Reviews* critic, "megaseller Johansen abandons the lush historical romances that have made her reputation and stakes out the proven market of Nora Roberts and Sidney Sheldon." The heroine, Nell, is the plain wife of a rich man who, along with their daughter, is murdered before her eyes; Nell herself is thrown off a cliff and survives, but is disfigured. Hero Nicholas, pursuing the drug dealers who killed Nell's family, takes her under his wing and sees that she receives state–of–the–art plastic surgery that turns her into a beauty. He also teaches her martial arts. Nell and Nicholas set out to destroy the villains and do so with the help of what the *Kirkus Reviews* critic called "inventive surprises." A *Publishers Weekly* reviewer called *The Ugly Duckling* "spectacular" and elaborated: "The romance here is suspenseful, and the suspense is romantic; for fans of each, this is a keeper." *Booklist's* Brad Hooper announced that, in *The Ugly Duckling,* "the romantic suspense genre is done a good turn."

Having achieved this new level of success, Johansen went on to create another successful thriller with her next book, *Long After Midnight,* a tale of scientific breakthroughs and corrupt corporations. The heroine, Kate, is a high–level working mother doing important research for top scientist Noah Smith and trying to give her nine–year–old son a good life at the same time. When Noah's lab blows up and attempts are made on Kate's life, Kate and Noah go into hiding to escape from the psychopathic hit man who is stalking them. Kate has two love interests, Noah and his solder–of–fortune friend, Seth. Noting that the plot premise contains some familiar, conventional elements, a *Publishers Weekly* critic added that "Johansen knows how to take the formula and run with it," appealing to readers with her believable characters, effective dialogue, and interesting plotting. The review also noted that a plot strand involving the heroine's father, an Alzheimer's patient, gives "the deft but somewhat protracted finish a moving, unexpected touch."

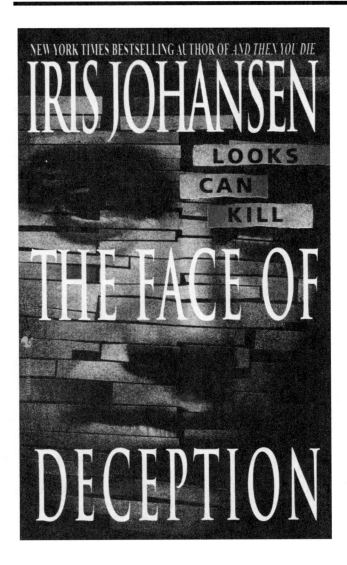

Johansen enters the modern crime lab in her 1998 thriller, as forensic sculptor Eve Duncan moonlights for a wealthy client whose request—to recreate the face of a skull in his possession—results in murder.

Segued Into Other Genres

Johansen continued to further her fiction horizons into the modern era with three new novels published by Bantam in 1998. *And Then You Die* is a contemporary medical/espionage thriller starring Bess Grady, a photojournalist who is recovering from a stressful working trip to war–torn Croatia. Vacationing with her sister Emily, a physician, Bess arrives in a small Mexican town with an easy assignment for a travel magazine. But they discover that all of the local residents have suddenly died, save for an infant girl. Soon, Bess is taken hostage

by a group of armed men, and learns that their leader has tested a biological weapon, the deadly anthrax virus, on the town. There are plans to unleash it on a much wider scale to further their political aims.

Drugged without her permission, Bess awakes and attempts an escape. She is caught and guarded by one of the rebel band, who also has orders to kill her. But Kaldak reveals himself as a renegade, frees her instead, and they flee. In reality, he is an undercover operative for the Central Intelligence Agency, and he insists that she and the surviving infant return home, since their blood obviously possesses

It began as a low–key assignment for a travel magazine, but in Johansen's hands photojournalist Bess Grady's trip to Mexico quickly becomes transformed into a nightmarish battle for survival in the author's 1998 medical thriller.

the natural antidote to anthrax. The action moves to Atlanta, where the National Center for Disease Control is situated, and then to Bess's apartment in New Orleans's French Quarter, where she and Kaldak fall into a tenuous romance. In their efforts to thwart the international terrorist conspiracy in the works, Bess finds that those she encounters are often not who they seem, and she is even wary about trusting Kaldak—a former doctor with a troubling secret. "Fans of conspiracy thrillers will enjoy the action," noted Kathleen Hughes in a *Booklist* review of *And Then You Die*. Arrye Rosser, critiquing the work for *Kliatt*, also praised Johansen's fifty–first novel, remarking, "The characters grow increasingly interesting and more complicated as the plot unfolds." A *Kirkus Reviews* assessment commended the author's skills as a contemporary storyteller. "Johansen continues the trend of creating female leads whose physical strength and personal courage are as well developed as the moral fiber they share with heroines of old," the review noted.

In 1998, Johansen also moved into the detective genre with an appealing female lead created for a pair of new books. *The Face of Deception* introduces Eve Duncan, a talented forensic sculptor with a national reputation. But Eve's personal triumphs have been hard–won, for she was raised in an abusive, neglectful home. In the course of this first novel, her eight–year–old daughter, Bonnie, is abducted. Though the body is never found, the killer is brought to justice at the end. Eve's story continues in *The Killing Game*, which finds her retired from her gruesome profession to a remote South Pacific island. Joe Quinn, her cop friend from the first novel, visits to inform her of the discovery of a mass grave of children in Georgia. Authorities believe her daughter's remains might be here.

Eve agrees to return home to help in the efforts, and there someone begins tormenting her. Her stalker, who calls himself Dom, claims he killed her daughter and threatens to murder her as well. Eve and the police realize that he may indeed be the culprit, a killer who has become so criminally insane that he now needs to interact with his future victims in order to achieve satisfaction. With the memory of her lost daughter always near, the intrepid Eve agrees to enter into a strategic but perilous plan to lure him near for capture. "An enthralling cat–and–mouse game ensues," noted a *Publishers Weekly* review of *The Killing Game*, "throughout which Johansen maintains perfect pacing, always revealing just enough to keep the reader turning the pages." Emily Melton, writing in *Booklist*, called the novel "a cross between [Stephen] King's nightmarish chillers and [Patricia] Cornwell's forensic thrillers," and full of "dozens of heartstopping plot twists."

If you enjoy the works of Iris Johansen, you might want to check out the following books:

Janet Dailey, *Masquerade,* 1990.
Tami Hoag, *Night Sins,* 1996.
Rosalind Laker, *Tree of Gold,* 1986.
Nora Roberts, *Public Secrets,* 1990.
Elizabeth Stuart, *Bride of the Lion,* 1995.

■ Biographical and Critical Sources

BOOKS

Vasudevan, Aruna, editor, *Twentieth–Century Romance and Historical Writers,* third edition, St. James Press (London), 1994, pp. 353–354.

PERIODICALS

Booklist, September 1, 1993, p. 34; March 1, 1996, p. 1076; November, 1997, Kathleen Hughes, review of *And Then You Die,* p. 435; August, 1998, Diana Tixier Herald, review of *The Face of Deception,* p. 1923; August, 1999, Emily Melton, review of *The Killing Game,* p. 1987.
Entertainment Weekly, October 29, 1999, Gillian Flynn, review of *The Killing Game,* p. 106.
Kirkus Reviews, February 15, 1996, p. 249; September 1, 1998, review of *The Face of Deception,* p. 1218; November 15, 1998, review of *And Then You Die,* pp. 1664–1665.
Kliatt, January, 1999, Arrye Rosser, review of *And Then You Die,* p. 41; March, 1999, Mary I. Purucker, review of *The Face of Deception,* p. 52.
Library Journal, December, 1993, pp. 174–175; May 15, 1994, p. 66; September 1, 1999, Adrienne Furness, review of *The Face of Deception,* p. 250.
Publishers Weekly, January 4, 1991, p. 68; April 26, 1991, p. 55; September 13, 1991, pp. 73–74; November 30, 1992, p. 49; July 26, 1993, p. 63; January 3, 1994, p. 78; July 4, 1994, p. 57; March 13, 1995, p. 65; December 4, 1995, p. 58; February 26, 1996, p. 84; May 18, 1996, p. 25; December 30, 1996, p. 54; November 10, 1997, p. 54; August 17, 1998, review of *The Face of Deception,* p. 45; July 12, 1999, review of *The Killing Game,* p. 75.

ON–LINE

Bantam, Doubleday, Dell Online Web site, located at http://www.bdd.com/ (January 29, 1999).
Books@Random Web site, located at http://www.randomhouse.com/ (January 29, 1999).*

William Joyce

phrey's Bear; Best Illustrated Award, *New York Times*, 1989, for *Nicholas Cricket*; Parents' Choice Award, 1991, for *A Day with Wilbur Robinson*; Silver Medal, Society of Illustrators, and Reading Magic Award, both 1992, both for *Bently and Egg*; Gold award, Society of Illustrators, 1993, for *Santa Calls*; Emmy Award nomination, Outstanding Special Class—Animated Program, National Academy of Television Arts and Sciences, and Certificate of Merit, San Francisco International Film Festival, and Gemini Award for Best Writing in a Children's of Youth Program, Academy of Canadian Cinema and Television, and Award of Excellence, Alliance for Children's Television, all 1999, all for animated television show *Rolie Polie Olie*.

■ Personal

Born December 11, 1957; married; wife's name, Elizabeth; children: Mary Katherine, Jack. *Education:* Graduated from Southern Methodist University.

■ Addresses

Home and office—3302 Centenary Blvd., Shreveport, LA 71104.

■ Career

Screenwriter, author, and illustrator. Continuing cover artist for the *New Yorker* magazine. Producer, co–screenwriter, and set designer for film *Buddy*, Columbia Pictures, 1997. Executive producer of animated children's television show *Rolie Polie Olie*, Disney Channel, 1998—. National Center for Children's Illustrated Literature, board member, 1999—.

■ Awards, Honors

Best Book Award, *School Library Journal*, 1985, for *George Shrinks*; Redbook Award, 1987, and Christopher Award (best illustration), 1988, both for *Hum-

■ Writings

AUTHOR AND ILLUSTRATOR

George Shrinks, Harper, 1985, special miniature edition, 1985.

Dinosaur Bob and His Adventures with the Family Lazardo, Harper, 1988.

A Day with Wilbur Robinson, HarperCollins, 1990.

Bently and Egg, HarperCollins, 1992.

Santa Calls, HarperCollins, 1993.

The Leaf Men and the Brave Good Bugs, HarperCollins, 1996.

Buddy (middle–grade novel), HarperCollins, 1997.

The World of William Joyce Scrapbook, HarperCollins, 1997.

Dinosaur Bob (board book), HarperCollins, 1998.

Life with Bob (board book), HarperCollins, 1998.

Baseball Bob (board book), HarperCollins, 1999.

Rolie Polie Olie, HarperCollins, 1999.

Snowie Rolie, HarperCollins, 2000.

ILLUSTRATOR

Catherine and James Gray, *Tammy and the Gigantic Fish,* Harper, 1983.

(Under name Bill Joyce) Marianna Mayer, *My First Book of Nursery Tales: Five Mother Goose Stories,* Random House, 1983.

Bethany Roberts, *Waiting–for–Spring Stories,* Harper, 1984.

Elizabeth Winthrop, *Shoes,* Harper, 1986.

Jan Wahl, *Humphrey's Bear,* Holt, 1987.

Joyce Maxner, *Nicholas Cricket,* Harper, 1989.

Stephen Manes, *Some of the Adventures of Rhode Island Red,* HarperCollins, 1990.

Also contributor of illustrations to periodicals, including cover art for the *New Yorker.*

OTHER

(With Caroline Thompson) *Buddy* (screenplay), Columbia Pictures, 1997.

■ Adaptations

A Day with Wilbur Robinson has been optioned as a feature–length animated film by Walt Disney Feature Animation; *Dinosaur Bob* has been optioned as a full–length motion picture by Walt Disney Feature Animation; *Santa Calls* has also been optioned for film.

■ Work in Progress

Producing and designing a feature length animated motion picture based on *Nicholas Cricket* for Warner Brothers Feature Animation.

■ Sidelights

Author–illustrator William Joyce has a dream: to be remembered for "a significant contribution to the cause of global silliness," as he told Sally Lodge in a *Publishers Weekly* interview. In books such as *Dinosaur Bob and His Adventures with the Family Lazardo, A Day with Wilbur Robinson, Bently and Egg, The Leaf Men and the Brave Good Bugs, Buddy,* and *Rolie Polie Olie* Joyce presents characters and settings that are colorful, magical and slightly wacky. Joyce's cast of players includes such unique characters as a base-ball–playing dinosaur, a frog who can sing and paint, a little boy who wakes up one morning to find himself becoming very, very small, an aging socialite who keeps a menagerie which includes three hundred St. Bernards and two gorillas on her New York estate, and a billiard–ball shaped robot who loves doing the rumba in his underwear.

> *"Picture books and movies have a lot in common in that they both tell their stories visually in color, movement, and composition. Often, when I'm working on my books, it plays as a movie in my head."*
>
> —William Joyce

Drawing on a wide range of influences, ranging from artists Maxfield Parrish, Maurice Sendak, and N. C. Wyeth to Technicolor movies, Joyce imbues his illustrations with vivid colors and painstaking detail. In Joyce's world, it is perfectly normal for a city family to adopt a friendly dinosaur or a "dull day" at a friend's house to include entertainment by jazz–playing frogs and a robot butler. Malcolm Jones, Jr., writing in *Newsweek,* summed up the author's appeal by noting that "looniness is Joyce's briar patch.... Reading Joyce is like hanging out with that slightly raffish uncle who came to town a couple of times a year, the one who drank martinis ... and always kept a few cherry bombs in the bottom of his suitcase. He was the guy who taught you that fun is the most important thing you can have."

Always Imaginative

Joyce became interested in drawing and storytelling at an early age. "I loved to draw and I loved to make things up," Joyce once remarked. "I always took play a little more seriously ... and I always liked to be the guy who got into the story part of

William Joyce at home, working on a Fourth of July creation.

love." Joyce's story of Billy and his pal—and the trouble that story got him into at school—will form the basis of an upcoming picture book.

While he enjoyed reading and watching movies and television, Joyce had ambivalent feelings about school—with the exception of art classes. "I hated [school] and loved it.... I hated getting up in the morning. I hated having to go there every day. I hated having to study. I hated having to sit there and learn mathematics.... I liked the social aspect of school—I mean I had a blast—but I hated the tyranny of learning," he once recalled. A self–admitted daydreamer, Joyce spent a lot of time imagining himself as a secret agent, until he realized that "secret agents sometimes get killed *and* kiss girls."

Joyce eventually decided to study filmmaking and illustration at Southern Methodist University. Part of his decision was based on a long–term fascination with movie imagery. "I got into movies," he once stated. "There were extraordinary things like Oz, Robin Hood, King Kong.... I was completely swept away.... Picture books and movies have a lot in common in that they both tell their stories visually in color, movement, and composition. Often, when I'm working on my books, it plays as a movie in my head."

"I'll see something that will trigger a series of thoughts or I'll just have some odd phrase words at the back of my mind. At some point, something strikes my fancy from my past, and ends up being in a book."

—William Joyce

---

the adventure." He received his first artistic kudos for a pictorial rendition of a dog and cat; soon after this success, Joyce moved on to bigger subjects, such as rampaging dinosaurs lopping off the heads and arms of cavemen. Joyce notes that, when sketching these later works, he "always ran out of red crayon and red pen faster than anything because of all the gore and blood."

Joyce wrote his first successful story while still in grade school. "Billy's Booger" chronicles the adventures of a young boy who "sneezes up" a talkative—and very smart—booger. Over the years, Billy's jovial, diminutive, "green and sort of slimy" pal has become a popular part of the author's school visits. Joyce observes in his interview: "Pandemonium ensues when I start drawing him.... [Billy's Booger] appeals to that sense of grotesque kids seem to

Joyce began sending samples of his work to publishers before his graduation from college; within a short time, he received a number of contracts for his illustrations. While happy to gain the practical experience, Joyce eventually found himself becoming a bit frustrated. He notes in his interview: "I began to enjoy it less and less as it went on. I began to work more and more of my own stories into [the assignments]."

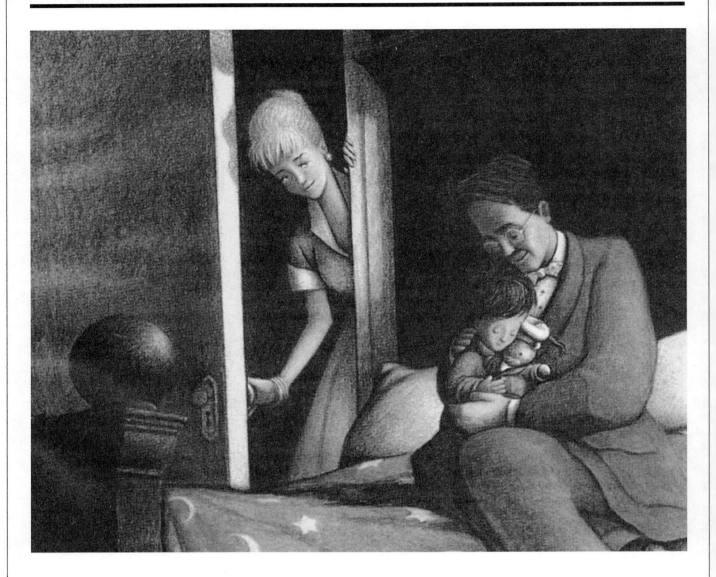

Joyce's gentle colored–pencil illustrations for Jan Wahl's 1987 picture book *Humphrey's Bear* **feature the comforting stability of family life as it was idealistically portrayed during the 1950s.**

Branches Out on His Own

Joyce wrote his first self–illustrated book in 1985. *George Shrinks* tells the story of a little boy who wakes up one day to find that he has shrunk several sizes. Instead of panicking, George uses a number of ingenious tricks to get his daily chores done, including feeding his goldfish by diving into their bowl and saddling his baby brother to take out the trash. Writing in the *New York Times Book Review*, Ralph Keyes called the story "a thoroughly charming piece of work." He added that the book's minimalist prose is "a perfect foil for Mr. Joyce's whim-

sical, perceptive illustrations." John Cech, reviewing this debut book in *Washington Post Book World*, noted that "Joyce gives this well–worn fantasy situation new wrinkles through illustrations that are generous in their sense of humor, character and clever pace." Cech went on to observe that these elements "hold the reader in the spell of young George's adventures."

Joyce introduced one of his most popular characters in the follow–up to *George Shrinks* entitled *Dinosaur Bob and His Adventures with the Family Lazardo*. Bob the dinosaur meets the Lazardos during their annual safari in Africa. The entire family is so taken by the gentle giant that they invite him to live with them in beautiful Pimlico Hills. Once he is happily settled in his new home, the good–natured dinosaur's baseball–playing skills make him popular with the entire neighborhood; unfortunately, his enthusiasm for chasing cars eventually gets him into trouble with the local police. After a series of adventures–on–the–lam, Bob is reunited with his adopted family and all is well. In a review of *Dinosaur Bob* for the *New York Times Book Review,* Mordecai Richler declared that Bob is "the most adorable of dinos." Richler went on to note that Joyce "managed the illustrations with considerable panache. His artwork makes it clear why Bob is such a hit with the Lazardos." A *Time* reviewer concurred, noting: "William Joyce's plot and pictures provide laughter, thrills, and most important, a happy ending." Several reviewers drew attention to Joyce's apparent love of Deco camp. A *Publishers Weekly* contributor noted the "illustrational style reminiscent of 1920s magazine advertising," while Michael Dirda commented in *Washington Post Book World,* "Not quite tongue–in–cheek, the story nonetheless offers up a number of little touches of Depression–era culture." Included among these are homages to Raymond Chandler, F. Scott Fitzgerald, and Bob the dinosaur himself, who "acts rather like a more benign King Kong, as he travels down the Nile." *Dinosaur Bob* has inspired two board book spin–offs, *Life with Bob* and *Baseball Bob.*

Joyce added to his repertoire of unique characters in *A Day with Wilbur Robinson,* which is based on some of the more unusual goings–on in his family. An eye–popping adventure full of music, magic, and mystery, *Wilbur Robinson* centers on a boy's day–long visit with his friend's unorthodox family. Action is the name of the game at the Robinson abode, where Uncle Art regales listeners with tales about his escapades in outer space and giant goldfish mingle with dog–riding frogs. In his commentary on *Wilbur Robinson* for the *New York Times Book Review,* David Leavitt wrote: "Painted in such a realistic way, the bizarre events in the pictures seem appealingly plausible.... This is a charming, new–fangled, old–fashioned book." Michael Cart, reviewing the book in the *Los Angeles Times Book Review,* announced "Joyce is arguably the most original talent working in the children's–book field today. Who else could have created a family as endearingly wacky as the Robinson's?"

More Offbeat Tales

The drawings in *Bently and Egg* marked a departure for Joyce. Instead of his usual palette of bold colors,

Joyce utilizes soft watercolor pastels reminiscent of Beatrix Potter's "Peter Rabbit" tales to tell the story of the frog Bently Hopperton and his efforts to save a duck friend's egg. Whether guarding the egg or sailing in a balloon, Bently's ingenuity never fails him. Jones, writing in *Newsweek,* found the high–spirited adventures of Joyce's amphibious protagonist highly enjoyable, calling the book "every bit as zestful as its predecessors.... Bently is never at a loss. Jubilantly resourceful, he has a swell time being a hero." *Horn Book*'s Nancy Vasilakis hailed the "playful language" as "full–bodied and musical," explaining that it is "a pleasure to read aloud." Cathy Collison praised the gentle, soft illustrations, writing in the *Detroit Free Press* that the artwork is "on the Caldecott Medal level."

Joyce's next book, *Santa Calls,* is "an extravagant homage to Hollywood as much as to the holidays," according to Roger Sutton in *Bulletin of the Center for Children's Books.* Art Atchinson Aimesworth and his adoring little sister, Esther, live with their aunt and uncle, who run a Wild West show. Art is too busy dreaming of invention, adventure, and heroism to be nice or even pay attention to Esther—until the day Santa sends a mysterious message to their Texas home asking them to come north. When Esther is seized by the Queen of the Dark during their travels, Art insists *he* will rescue her alone—and does, in a madcap adventure reminiscent of Hollywood serials. "Joyce combines fast–paced narrative with his witty, infectious illustrations, which ... look like a child's Technicolor dreams," Michael Anderson remarked in the *New York Times Book Review.* "The whole book has a 1930s feel," Ilene Cooper explained in *Booklist,* "from the stylized art to the very nature of the adventure, with its overtones of Saturday movie serials." As Jane Marino concluded in *School Library Journal, Santa Calls* is "a tour de force that should not be missed."

Joyce's next book, *The Leaf Men and the Brave Good Bugs,* had its genesis in a story the artist told his young daughter. As he related to Lodge in *Publishers Weekly,* he had just returned home after caring for a terminally ill friend. "I was sad and she could tell. She asked me to tell her a story, which is something she almost never asks and something I almost never do. And *The Leaf Men* tumbled out of my mouth, pretty much fully formed. Months later I realized that the story was about loss and how memories of people you've lost who are dear to you can keep them alive."

The Leaf Men and the Brave Good Bugs tells of the battle for both the life of an elderly woman and the health of her garden. When the woman takes ill, she is confined to bed and unable to tend her garden. Her rosebush grows sickly at the same time, and the insects in the garden decide to summon the mysterious Leaf Men to help them battle the evil Spider Queen and restore the garden. While a *Reading Time* contributor noted that "there are multiple layers to this complex story," other critics found that Joyce's "characteristically offbeat and occasionally eerie illustrations carry the day," as a *Publishers Weekly* writer stated. In a *Booklist* review, Susan Dove Lempke praised the artist's unique perspective which presents characters "depicted in lush green, enticing paintings filled with fascinating detail."

Film and Television Work

Although very busy with writing and illustrating books, Joyce has found time to do work in motion pictures as well. He was one of several illustrators who contributed designs to the Disney computer–animated film *Toy Story*, and he co–wrote and co–produced the 1997 film *Buddy*, a real life story about Gertrude Lintz, an eccentric socialite who attempted to raise a gorilla on her New York estate in the 1930s. *Buddy* was also turned into a chapter book. "I came across Mrs. Lintz's life by accident while researching something else," Joyce told Lodge. "I was thrilled, since it blends my three big enthusiasms: the 1930s, King Kong and eccentric households." Lintz raised the gorilla named Buddy only to discover the animal was not made for city living. Joyce adapted his tale from this actual situation.

"Once you enter Joyce's world, you'll never want to leave."

—Malcolm Jones, Jr.

In the book, Buddy sports ties, eats at a formal table, and shops at Bergdorf's. Gertie raises him from infancy and takes him with her everywhere she goes. But on a trip to the World's Fair in 1933, she finally realizes that Buddy cannot deal with the close quarters of even the most sumptuous of hotels. He makes a bid for freedom on the African Safari ride at the Fair, and this finally lets Gertie know that her charge is ready for a change of life. She decides to

sacrifice her feelings and finds the perfect environment for him at the Philadelphia Zoo. Carol Ann Wilson, writing in *School Library Journal*, remarked, "Youngsters will empathize with Gertie, who must wistfully temper her childlike enthusiasm when faced with reality." Wilson also drew attention to Joyce's "sepia–toned drawings" which "serve as visual vignettes of the period." *Booklist*'s Cooper noted that the "whole book has the deco feel of the 1930s in which the events took place."

Joyce has also completed full–length screenplays for *A Day with Wilbur Robinson* and *Santa Calls,* and hopes for productions some time in the future. Also in the works are a series of holiday specials for Fox Television. Joyce also continues his career as a children's book writer and illustrator. As he told Lodge, "No matter what happens, I know I always have three or four books in the works to come home to." One of those books was the 1998 *The World of William Joyce Scrapbook,* an assemblage of "interesting tidbits and artistic insights," according to *Booklist*'s Cooper, that "will be of particular interest to budding artists."

In 1999 Joyce issued a picture book titled *Rolie Polie Olie*. Based on an Emmy Award–winning television program of the same name that Joyce produced, the book tells the tale of a round robot living on a planet where everything, but everything is round. For the projects, Joyce and his friends collaborated with three hundred animators on several continents to develop computerized animation over the Internet to tell the story of his intergalactic robots. In the book, after a day of adventures with his family, including Mom, Dad, sister Zowie, and dog Spot, Olie is too excited to go to bed. Dancing in his underpants and having fun with chores have taken their toll. Michael Cart, writing in *Booklist*, called the book "a sweet, spirited story, told in verse." The characters are all spherical, with bodies reminiscent of billiard balls, while computer–generated backgrounds add a sort of three–dimensional, science fiction look to the enterprise.

Joyce says that many of his story and character ideas come "out of nowhere." "I'll see something that will trigger a series of thoughts or I'll just have some odd phrase words at the back of my mind," he explained. "At some point, something strikes my fancy from my past, and ends up being in a book." Joyce often turns to his family for inspiration; in fact, he notes that developing characters is often a family affair: "Elizabeth [his wife] actually posed for a lot of my characters.... My nephews would pose for me, my dad would pose for me, whoever's around. I'll say 'Stand here, put on this cap, do this.'" Joyce's works appeal to both young and old.

"They strike a playful chord that grownups remember from their own childhoods," Joyce stated. "[The books] ... harken back to the sort of shared popular culture that we all grew up with on television—Flash Gordon from the thirties, the Stooges from the forties, Bugs Bunny from the fifties. Growing up watching television, you would see this constant barrage of cool stuff ... it's become a sort of shared sensibility." Jones voiced the sentiment of a legion of the author–illustrators fans in *Newsweek:* "Once you enter Joyce's world, you'll never want to leave."

If you enjoy the works of William Joyce, you might want to check out the following:

Florence Parry Heide's *The Shrinking of Treehorn,* illustrated by Edward Gorey, 1971.

The works of Jon Scieszka and Lane Smith, including *The Stinky Cheese Man and Other Fairly Stupid Tales,* 1992, and *Math Curse,* 1995.

The works of Maxfield Parrish and N. C. Wyeth, two artists who influenced Joyce.

■ Biographical and Critical Sources

BOOKS

Children's Literature Review, Volume 26, Gale, 1992.

Silvey, Anita, editor, *Children's Books and Their Creators,* Houghton, 1995.

Sixth Book of Junior Authors and Illustrators, Wilson, 1989.

St. James Guide to Children's Writers, 5th edition, St. James Press, 1999.

PERIODICALS

Booklist, August, 1993, Ilene Cooper, review of *Santa Calls,* p. 2060; October 1, 1996, Susan Dove Lempke, review of *The Leaf Men and the Brave Good Bugs,* pp. 358–59; August, 1997, Ilene Cooper, review of *Buddy,* p. 1901; January 1, 1998, Ilene Cooper, review of *The World of William Joyce Scrapbook,* p. 805; November 1, 1999, Michael Cart, review of *Rolie Polie Olie.*

Bulletin of the Center for Children's Books, October, 1993, Roger Sutton, review of *Santa Calls,* pp. 48–49; September, 1997, p. 165; February, 1998, p. 208.

Detroit Free Press, March 18, 1992, Cathy Collison, review of *Bently and Egg.*

Horn Book, March–April, 1992, Nancy Vasilakis, review of *Bently and Egg,* pp. 191–92.

Los Angeles Times Book Review, November 25, 1990, Michael Cart, "Picture Windows to the World," pp. 24–25.

Magpies, March, 1997, p. 29; July, 1997, p. 30.

Newsweek, March 16, 1992, Malcolm Jones, Jr., "Make Room for Bently," p. 72.

New York Times Book Review, December 29, 1985, Ralph Keyes, review of *George Shrinks,* p. 23; November 13, 1988, Mordecai Richler, review of *Dinosaur Bob,* p. 60; November 11, 1990, David Leavitt, "Can I Go Over to Wilbur's?," p. 29; December 19, 1993, Michael Anderson, review of *Santa Calls,* p. 16.

Publishers Weekly, June 24, 1988, review of *Dinosaur Bob and His Adventures with the Family Lazardo,* p. 111; July 15, 1996, review of *The Leaf Men and the Brave Good Bugs,* p. 73; September 16, 1996, Sally Lodge, "William Joyce Goes Hollywood—Sort Of," pp. 28–29; February 1, 1999, p. 86; September 6, 1999, p. 101.

Reading Time, May, 1997, review of *The Leaf Men and the Brave Good Bugs,* p. 22.

School Library Journal, October, 1993, Jane Marino, review of *Santa Calls,* pp. 44–45; January, 1997, p. 37; August, 1997, Carol Ann Wilson, review of *Buddy,* p. 136; February, 1998, p. 100.

Southern Living, December, 1996, p. 102.

Time, December 12, 1988, review of *Dinosaur Bob and His Adventures with the Family Lazardo,* p. 87.

Variety, June 9, 1997, p. 69.

Washington Post Book World, November 10, 1985, John Cech, "A Palette of Picture Books," pp. 19, 22; October 9, 1988, Michael Dirda, review of *Dinosaur Bob and His Adventures with the Family Lazardo,* pp. 10–11.

Joan Lingard

Scriptwriter for the Scottish Television network and the British Broadcasting Corporation (BBC). Has also worked in a bank in Belfast and as a library assistant in Edinburgh.

■ Personal

Born April 8, 1932, in Edinburgh, Scotland; daughter of Henry James (Chief Yeoman of Signals in the Royal Navy) and Elizabeth (a homemaker; maiden name, Beattie) Lingard; married first husband, c. 1954 (divorced, 1970); married second husband, Martin Birichaws (an architect and lecturer), c. 1972; children: (first marriage) Kersten, Bridget, Jenny. *Education:* Attended Bloomfield Collegiate School, Belfast; Moray House Training College of Education, Edinburgh, General Certificate of Education, c. 1954. *Religion:* Raised Christian Scientist. *Hobbies and other interests:* Being a grandmother, reading, walking, travel.

■ Addresses

Home—72 Great King St., Edinburgh EH3 6QU, Scotland. *Agent*—c/o David Higham Assoc., 5/8 Lower John St., London W1R 4HA, England.

■ Career

Author, scriptwriter, and educator. Teacher in Belfast, Ireland, c. 1948, and Midloathian district, Edinburgh, Scotland, 1953–61; freelance writer, 1963—.

■ Member

International PEN, Society of Authors.

■ Awards, Honors

Scottish Arts Council bursary, 1969; Junior Literary Guild selection, 1983, for *Stranger in the House*; Buxtehude Bulle Prize for Children's Literature (West Germany), 1986, for *Across the Barricades*; Federation of Children's Book Group Award, Sheffield Book Award, and Carnegie Medal shortlisting, 1989, and Lancashire Children's Book Club Book of the Year Award runner–up, 1990, all for *Tug of War*; Scottish Arts Council Award, 1994, for *After Colette*; Scottish Arts Council Award, 1999, for *Tom and the Treehouse*. Lingard was made a member of the Civil Division of the Most Excellent Order of the British Empire (OBE), 1998.

■ Writings

JUVENILE FICTION AND PICTURE BOOKS

Frying as Usual, illustrated by Priscilla Clive, Hamish Hamilton (London), 1973, illustrated by Kate Rogers, Puffin (Harmondsworth), 1986.

Snake among the Sunflowers, Thomas Nelson (Nashville), 1977.

The Gooseberry, Hamish Hamilton, 1978, published in the United States as *Odd Girl Out*, Elsevier/Nelson Books (New York), 1979, illustrated by Dyfed Rowlands, Gomer (Llandysul, Wales), 1990.

The File on Fraulein Berg, Elsevier/Nelson Books (New York), 1980, Julia MacRae (London), 1980.

Strangers in the House, Hamish Hamilton, 1981, Dutton (New York), 1983.

The Winter Visitor, Hamish Hamilton, 1983.

The Freedom Machine, Hamish Hamilton, 1986.

The Guilty Party, Hamish Hamilton, 1987, illustrated by John Rowlands, Gomer (Wales), 1988.

Rags and Riches, Hamish Hamilton, 1988.

Tug of War, Hamish Hamilton, 1989, Dutton Lodestar, 1990.

Glad Rags, Hamish Hamilton, 1990.

Between Two Worlds, Hamish Hamilton, 1990, Dutton, 1991.

Can You Find Sammy the Hamster?, illustrated by Jan Lewis, Walker (London), 1990.

Morag and the Lamb, illustrated by Patricia Casey, Walker, 1991.

Hands Off Our School! illustrated by Mairi Hedderwick, Hamish Hamilton, 1992.

Night Fires, Hamish Hamilton, 1993.

Lizzie's Leaving, Hamish Hamilton, 1995.

Dark Shadows, Hamish Hamilton, 1998.

A Secret Place, Hodder & Stoughton (London), 1998.

Tom and the Tree House, illustrated by Paul Howard, Hodder & Stoughton, 1998.

The Egg Thieves, Hodder & Stoughton, 1999.

"KEVIN AND SADIE" SERIES; YOUNG ADULT FICTION

The Twelfth Day of July, Hamish Hamilton, 1970, Thomas Nelson (Nashville), 1972, illustrated by Kenny McKendry, Puffin (London), 1996.

Across the Barricades, Hamish Hamilton, 1972, Thomas Nelson, 1973.

Into Exile, Thomas Nelson, 1973.

A Proper Place, Thomas Nelson, 1975.

Hostages to Fortune, Hamish Hamilton, 1976, Thomas Nelson, 1977.

"MAGGIE" SERIES; YOUNG ADULT FICTION

The Clearance, Hamish Hamilton, 1973, Thomas Nelson, 1974.

The Resettling, Thomas Nelson, 1975.

The Pilgrimage, Thomas Nelson, 1976.

The Reunion, Hamish Hamilton, 1977, Thomas Nelson, 1978.

Maggie, illustrated by Rhian Pierce Jones, Gomer (Wales), 1993.

"FLIPPERS" SERIES; ILLUSTRATED BY JACQUI THOMAS

Secrets and Surprises, Macmillan (London), 1991.

Clever Clive and Loopy Lucy, Macmillan, 1993.

Slow Flo and Boomerang Bill, Macmillan, 1994.

Sulky Suzy and Jittery Jack, Macmillan, 1995.

ADULT FICTION

Liam's Daughter, Hodder & Stoughton (London), 1963.

The Prevailing Wind, Hodder & Stoughton, 1964.

The Tide Comes In, Hodder & Stoughton, 1966.

The Headmaster, Hodder & Stoughton, 1967.

A Sort of Freedom, Hodder & Stoughton, 1968.

The Lord on Our Side, Hodder & Stoughton, 1970.

The Second Flowering of Emily Mountjoy, Paul Harris (Edinburgh), 1979, St. Martin's, 1980.

Greenyards (historical fiction), Putnam (New York), 1981.

Sisters by Rite, St. Martin's, 1984, Hamish Hamilton, 1984.

Reasonable Doubts, Hamish Hamilton, 1986, Trafalgar Square, 1987.

The Women's House, St. Martin's, 1989.

After Colette, Sinclair–Stevenson (London), 1993, Trafalgar Square, 1995.

Dreams of Love and Modest Glory, Sinclair–Stevenson, 1995.

OTHER

Also author of television scripts for the British Broadcasting Corporation (Scotland), including "Maggie," an eighteen–part serial based on her novels that was broadcast in 1981 and 1982; author of scripts for the Scottish Television network, including those for the soap opera "High Living." Author of television plays "The Sandyford Place Mystery" and "A Kiss, A Fond Embrace," both adapted from the novel *Square Mile of Murder* by Jack House, 1980, and "Her Mother's House," 1982. Some of Lingard's books have been translated into Danish, Finnish, French, German, Japanese, Norwegian, Polish, Slovak, Swedish, and Welsh.

■ Adaptations

Across the Barricades was adapted as a play script by David Ian Neville and published by Oxford University Press, 1990.

■ Work in Progress

"A novel for children set in present–day Scotland and in Russia during the 1917–18 Revolution."

■ Sidelights

Considered one of Scotland's most accomplished contemporary writers for children and young adults, Joan Lingard is regularly praised for creating works that are characterized by challenging themes, authentic portrayals of current and historical events, and perceptive depictions of people and relationships. The author of picture books for preschoolers, stories for primary and middle graders, novels for young adults, and fiction for adults, she is regarded as an exceptional storyteller whose books are candid and thought–provoking, interesting and accessible.

> "I wanted to cross frontiers, live in the country, at the sea, in the city, climb the Himalayas, track down smugglers, go up the Amazon in pursuit of Colonel Fawcett. One way to do it was through books. When I read, I inhabited different worlds, lived inside different skins."
>
> —Joan Lingard

Lingard is often recognized for the objective, impartial stance that she takes toward the difficult issues that she presents in her works. For example, her "Kevin and Sadie" series of young adult novels, which are some of the author's best–known books, features a Catholic boy and Protestant girl who try to maintain their love against the background of "the Troubles," Northern Ireland's violent religious war. The author, who spent her formative years in Belfast, is credited with presenting her subject realistically and without judgment. In her other works, Lingard addresses such issues as the implications of producing nuclear weapons; displacement, both physical and emotional; adjustment to a new homeland; balancing personal desire and family responsibility; and dealing with the remarriage of a parent.

Lingard is often commended for her skill in depicting place and period; in addition to Northern Ireland, she has set her books in Scotland, France, Latvia, and Canada. The author is also recognized for making specific experiences universal and relevant; for her characterizations, especially of vibrant young women; for her understanding of her audience; and for presenting sober issues with restraint, humor, and optimism. In addition, several of the author's works are considered important books that discuss problems not often considered in titles for their respective age groups.

Lingard is generally recognized as an author whose unique perspective, literary talents, and appreciation for young readers has given her a strong critical and popular reputation. Writing in *Twentieth–Century Children's Writers*, Gillian Klein stated, "Joan Lingard is tough and uncompromising, also lively, humorous, and unfailingly accessible. It is partly her honesty that evokes, within a few opening pages of each novel, a sharply realised world peopled by real, flawed humans. No one better expresses prejudice without falling into the all–too–common trap of merely expressing it." Writing in the *St. James Guide to Young Adult Writers*, Eileen Dunlop and Judson Knight added that Lingard has "a natural empathy with adolescent readers, understanding their hopes, aspirations, and emotional uncertainties, yet paying her readers the compliment of engaging them on an intellectual level as adults. . . . She creates a world which young readers instantly recognize as their own, and they compliment her in return: she is one of the few quality writers whose books teenagers, notoriously unbookish, eagerly buy for themselves."

A Scottish and Irish Upbringing

Lingard told Jennie Renton of *Capital Letters*, "The stories I have created have mostly come out of the backgrounds of my life or of people close to me." Born in Edinburgh, Scotland, Lingard arrived in the world in a taxi cab traveling down the city's Royal Mile. In her essay in the *Something about the Author Autobiography Series* (SAAS), she wrote, "I've always been pleased about the circumstances of my birth. . . . I like the idea of the taxi, for it suggests mobility, and of the Royal Mile, for it is redolent with memories of the past, being the ancient High Street of Edinburgh which dates back to the sixteenth century."

When she was two, Lingard moved to Belfast, Northern Ireland, where her father, Henry, a Londoner who joined the Royal Navy Volunteer Reserve after nearly thirty years of service to the Royal Navy, was sent to be in charge of communications on a trading ship. Joan lived in Belfast until she was eighteen. She wrote in the *Fifth Book of Junior Au-*

thors and Illustrators (FBJAI), "[A]ll my formative years were spent in that city. This is reflected in my writing. I would say, in fact, that it is reflected in my life also, for the experiences, sights, sounds, and smells of childhood are so intense that they stay with one forever afterwards."

While living in Belfast, Lingard's mother, Elizabeth—"Edinburgh born and bred," according to her daughter in *SAAS*—learned from friends in the next street about Christian Science, a religion that teaches that there is no sin, disease, or death and that the mind can control matter. Lingard wrote in *SAAS* that she "was a fervent believer right through my teens." Since Henry Lingard was often away from home and was recalled to active service in the Royal Navy in 1939, Elizabeth Lingard often played the role of single parent to Joan and her older sister, Doris; when Doris, who was eleven years Joan's senior, left to work in London at seventeen, Joan, as she noted, "led the life of an only child."

Lingard wrote in her autobiographical essay, "I was crazy about books as a child. I read and read and read—school stories, adventure novels, *Grimms' Fairy Tales, The Wind in the Willows, Alice in Wonderland, Little Women, Anne of Green Gables,* anything I could get my hands on. I borrowed them from friends or from the library. For birthdays and Christmas, I always asked for books. . . ." She added in *FBJAI,* "My own life seemed too limited; I wanted to cross frontiers, live in the country, at the sea, in the city, climb the Himalayas, track down smugglers, go up the Amazon in pursuit of Colonel Fawcett. One way to do it was through books. When I read, I inhabited different worlds, lived inside different skins."

The Writing Bug

Lingard once stated, "I started to write because I loved reading so much and could never get enough to read, so when my mother suggested I write a book of my own I thought, 'Why not?' So I got lined, foolscap paper, filled my fountain pen with green ink—since that, I thought, would be suitable for an author—and began. The books that I wrote were of the improbable adventure type, much in the mode of British children's author Enid Blyton. I didn't write anything set in Belfast. Later, I came to realize that I would write more convincingly if I wrote about people and places I knew and understood." After completing her first book at the age of eleven, Lingard wrote in *FBJAI* that she "had only one ambition, as regards a career anyway."

As a teenager, Lingard continued to write her own books, works set in places such as Brazil, the Yorkshire moors, and the northwest of Scotland. She

once wrote, "[O]ne reason why I am sure I read so much and then began to write was that I wanted to push out the boundaries of my life. I could not accept that it was enough to live in this one body, inhabit this one house in this one city." However, as she matured Lingard realized that she would write more convincingly "[i]f I knew my backgrounds at first–hand and understood the kind of people who inhabited them. And so it proved."

During World War II, Lingard lived both in Belfast and on her paternal grandmother's farm twenty–five miles outside of London. She wrote in *SAAS,* "We were encouraged to hate Germans, all Germans. . . . And so, when I went to secondary school, which was a small school for girls only, and a new teacher arrived to teach us German, and she turned out to be German herself, we were flabbergasted. We were convinced, of course, that she must be a spy. What else?" Joan and two of her classmates spied on their teacher, copying down every detail that they could find, "which," Lingard wrote "was not a lot. . . . We must have been truly horrible and she must have known that we were following her. . . . When the war ended we learned something which turned our ideas about her upside down and made us feel ashamed." This incident later inspired *The File on Fraulein Berg,* a young adult novel about three girls who believe that their German teacher is a Nazi spy. Autobiographical material also comprises a great part of one of Lingard's novels for adults, *Sisters by Rite,* which describes the friendships of three girls—a Protestant, a Catholic, and a Christian Scientist—from 1943 to 1970. The war, Lingard wrote, "had dominated my childhood, coloured it, and is inextricably entwined with my recollections of it."

As an adolescent, Lingard read the works of such authors as Dickens, Tolstoy, Flaubert, Hemingway, Grahame Greene, and Jane Austen. She also had an active social life, forming a close–knit group called "the Gang" with seven other girls from her school. Despite these happy times, Lingard's adolescence, as she wrote in *SAAS,* "was troubled with anxiety and, subsequently, grief." When she was fourteen, her mother was diagnosed with breast cancer and died eighteen months later. Lingard wrote, "This was the most traumatic event of my life. I was devastated and so was my father." The summer after the death of her mother, Lingard traveled from place to place, staying with her sister or her father; the author noted, "I felt completely disorientated." After returning to Belfast, she got a job at sixteen as a primary school teacher in a poor area of the city: "Totally untrained," she recalled "I stood before a class of fifty–four six–year–olds." The conditions at the school were deplorable, and some of the children had tuberculosis. The author noted, "It was like something out of a novel by Charles Dickens."

Although she enjoyed her pupils, Lingard left her position after a year and went to work in the head office of the Ulster Bank. Shortly thereafter, she left Belfast to return to her birthplace, Edinburgh, where her father was living. Lingard said that this move "marked very definitely the end of the first part of my life."

For six months after moving to Edinburgh, Lingard worked as an assistant in the public library and lived in a boarding house; there, she became friends with the landlady's two daughters, who were Christian Scientists. Although she went to church and joined the youth club, Lingard's views were changing. She decided at eighteen that she could no longer accept the Christian Scientist tenet that there is no sin, disease, or death; consequently, Lingard stopped going to church. "That was," she wrote in *SAAS*, "the next big traumatic event in my life for it meant more than just not going to church; it meant giving up a way of life, and friends." The author added, "I felt like the sinner who has fallen. I felt as if I had gone out into the wilderness." Lingard entered the Moray House Training College of Education in Edinburgh. She once wrote that "the three years that I spent there turned out to be the three most stultifyingly boring years of my life."

After graduation, Lingard got a job teaching in a primary school in the city. At the end of that year, she married and went to live in a cottage in Temple, a small village twelve miles outside of Edinburgh. While working as a teacher in the Midlothian district of Edinburgh, Lingard began writing. Her first book was an eighty thousand word novel about a teacher's training college with a fictitious name. She mused in *SAAS*, "It was thinly disguised . . . and had the book ever been published I might well have been brought up on libel charges." The fledgling author ended up burning what she called her "hymn of hate."

In 1961, Lingard's first child, her daughter Kersten, was born. When Kersten was five or six weeks old, Lingard received notice that her adult novel *Liam's Daughter* had been accepted for publication. "I did feel lucky," Lingard wrote. "I had a child, and I was to be a published writer. My only sadness was that my mother was not alive to share the happiness." In 1963, Lingard had her second daughter, Bridget; the next year, her daughter Jenny was born. Lingard noted, "When I look back on those years I wonder how I did manage to produce the work that I did. I published another four novels in the sixties, all for adults, and that marked the end of the first phase of my published writing career."

"One reason why I am sure I read so much and then began to write was that I wanted to push out the boundaries of my life. I could not accept that it was enough to live in this one body, inhabit this one house in this one city."

—Joan Lingard

In 1967, Lingard and her family moved from the Edinburgh countryside back to the city; three years later, her marriage broke up. Short of money, she decided to try writing for a more lucrative market: television. Lingard became part of the team that wrote the soap opera "High Living" for the Scottish Television network. She noted in *SAAS*, "It was all good experience and it stood me in very good stead when I came to write original plays of my own and to adapt my 'Maggie' books into eighteen parts for BBC television." In 1970, Lingard published *The Lord on Our Side*, an adult novel about the religious and political divisions in Ulster from the 1940s to the 1960s. She noted, "What had started as a civil rights movement for Catholics in 1968 had swollen into something approaching civil war." A friend of Lingard's, Honor Arundel, herself a respected author of children's literature, had read *The Lord on Our Side* and made the suggestion that she write a book for young people about what was happening in the province. Lingard recalled "I thought about it and realised that I had a book almost waiting in my head, as it were, to come out." That book, *The Twelfth Day of July*, was the first of Lingard's series of "Kevin and Sadie" books.

Examines "The Troubles"

Set at the beginning of "the Troubles," *The Twelfth Day of July* describes how two Catholic children, fourteen–year–old Kevin McCoy and his younger sister, Brede, and two Protestant children, thirteen–year–old Sadie Jackson and her younger brother, Tommy, become embroiled in the prejudice and tension that surrounds preparations for the day referred to in the book's title. On that day in 1690, King William of Orange, a Protestant, defeated the Catholic army in the Battle of the Boyne, and since then Orange supporters have celebrated the victory. When Kevin and his friend Brian vandalize the picture of William on a wall in the Protestant section of Belfast, Sadie and her friends change the slogan "God Bless the Pope" to "God Bless King Billy" on a poster in the Catholic section of town. The Jackson house is burned down, and arson by Catholics is suspected. On the eleventh of July, a bonfire night for Orange supporters, Sadie and Tommy and their friends go to the stretch of ground that separates the Protestant and Catholic sides. Kevin, Brian, and their friends take positions across the divide. Stones are thrown, and a battle takes place; Brede, Kevin's sister, is struck on the head and severely wounded. Meeting in the middle of the road, Kevin, Sadie, and Tommy take Brede to the hospital. Later, the children spend the next day at the seaside. A reviewer for the *Times Literary Supplement* called *The Twelfth Day of July* "a good and important book. . . . [I]t is no tract but a fully realized and moving work of fiction. . . . Lingard sees that the only real hope of peace is in getting the two sides together, and this she manages with a naturalness that is itself a cause for hope. . . . This book should be compulsory reading in the Six Counties and, for its wider implications, far beyond." Writing in the *Bulletin of the Center for Children's Books*, Zena Sutherland added that, for American readers, the book "may clarify to some extent the bitterness rampant in Northern Ireland today."

Across the Barricades takes place three years after the conclusion of *The Twelfth Day of July.* Although they have not kept in touch during this time, Kevin and Sadie bump into each other and become friends again. They fall in love, but the stones and paint pots of the first book have given way to guns, and the animosity between Catholics and Protestants has escalated. Sadie defies her parents and friends to go out with Kevin, who is beaten by former schoolmates for dating a Protestant. Sadie's former teacher Mr. Blake offers the girl a job as his housekeeper and allows the young couple to meet in his home. When his house is bombed, Mr. Blake is killed for his kindness. At the end of the novel, Kevin and Sadie leave Belfast for Liverpool. Several critics have noted that *Across the Barricades* is the finest novel of the series. *Twentieth-Century Children's Writers* contributor Gillian Klein called it "arguably the best in the series," while Eileen Dunlop and Judson Knight stated in the *St. James Guide to Young Adult Writers* that *Across the Barricades* is "[p]robably the best and most powerful of these novels," adding that the development of the protagonists's love "against a bitter background of family disapproval and civil disintegration is a moving variation on a classic theme of young love under a comfortless star." Writing in *Library Journal*, Carole L. Stanke concluded that the book "will bring alive the current situation in Ireland."

In the third novel of the series, *Into Exile,* Kevin and Sadie are married, living in London, and, in the words of a critic in *Times Literary Supplement*, "trying to make a home for themselves in one room and to keep their marriage alive in poverty and stress." When his father is killed by a bomb in Belfast, Kevin is called back home, where he finds that his mother is still hostile toward his marriage. Sadie, who is feeling insecure in her relationship, is almost led astray by some friends. Finally, the two realize that they must go off on their own if their union is to withstand the pressure. The reviewer for the *Times Literary Supplement* continued, "There is a simplicity and sadness about the way *Into Exile* is written that reflects the limitations and background of all the characters," while Stanke called *Into Exile* "a timely novel that will appeal to teenagers because of its exploration of the problems of young marriage and the current conflict in Northern Ireland."

"It seems to me that the only way a situation such as the Ulster one will ever change will be when the young rebel against its continuing and decide to reject the prejudices of their parents and grandparents and great-grandparents."

—Joan Lingard

In the fourth volume of the series, *A Proper Place,* Kevin has returned from Ireland, and he, Sadie, and their new son, Brendan, have moved to a cramped flat in Liverpool. Their marriage is tested when Sadie's bigoted mother comes to visit and when Gerald, Kevin's problematic younger brother, comes to stay. Finally, Kevin finds work as a farmhand on an estate in Cheshire, a situation that brings with it a house to live in and an easing of some of the tension. Lesley Croome wrote in the *Times Literary Supplement* that Lingard's books "reflect the complexities of the inflammable situation in Northern Ireland with a rare accuracy. . . . Joan Lingard has a gift for conveying the authentic sense of the places she is describing, though this would count for little were she not so well attuned to the changing emotional states of her characters." Croome added, "Her latest novel is quieter in tone than the earlier ones but it is still not lacking in dramatic conflict."

Hostages to Fortune is the fifth volume of the "Sadie and Kevin" series. In this work, the couple and Brendan have moved to their cottage on a Cheshire farm; however, when Kevin's employer dies, they are forced to relocate once again. They go to a village in Wales to fill in for a pubkeeper who is ill and decide to settle there. However, the couple faces a number of domestic crises, including the presence of Kevin's runaway sister Clodagh, whom Cecilia Gordon described in the *Times Literary Supplement* as "unforgivably perverse," and Sadie's biased mother. The couple's marriage is further tested when Sadie has a stillborn daughter. However, by the end of the novel Kevin and Sadie have weathered their trials and have begun to communicate more openly. Gordon noted, "Those who help and support Kevin and Sadie are all older people, even elderly. Typically, Joan Lingard underlines differences and then shows how barriers can be crossed. Many children will recognize such bridging of the generation gap and will appreciate the picture of loving mothers who are much less help than outsiders." Writing in the *Bulletin of the Center for Children's Books*, Zena Sutherland stated, "Lingard has created well–defined, sympathetic characters in this series, she writes about them with practiced ease and consistent candor, and she touches on problems that are discussed in few books for young readers." *Junior Bookshelf* contributor M. Hobbs called the events of the novel "laudably absorbing and relevant to today, for those who have followed the McCoys' adventures so far. The style is so naturally Belfast in grammar and idiom that one can hear the accents."

Lingard once remarked that she wrote *The Twelfth Day of July* "basically as an appeal for tolerance, to try to show children that they need not accept their parents' prejudices, because I believe that the only hope for peace must come through changing the attitudes of children first. Indoctrination and prejudice begin so young; this is seen very clearly in the Ulster situation. It is pathetic how young some of the children who have been involved are." She added in *SAAS*, "It seems to me that the only way a situation such as the Ulster one will ever change will be when the young rebel against its continuing and decide to reject the prejudices of their parents and grandparents and great–grandparents. And if I have been successful in writing it in an unbiased way then I believe it is due to my upbringing as a Christian Scientist and also because I have left Belfast and can look back more objectively than if I were caught up in the middle of the trouble itself." Lingard did not intend to write any more about Kevin and Sadie after she finished her first novel about them. However, as she wrote in *SAAS*, "they turned out to be the kind of characters who won't lie down in one's head. I kept wondering what would have happened to them afterwards so I just had to go on and find out."

The "Maggie" Tales

In addition to her series about Sadie and Kevin, Lingard is the creator of another popular series of young adult novels about Maggie McKinley, an independent, enterprising, and high–spirited adolescent from working–class Glasgow who wants to attend college and be a social anthropologist. Begun as a respite from writing about Ulster and its problems, the series—which includes four novels, *The Clearance, The Resettling, The Pilgrimage,* and *The Reunion*—is lighter and more humorous than the works about Kevin and Sadie; however, Lingard is generally credited with exploring themes such as class distinction, family responsibility, and early marriage with her usual insightfulness. A critic noted in a *Times Literary Supplement* review of the first novel in the series, *The Clearance,* "Joan Lingard has always revealed a sure touch in describing the tensions and cross–currents of family relationships. Now she also shows a sympathetic understanding of the varied roles a girl is forced to play vis–a–vis her family, her school and her boy friends." In another issue of the same periodical, Gillian Cross called the third volume of the series, *The Pilgrimage,* "a very skillful piece of work. . . . It is extremely entertaining, and its humour and unpretentiousness should not blind one to the author's skill in describing unstereotyped relationships, nor to the depth of her discussion of marriage at an early age."

Assessing the final volume in the series, *The Reunion,* D. A. Young mused in the *Junior Bookshelf,* "I cannot help feeling that a resourceful girl like Maggie will find a way of getting into print again." Writing about the series in the *St. James Guide to Young Adult Writers,* Eileen Dunlop and Judson Knight noted, "Nowhere does Lingard display her talent for seeing the world through young eyes more amusingly than she does in these books." Lingard wrote in *SAAS* that the theme of the quartet of stories about Maggie "is that of being displaced—or cleared—from one's environment against one's will and having to resettle. I am interested in characters caught at a point of social or historical change." Lingard wrote the scripts for the eighteen–part television adaptation of the "Maggie" books that was shown on the Scottish Television network in 1981 and 1982; she also bought a cottage in Inverness, Scotland, that figures prominently in the series to use as a summer home.

In the early 1970s, Lingard married her second husband, Martin Birichaws, a Latvian–born Canadian architect and lecturer. Twenty years later, she used his childhood experiences as the background for two stories, *Tug of War* and *Between Two Worlds,* that are directed at young adults. These books describe how the Peterson family, forced to flee their home in Latvia during the Soviet Invasion of 1944, survive displacement to reunite in Canada, where their struggle continues. Lingard shows the difficulties faced by strangers in a foreign country—such as hostility, fear, distrust, and grueling work—while depicting a close, resilient family. At the end of the second novel, the Petersons are able to buy a plot of land on which to build a house and have begun to make friends in their new homeland. Zena Sutherland of the *Bulletin of the Center for Children's Books* called *Tug of War* "a narrative of fear and courage," while Marcus Crouch of *Junior Bookshelf* dubbed *Between Two Worlds* "a remarkable piece of historical writing."

Lingard is also the author of another well–received book for young people that is set in Eastern Europe, *Night Fires.* Set in the 1980s in an unnamed country, the story portrays two children caught up in a revolution to overthrow the harsh regime that has ruled their country since the 1930s. The youngsters, Laura and Nik, are among the eldest wards of a state–run orphanage. Left on their own, they go into the city and become committed to an underground movement. The children put themselves in danger, but find friends and comrades in their search for freedom. *Books for Keeps* critic David Bennett called *Night Fires* "[o]ne of the most approachable political novels of recent years," while John Murray noted in *Magpies* that the book "conveys something of the fear and distrust of living under a totalitarian regime."

If you enjoy the works of Joan Lingard, you might want to check out the following books:

Nancy Bond, *The Love of Friends*, 1997.
Trudie Krisher, *Spite Fences*, 1994.
Catherine Sefton, *Frankie's Story*, 1988, and *Tango's Baby,* 1995.

Lingard once stated, "I have . . . published three books, all in a short space of time, on different themes, in different settings, and for different ages. *Tom and the Tree House* (for seven–to–nine year olds) is about a boy who is adopted trying to come to terms with his adoptive parents producing a child of their own whom he classes as their 'real' child while he is the 'unreal' one. In *A Secret Place* (for readers nine to twelve), a Spanish father, frustrated because his former wife is blocking his success to his children, snatches them from their school gate in Scotland and takes them to a white village high in the mountains of Spain. And in *Dark Shadows* (for ten–to–fourteen year olds), I returned to Belfast to tell the tale of Jess and Laurie, two cousins of different religions who meet for the first time when they are fifteen years old. Their families had fallen out twenty years previously and the girls decide to try to bring about a reconciliation, which does not prove to be easy. The divisions between the two families are deep, just as they are in Northern Ireland itself." Lingard concluded, "I like variety in my writing, just as I do in my reading. I have published more than thirty books now for young people and thirteen adult novels. But I enjoy writing especially for young people. They are so much more responsive and appreciative than their elders. They don't hesitate to tell you that they thought your book was fantastic. Any author enjoys hearing that!"

■ Biographical and Critical Sources

BOOKS

Fifth Book of Junior Authors and Illustrators, edited by Sally Holmes Holtze, Wilson, 1983, pp. 195–96.
Lingard, Joan, essay in *Something about the Author Autobiography Series,* Volume 5, Gale, 1988, pp. 223–36.
Major Authors and Illustrators for Children and Young Adults, Gale, 1993, pp. 1477–79.
St. James Guide to Young Adult Writers, edited by Tom Pendergast and Sara Pendergast, 2nd edition, St. James, 1999, pp. 517–19.
Twentieth–Century Children's Writers, edited by Tracy Chevalier, 3rd edition, St. James, 1989, pp. 591–92.

PERIODICALS

Books for Keeps, January, 1996, David Bennett, review of *Night Fires,* p. 12.
Bulletin of the Center for Children's Books, April, 1973, Zena Sutherland, review of *The Twelfth Day of July,* p. 128; July–August, 1977, Zena Sutherland, review of *Hostages to Fortune,* pp. 176–77; September, 1990, Sutherland, Zena, review of *Tug of War,* pp. 11–12.
Junior Bookshelf, April, 1977, M. Hobbs, review of *Hostages to Fortune,* p. 117; June, 1978, D. A. Young, review of *The Reunion,* p. 156; February, 1992. Marcus Crouch, review of *Between Two Worlds,* p. 56.

Library Journal, July, 1973, Carol L. Stanke, review of *Across the Barricades,* p. 2202.

Lion & the Unicorn, September, 1997.

Magpies, November, 1994, John Murray, review of *Night Fires,* p. 33.

School Librarian, summer, 1999, p. 89.

School Library Journal, February, 1974, Carol L. Stanke, review of *Into Exile,* p. 71.

Scottish Book Collector, Volume 5, number 4, 1996, p. 30.

Times Educational Supplement, July 3, 1998, p. 19.

Times Literary Supplement, December 11, 1970, review of *The Twelfth Day of July,* p. 1457; September 28, 1973, review of *Into Exile,* p. 1118; July 5, 1974, review of *The Clearance,* p. 721; July 11, 1975, Lesley Croome, "Progression from Childhood," p. 766; July 16, 1976, Gillian Cross, "Past Presences," p. 885; December 10, 1976, Cecilia Gordon, review of *Hostages to Fortune,* p. 1548.

ON—LINE

Additional Literature: Joan Lingard, located at http://www.englisch.schule.de/cal.addition.html.

James Thin Home Page, located at http://www.jamesthin.co.ud/lingard.htm (contains Joan Lingard interview with Jennie Renton in *Capital Letters*).

Puffin Author I.D. Card: Joan Lingard, located at http://www.puffin.co.uk/living/aut_30.html.

—Sketch by Gerard J. Senick

Andrew Lloyd Webber

■ Personal

Born March 22, 1948, in London, England; son of William Southcombe (a composer and music college director) and Jean Hermione (a piano teacher; maiden name, Johnstone) Lloyd Webber; married Sarah Jane Tudor Hugill (a singer and musician), July 24, 1971 (divorced, 1983); married Sarah Brightman (a singer and actress), March 22, 1984 (divorced, 1990); married Madeleine Gurdon, February 9, 1991; children: (first marriage) Nicholas, Imogen, (third marriage) Alastair Adam, William Richard, and a third child. *Education:* Attended Westminster School, London, 1960–65; attended Magdalen College, Oxford, 1965; attended Guildhall School of Music and Drama, 1966–67; attended the Royal College of Music, 1967–68. *Religion:* Church of England.

■ Addresses

Home—2 Tower Street, London, WC2H 9NS. *Office*—The Palace Theatre, Shaftesbury Ave., London W1V 8AY, England.

■ Career

Composer, author, and producer. Composed stage scores, including *Joseph and the Amazing Technicolor Dreamcoat*, 1968; *Jesus Christ Superstar*, 1971; *By Jeeves*, 1975; *Evita*, 1978; (and producer) *Cats*, 1981; *Song and Dance*, 1982; *Starlight Express*, 1984; *The Phantom of the Opera*, 1986; *Aspects of Love*, 1989; and *Sunset Boulevard*, 1993. Composer of the musical pieces including *Variations*, 1977, and *Requiem*, 1985; composer of film scores, including *Gumshoe*, Columbia, 1972, and *The Odessa File*, Columbia, 1974; producer of plays in London, England, including *Daisy Pulls It Off*, 1983; *The Hired Man*, 1984; *Lend Me a Tenor*, 1986; and *The Resistible Rise of Arturo Ui*, 1987; also composer of unproduced musicals, including *The Likes of Us, Come Back, Richard, Your Country Needs You,* and *Cricket.* Founder of The Really Useful Theatre Company (now The Really Useful Theatre Group), London, England.

■ Member

Royal College of Music (fellow).

■ Awards, Honors

Drama Desk Award, 1971, for *Jesus Christ Superstar*; Gold Record, London, 1977, for *Variations*; New York Drama Critics Circle Award for Best Musical, 1979, for *Evita*; two Antoinette Perry Awards (Tony) for *Evita*, 1980, two for *Cats*, 1982, seven awards, including Best Musical, for *The Phantom of the Opera*,

1988; Grammy Award from the National Academy of Recording Arts and Sciences, 1981, for Best Cast Show Album of the Year for *Evita,* and 1986, for Best Classical Contemporary Composition, *Requiem;* Lawrence Olivier Award, *Plays and Players* Award, *London Standard* Award, all for Best Musical, all 1986, all for *The Phantom of the Opera;* named a Living Legend Grammy, 1989; knighted by Queen Elizabeth II, 1992; Tony award for best score, best musical, 1995, for *Sunset Boulevard;* Praemium Imperiale Award for Music, 1995; Best Original Song, Academy of Motion Picture Arts and Sciences, 1997, for "You Must Love Me," from the film version of *Evita;* named peer of the realm by Queen Elizabeth II, 1997.

■ **Writings**

STAGE SCORES

(With Tim Rice) *Joseph and the Amazing Technicolor Dreamcoat,* first produced at St. Paul's Junior School, London, 1968, first produced in United States at the College of the Immaculate Conception, Douglaston, NY, 1970, also produced at the Albery, London, 1973, at the Brooklyn Academy of Music, December 23, 1976, at Entermedia Theatre (off–Broadway), and the Royale Theatre (Broadway), November 18, 1981.

(With Tim Rice) *Jesus Christ Superstar* (adapted from the Gospels), produced at Mark Hellinger Theatre, New York City, October 12, 1971.

(With Alan Ayckbourn) *By Jeeves,* produced in London, 1975.

(With Tim Rice) *Evita,* produced at the Prince Edward Theatre, London, June 21, 1978, at the Dorothy Chandler Pavilion, Los Angeles, spring, 1979, and Broadway Theatre, New York City, September 25, 1979.

(And producer) *Cats* (adapted from T. S. Eliot's *Old Possum's Book of Practical Cats*), produced at the Palace Theatre, London, May, 1981, and Winter Garden Theatre, New York City, October 7, 1982.

Song and Dance (includes "Tell Me on a Sunday," with lyrics by Don Black, and "Variations"), produced at Palace Theatre, London, 1982, produced on Broadway at Royale Theatre, September, 1985.

(With Richard Stilgoe) *Starlight Express,* produced at Apollo Theatre, London, 1984, and Gershwin Theater, New York City, 1986.

(With Richard Stilgoe and Charles Hart) *The Phantom of the Opera* (based on the book by Gaston Leroux), produced at Her Majesty's Theatre, London, October 9, 1986, and Majestic Theater, New York City, January 26, 1988.

(With Charles Hart and Don Black) *Aspects of Love* (based on the novel by David Garnett), produced in London, 1989, premiered on Broadway, 1990.

Sunset Boulevard (based on the film directed by Billy Wilder), produced on Broadway, 1993.

(With Jim Steinman) *Whistle Down the Wind* (based on the film directed by Bryan Forbes), produced at Aldwych Theatre, London, 1998.

(With Ben Elton) *The Beautiful Game,* produced at Cambridge Theatre, London, 2000.

Also composer of several unproduced plays, including *The Likes of Us* (lyrics by Tim Rice), *Come Back Richard, Your Country Needs You,* (with Tim Rice), and *Cricket;* author of a food column for the British *Daily Telegraph* since the mid–1990s.

COMPOSITION

Variations (based on A minor Caprice No. 24 by Paganini), Chappell, 1977.

Requiem, Angel, 1985.

FILM SCORES

Gumshoe, Columbia, 1972.

The Odessa File, Columbia, 1974 (single "Christmas Dream" performed by Perry Como and the London Boys, EMI, 1977).

RECORDINGS

Jesus Christ Superstar (cast album featuring Yvonne Elliman's "I Don't Know How to Love Him"), Decca, 1971, MCA Records, 1973.

Joseph and the Amazing Technicolor Dreamcoat (first record of completed work), MCA Records, 1974, with original Broadway cast, Chrysalis, 1982.

Evita (London cast recording with Julie Covington), MCA Records, 1976, Broadway cast album featuring Patti LuPone and Mandy Patinkin, MCA Records, 1979.

Variations (two recordings), MCA Records, 1978.

Tell Me on a Sunday (one–act musical featuring Marti Webb), Polydor, 1980.

Cats (London cast album), Geffen Records, 1981, Polydor, 1981, with Broadway cast featuring Betty Buckley's "Memory," Geffen Records, 1983.

Starlight Express (London cast album), Polydor, 1984, music and songs from *Starlight Express,* MCA Records, 1987.

Requiem (performed by Placido Domingo, Sarah Brightman and the Winchester Cathedral Choir; conducted by Lorin Maazel), EMI Angel, 1985.

Song and Dance: The Song (featuring Bernadette Peters), RCA Records, 1985, with original London cast as *Song and Dance*, Polydor, 1992.

The Phantom of the Opera (original London cast with Sarah Brightman and Michael Crawford), Polydor, 1987.

The Premiere Collection, MCA, 1988.

The Songs That Got Away, Polydor, 1989.

Aspects of Love (London cast recording), Polydor, 1989.

Laclede Quartet Plays Andrew Lloyd Webber, Laclede Records (St. Louis, MO), 1991.

Essentials, Koch International, 1992.

The Premiere Collection Encore, Polydor, 1992.

Sarah Brightman Sings the Music of Andrew Lloyd Webber, Polydor, 1992.

Sunset Boulevard (world premiere recording), Polydor, 1993, featuring Glenn Close, Polydor, 1994, featuring Petula Clark, Polydor, 1996.

The Very Best of Andrew Lloyd Webber, Polydor, 1994.

By Jeeves (original London cast), Polydor, 1996.

The Very Best of Andrew Lloyd Webber: The Broadway Collection, Polydor, 1996.

The Andrew Lloyd Webber Collection, Polydor, 1997.

Whistle Down the Wind (original London cast), Polydor, 1998, with performances by various artists as *Whistle Down the Wind: Concept Album*, Polydor, 1998.

The Beautiful Game (original cast), Telstar, 2000.

TELEVISION

Tell Me on a Sunday, BBC–TV, 1980.

Requiem, premiere at St. Thomas Church, New York City, on April 3, 1985, presented on BBC–TV.

BOOKS

(With Tim Rice) *Evita: The Legend of Evita Peron, 1919–1952*, Drama Book Specialists (New York), 1978.

Cats: The Book of the Musical, with photographs and drawings by John Napier, Faber & Faber (Winchester, MA), 1981.

(With Tim Rice) *Joseph and the Amazing Technicolor Dreamcoat*, illustrated by Quentin Blake, Holt (New York), 1982.

(Foreword) George Perry, *Sunset Boulevard: From Movie to Musical*, Holt (New York City), 1993.

The Musicals of Andrew Lloyd Webber: His Life and Works, Virgin Publishing, 1995.

Many of Lloyd Webber's compositions have been collected and published, including *Andrew Lloyd Webber* (arranged for the harp by Sylvia Woods), Woods Music and Books (Montrose, CA), 1991, and *Andrew Lloyd Webber: The Essential Collection*, Hal Leonard, 1998.

■ Adaptations

Joseph and the Amazing Technicolor Dreamcoat was produced for television in 1972; a film version of *Jesus Christ Superstar* was made by Universal Films in 1973; *Requiem* was performed by American Ballet Theater, Chicago, IL, February 7, 1986; a film version of *Evita* was made by Hollywood Pictures, 1996.

■ Sidelights

British composer Andrew Lloyd Webber is best known for creating the music to some of the world's most popular contemporary theatrical productions. His collaborations with lyricist Tim Rice include *Joseph and the Amazing Technicolor Dreamcoat, Jesus Christ Superstar*, and *Evita*; with other lyricists he has created the blockbusters *Cats, The Phantom of the Opera*, and *Sunset Boulevard*. Lloyd Webber has garnered many of the stage's top honors for his work, including several Antoinette Perry (Tony) Awards. Critical opinion of his musicals has, however, differed widely. Some experts credit Lloyd Webber and his collaborators with infusing new life into musical theater and resurrecting a dying genre; others say that he has been largely responsible for a trend towards great stage spectacle with little content. Whatever the critical evaluation, Lloyd Webber's music is known for the way it blends various styles, from classical, to rock, to country, to calypso.

Lloyd Webber was born in London in 1948. His father was a composer who directed the London College of Music, and his mother was a piano teacher, but the Lloyd Webbers were not as classically oriented as might be presumed. "I always heard music of all kinds, side by side," Lloyd Webber told Leslie Bennetts in the *New York Times*. "Nobody ever suggested there was any barrier." He took lessons in violin, piano, and French horn but became fascinated with musical theater early in life. He made model stages with puppets and other figures, and by age nine had written his first musical, based on Oscar Wilde's play *The Importance of Being Earnest*. At the age of twelve, Lloyd Webber wrote a fan letter to famed musical composer Richard Rodgers and was invited to meet him. At roughly the same time, he won a scholarship to Westminster School in London, where he continued writing musicals.

Winner of the 1971 Drama Desk Award, Lloyd Webber's *Jesus Christ Superstar* featured Yvonne Elliman as Mary Magdalene and Tim Rice, both pictured here, during the show's successful Broadway run.

Some of the songs he later developed in his major works, but, as he revealed in an interview with Catherine Courtney for *Authors and Artists for Young Adults,* Lloyd Webber was also developing an interest in architecture. "I really did think that perhaps I wouldn't go in for music at all, but something to do with architecture. I was always intrigued. I was interested in paradoxes within buildings."

Collaborates with Tim Rice

Lloyd Webber entered Oxford University in 1965 but withdrew after one term and returned to London. There he met Tim Rice, with whom he began collaborating on musical works. Their first effort, entitled *The Likes of Us,* was based on the life of Victorian orphanage founder Dr. Thomas Barnardo and has never been produced. A friend who was a local schoolmaster, however, commissioned them to create a musical play for production by the children

of his school. The result became *Joseph and the Amazing Technicolor Dreamcoat.* The play is based on the biblical story of Joseph, who is sold into slavery in Egypt by his brothers, but nevertheless finds success through his dream–reading ability. Though biblical in its origins, the musical combined many styles of modern music such as jazz and country, and portrayed the Pharaoh of Egypt as an Elvis Presley–like entity. *Joseph and the Amazing Technicolor Dreamcoat* proved so successful in its original setting that it also played at the Central Hall in Westminster, where it was seen by Derek Jewell, a critic for the London *Sunday Times.* His praise of the piece resulted in a recording being made and a full–scale production of the work in London. *New York Times* contributor Clive Barnes, after viewing a British production of *Joseph* called it "an understandable knockout" and "totally charming"; Nick Tosches in *Rolling Stone* hailed it as "a highly moving . . . testimony of one man's unswerving fidelity to God." Later revivals of *Joseph,* expanded and ornamented to fit with Lloyd Webber's subsequent reputation for theatrical blockbusters, have not fared as well. Lloyd Webber and Rice later authored a children's book version of the musical.

Lloyd Webber and Rice again chose a biblical theme for their next musical, *Jesus Christ Superstar.* At first unable to find sponsorship for a theatrical production of the work, the pair released an album of the songs they had written for it. The album became very popular in both Great Britain and the United States, the title song becoming a hit single and creating a demand for the stage show. When it finally arrived, controversy came with it. Though *Jesus Christ Superstar* drew large audiences, protesters often picketed the theaters where it played. The very title aroused conservative ire, and some Christian groups were angered both by the fact that Lloyd Webber and Rice's story leaves out the Resurrection and by their portrayal of Jesus as a sometimes troubled human being. Some Jewish groups felt that the work's depiction of the Pharisees was anti–Semitic. On the first point, James R. Huffman in the *Journal of Popular Culture* argued, "Works like *Jesus Christ Superstar,* which 'ask the right questions' but allow each individual to provide his own answers, will be appropriated by nearly all—the atheist, the agnostic, and the believer. Only the indifferent will remain unimpressed; only the devout and the aesthetically critical may be offended." As for the Jewish issue, James M. Wall, reviewing the later 1973 film version in *Christian Century,* asserted that "the Pharisees, obviously villains in this opera, are far from being 'Jewish' villains. They constitute the establishment, troubled by the admiration evoked by the reckless life style of Jesus."

Following its debut in London in 1981, *Cats* became the longest–running show in theater history, earning its author two Tony awards before it closed in late 2000.

Critical opinion of *Jesus Christ Superstar*—as was to become common for Lloyd Webber's works—was mixed. Jonathan Cott of *Rolling Stone* panned the stage show, dismissing the words and music as having a tone of "forced hipness and sentimentality, that of an egregiously over–sweet rock–coated Broadway musical." Richard Williams in *Melody Maker*, however, hailed it as "an honest attempt at a very hard job, and the amount of artistic success which is already definitely apparent is surprising and pleasing. The work demands more serious listening than it'll probably get." Clifford Edwards in *Catholic World* defended Rice and Lloyd Webber's portrayal of Jesus as a "flesh–and–blood human being," and noted that "a common reaction to *Superstar* is: 'It was the first time I ever thought of Jesus

as a real person.'" Malcolm Boyd in the *New York Times*, conversely, took issue with what he sarcastically called "a confused, tired but plucky Jesus who is going to the cross even if it kills him," and concluded of the show as a whole that "it doesn't have a soul." The play's sympathetic portrayal of Judas Iscariot was often discussed by critics as well, in both favorable and unfavorable terms. *Jesus Christ Superstar* garnered the 1971 Drama Desk Award, and, as William Bender observed in *Time*, "whatever the reaction to *Superstar* may be, [Lloyd] Webber and Rice have fused words and music into such a convincing narrative style that rock may never be quite the same again." Besides the hit title song, the musical also included the memorable lament of Mary Magdalen, "I Don't Know How to Love Him."

Vocalist Michael Crawford portraying the disfigured music patron in love with a beautiful chanteause in Lloyd Webber's version of *The Phantom of the Opera*, which thrilled theatergoers with its opulent sets and romantic storyline.

Lloyd Webber had his first real flop with *By Jeeves* in 1975. Rice had begun the project with him but backed out early. The pair did collaborate on one final success, however, with 1978's *Evita*. The story of Argentine dictator Juan Peron's first wife, Eva, the musical was narrated by a character known only as Che, but whom most reviewers interpreted as a representation of Latin American revolutionary Che Guevara. *Evita* follows Eva Peron from her beginnings as an ambitious small–town girl through her marriage to Peron, and her overwhelming popularity with the Argentinean people, to her death while still in her thirties from cancer. Lloyd Webber also collaborated with Rice on a book that listed the brief historical facts of Eva Peron's life.

Again, critical opinion of *Evita* the musical was divided. Walter Kerr, in the *New York Times*, complained about the use of a narrator, saying it kept the audience too distant from the characters. He called it "a chilly and left–handed way to write a character–musical." Clive Barnes's opinion in the

New York Post was itself divided—he told readers that "*Evita* is a stunning, exhilarating theatrical experience, especially if you don't think about it too much." Eric Salzman in *Stereo Review* panned at least the second part of *Evita* as being "full of draggy, bad modern–opera–isms and fake Caribbean tunes along with endless repetitions of music from Part I, some of it pasted up in mawkish, awkward collage." Martin Gottfried, however, critiquing the musical in *Saturday Review,* hailed it as something that had "never been seen before; while it uses techniques developed in such Broadway shows as *Cabaret* and *Follies,* it rises to still higher theatrical purpose." *Evita* won two Tony awards in 1980; "Don't Cry for Me, Argentina" is considered its most memorable song. About the same time that *Evita* came to the stage, Lloyd Webber founded The Really Useful Theatre Company, which became The Really Useful Group. Through this company he produced plays by various authors and eventually purchased the Palace Theatre in London—the site of his boyhood meeting with Richard Rodgers.

Cats and *The Phantom*

One of Lloyd Webber's biggest successes came with *Cats,* his musical stage adaptation of T. S. Eliot's verse collection *Old Possum's Book of Practical Cats.* The composer recalled for Courtney: "I remembered reading the cat poems in bed during childhood. Later, I'd play them on the piano for reaction from interviewers or friends. Finally, I put them together." He also discovered additional materials by Eliot that provided inspiration for the play's central "Jellicle Ball," and the story of Grizebella, the character that sang the popular "Memory." *Cats* premiered in London in 1981 and ran for several years both there and in New York, in addition to having tours in many different countries. Like *Evita,* the play drew two Tony Awards. Lloyd Webber authored an accompanying book that appeared in 1981 entitled *Cats: The Book of the Musical.*

Lloyd Webber's 1986 collaboration with Richard Stilgoe and Charles Hart, *The Phantom of the Opera,* garnered seven Tony Awards. Taken from a 1910 novel by Gaston Leroux, the story concerns a severely disfigured man hiding out beneath the Paris Opera House. He falls in love with a beautiful singer and manipulates her career. Lloyd Webber asserted to Courtney that *Phantom* is his "most mainstream romantic score." Both the London and New York openings of the musical featured Lloyd Webber's second wife, Sarah Brightman, in the lead female role of Christine. Her soprano range reportedly inspired much of the music for the show. The couple divorced, however, in 1990, and Lloyd Webber married his third wife, Madeleine Gurdon, the following year.

Pop singer Madonna set aside her usual attention–getting gimmicks to play it straight as a talented vocalist and actress, earning Lloyd Webber his first Oscar for Best Original Score in the 1996 film version of the composer's *Evita*.

Many critics agree that *Phantom of the Opera* is Lloyd Webber's most impressive production as a whole, speaking in terms of music, story, and spectacle. However, not everyone liked it. Robert Brustein in the *New Republic* labeled the play "a vulgar glitzorama, a parade of conspicuous consumption, a display of fake rococo for a trans–Atlantic audience glutted with material goods." Barrymore Laurence Scherer, by contrast, in *Opera News*, hailed *Phantom* as "an important musical drama, adapted with elegance and good humor," and declared that the score was Lloyd Webber's "most satisfying to date."

Aspects of Love, Lloyd Webber's 1989 collaboration with Hart and Don Black, is something of a departure from his usual big, dramatic, plays. Based on the novel of the same name by Bloomsbury Group author David Garnett, it concerns the interwoven love relationships of five characters—one bisexual, one only fourteen. Jack Kroll in *Newsweek* explained,

however, that "this erotic pretzel is actually a story of considerable sweetness and charm." He also reported that the play was Lloyd Webber's "most personal, deeply felt work." While Thomas M. Disch in the *Nation* had reservations about parts of the play, he noted that "*Aspects* does one thing quite well: It tells a good story with exceptional speed."

Lloyd Webber's 1993 effort, *Sunset Boulevard*, has proved quite popular with theater audiences. When it opened on Broadway, Vincent Canby announced in the *New York Times:* "It's here and it's a stunner. If you have to ask what 'it' is, you haven't been paying attention." As Canby went on to report, the musical is based on a Billy Wilder film made in 1950. Both the film and the musical tell the story of Norma Desmond, a fictional former silent screen star displaced by the introduction of sound to the movie business. John Simon in *New York* judged that *Sunset* "is neither as bad as the gossips may have wished nor as good as the gullible must have hoped." William A. Henry III in *Time,* however, praised the show, particularly its comic treatment of characters and subject matter.

Wins Oscar for *Evita*

Lloyd Webber enjoyed another successful transition to film with *Evita,* released in 1996 with Madonna in the title role. The work won the composer his first Oscar, in the Best Original Song category. The following year brought numerous career triumphs in addition to the Oscar: in June, *Cats* became the longest–running musical on Broadway; Lloyd Webber advanced from the British honorific "Sir" to "Lord" after Queen Elizabeth II granted him a seat in the British House of Lords, and he surpassed the number of musicals done by Richard Rodgers and Oscar Hammerstein, a career achievement that had helped him amass a reported wealth of $500 million. Yet Lloyd Webber also faced several other obstacles, including some severe financial crises at the Really Useful Group headquarters. Two stars from *Sunset Boulevard* sued over contractual issues related to the musical, and the producer had to pay Patti LuPone and Faye Dunaway large court judgments.

Lloyd Webber also began work on another musical, which opened to poor reviews in Washington, D.C., in 1996. *Whistle Down the Wind* was then revised for a more successful London opening in collaboration with a new lyricist, Jim Steinman, the veteran rock professional best known for his work on Meat Loaf's *Bat Out of Hell.* The story, based on a book written by the mother of British actress Hayley Mills, who starred in the 1961 film version, centers around an escaped convict whom three children discover hiding out in a barn in their Deep South town; they become convinced that he is the new messiah. The work, wrote *Time*'s Richard Zoglin, "has a welcome modesty and warmth, a far cry from the chilly Gothic pretensions" of some earlier musicals from Lloyd Webber; Zoglin described *Whistle Down the Wind* as "more emotionally accessible and musically alive than anything Lloyd Webber has done in a long while." Despite its shaky debut, the show enjoyed a long run in London, closing on January 6, 2001. On his Web site "The Really Useful Group," Lloyd Webber stated, "I am sad to see *Whistle Down the Wind* go, though a two–and–one–half–year run is pretty good. Although with hindsight I feel I might have been treading water, the show did contain 'No Matter What,' my biggest ever Number One hit in the UK, and many other songs of which I am extremely proud."

Lloyd Webber's *The Beautiful Game* premiered in London in September 2000. The show concerns a group of teenagers in Belfast, Northern Ireland, dur-

ing the late 1960s and early 1970s. The drama follows the teens as they come of age during a time of great violence and conflict. On "The Really Useful Group" Web site, Lyricist Ben Elton commented that *The Beautiful Game* "is dedicated to all those innocent and defenceless people who every day are forced to struggle simply to be left alone. Simply to be allowed to live and love in peace."

If you enjoy the works of Andrew Lloyd Webber, you might want to check out the following:

The stage musical *Rent* by Jonathan Larson.
Oliver!, an Academy Award–winning film, 1968.
West Side Story, an Academy Award–winning film, 1961.

Lloyd Webber seems certain to continue his work in musical theater. In 1998, on the occasion of his fiftieth birthday, he was honored with a performance of his greatest songs at London's Royal Albert Hall. Addressing the audience, Lloyd Webber stated, "Above all I thank everyone who has supported my work in music and musicals. You have made my career possible in the world which I hold dearest."

■ Biographical and Critical Sources

BOOKS

Contemporary Literary Criticism, Volume 21, Gale, 1982.
McKnight, Gerald, *Andrew Lloyd Webber,* St. Martin's, 1985.
Walsh, Michael, *Andrew Lloyd Webber: His Life and Works,* Abrams, 1989, expanded edition, 1997.

PERIODICALS

American Spectator, August, 1997, Mark Steyn, "Andrew Lord Hyphen," pp. 50–51, 79.
Catholic World, August, 1971, Clifford Edwards, review of *Jesus Christ Superstar,* pp. 217–21.

Christian Century, June 27, 1973, James M. Wall, review of *Jesus Christ Superstar*, pp. 693–94.

Entertainment Weekly, March 8, 1996, Kipp Cheng, "This Week: Websites," p. 71.

Journal of Popular Culture, fall, 1972, pp. 259–69.

Melody Maker, October 10, 1970, Richard Williams, review of *Jesus Christ Superstar*, p. 8.

Nation, May 7, 1990, Thomas M. Disch, review of *Aspects of Love*, p. 643.

New Republic, March 14, 1988, Robert Brustein, review of *Phantom of the Opera*, pp. 33–34, 36.

Newsweek, April 16, 1990, Jack Kroll, review of *Aspects of Love*, p. 91.

New York, November 28, 1994, John Simon, review of *Sunset Boulevard*, p. 75; August 7, 1995, John Simon, "*Sunset* Sunrise," pp. 72–73.

New York Post, September 26, 1979, Clive Barnes, review of *Evita*.

New York Times, October 24, 1971, sec. 2, pp. 1, 7; September 5, 1972, p. 45; September 26, 1979; September 1, 1982; November 27, 1994, pp. 1, 5; June 20, 1996, p. B1.

Opera News, June, 1988, Barrymore Laurence Scherer, review of *Phantom of the Opera*, p. 32.

People, December 23, 1996, Tom Gliatto, review of *Evita*, p. 17.

Rolling Stone, December 2, 1970, p. 10; June 24, 1971, p. 43.

Saturday Review, October 14, 1978, Martin Gottfried, review of *Evita*, p. 57.

Stereo Review, April, 1977, Eric Salzman, review of *Evita*, p. 108.

Time, November 9, 1970, p. 47; December 20, 1993, p. 66; July 27, 1998, Richard Zoglin, review of *Whistle Down the Wind*, p. 62.

Variety, December 15, 1997, Matt Wolf, "Curtain Up on Act Two," p. S33; January 26, 1998, David Mermelstein, "The Music of the Knight Continues to Slay Fans," p. 58; April 13, 1998, Matt Wolf, "Starry Night," p. 33; July 13, 1998, Matt Wolf, "Which Way Will 'Wind' Blow?" p. 59.

ON—LINE

Sir Andrew Lloyd Webber's Web site, "The Really Useful Group," is located at http://www.reallyuseful.com (2000).*

Janet Lunn

gina Public Library, Regina, Saskatchewan, 1982–83; writer in residence, Kitchener Public Library, Ontario, 1988, Ottawa University, 1993.

■ Personal

Born December 28, 1928, in Dallas, TX; naturalized Canadian citizen, 1963; daughter of Herman Alfred (a mechanical engineer) and Margaret (maiden name, Alexander) Swoboda; married Richard Lunn (a teacher), 1950 (died, 1987); children: Eric, Jeffrey, Alexander, Katherine, John. *Education:* Attended Queen's University of Kingston, 1947–50. *Politics:* New Democratic Party. *Hobbies and other interests:* Art, archeology, history, sketching, gardening, and compulsive reading.

■ Addresses

Home—115–3260 Southgate Rd., Ottawa, Ontario K1V 8W9, Canada. *Agent*—Lee Davis Creal, 187 Browning Ave., Toronto, Ontario M4K 1W7, Canada.

■ Career

Freelance editor and writer, editorial consultant, and lecturer. Clarke Irwin & Co., Toronto, Ontario, children's editor, 1972–75; writer in residence, Re-

■ Member

International Board on Books for Young People (IBBY), PEN, Writers Union of Canada (chair, 1984–85), Canadian Society of Children's Authors, Illustrators, and Performers.

■ Awards, Honors

Canada Council grant, 1978; Ontario Arts grants, 1978, 1980, and 1983; *The Twelve Dancing Princesses* was named one of the ten best children's books of 1979 by the Canadian Library Association, and was awarded the children's book award from the Toronto branch of International Order of Daughters of the Empire, 1980; Vicki Metcalf Award for body of work from Canadian Authors Association, 1981; Book of the Year for Children Medal, Canadian Library Association, 1981, first honorable mention for the prize awarded by the Canada Council of Children's Literature, 1982, Notable Book, American Library Association, 1983, Outstanding Science Trade Book for Children, National Science Teachers Association and Children's Book Council, Honor List selection, International Board on Books for Young

People (IBBY), 1984, and California Young Readers' Medal, 1988, all for *The Root Cellar*; Children's Literature Award, Canada Council, Young Adult Book of the Year, Saskatchewan Library Association, and Book of the Year for Children Medal, Canadian Library Association, all 1986, and Honor List, *Horn Book,* 1989, all for *Shadow in Hawthorn Bay;* Mr. Christie's Award, 1992, for *The Story of Canada;* Governor General's Award for Literature, 1998, for *The Hollow Tree.* Lunn was awarded an Honorary Doctorate of Laws, Queen's University, 1992; Honorary Diploma, Loyalist College of Applied Arts and Technology, 1993; Order of Ontario, 1996; and Order of Canada, 1997.

■ Writings

FOR CHILDREN

(Adapter) Jakob Ludwig Karl and Wilhelm Karl Grimm, *The Twelve Dancing Princesses,* illustrated by Laszlo Gal, Methuen, 1979.

Amos's Sweater (picture book), illustrated by Kim LaFave, Groundwood, 1988, Camden House, 1991.

One Hundred Shining Candles, illustrated by Lindsay Grater, Lester & Orpen Dennys, 1989, Scribner, 1991.

Duck Cakes for Sale (picture book), illustrated by Kim LaFave, Groundwood (Toronto), 1989.

Come to the Fair (picture book), illustrated by Gilles Pelletier, Tundra (Toronto), 1997.

The Umbrella Party (picture book), illustrated by Kady MacDonald Denton, Douglas & McIntyre (Vancouver), 1998.

Charlotte, illustrated by Brian Deines, Tundra, 1998.

FICTION; FOR YOUNG ADULTS

Double Spell (mystery), illustrated by Emily Arnold McCully, Peter Martin, 1968, published with illustrations by A. M. Calder, Heinemann, 1985, also published as *Twin Spell,* illustrated by McCully, Harper, 1969.

The Root Cellar, Lester & Orpen Dennys, 1981, Scribner, 1983.

Shadow in Hawthorn Bay, Lester & Orpen Dennys, 1986, Scribner, 1987.

One Proud Summer, Penguin, 1988.

The Hollow Tree, Knopf, 1997, Viking, 2000.

OTHER

(With husband, Richard Lunn) *The County* (history of Prince Edward County, Ontario), County of Prince Edward, 1967.

Larger Than Life (Canadian historical profiles), illustrated by Emma Hesse, Press Procepic, 1979.

(With Christopher Moore) *The Story of Canada* (history), illustrated by Alan Daniel, Key Porter/ Lester, 1992.

(Editor) *The Unseen,* Lester (Toronto), 1994, Puffin, 1997.

Also author of scripts for Canadian Broadcasting Co. Contributor of articles and short stories to periodicals, including *Starting Points in Language Arts.* Many of Lunn's books have been translated into Danish, French, German, Spanish, and Swedish.

■ Sidelights

Janet Lunn has staked out the past as her special literary territory. The American–born Canadian author has mined aspects of the Revolutionary War, the American Civil War, and frontier life in Canada in her fifteen novels, picture books, and histories. Employing time travel and telepathy in her stories, Lunn has attracted a wide variety of readers in both Canada and the United States with such award–winning novels as *The Root Cellar, Shadow in Hawthorn Bay,* and *The Hollow Tree.* In illustrated books for older readers, *Charlotte* and *One Hundred Shining Candles,* Lunn has also brought historical times to life, and in her picture books she has told of sweaters, cheeky ducks, umbrellas, and fairs.

Born in 1928, in Dallas, Texas, Lunn was raised in Vermont and in the suburbs of New York City. She recalled her childhood home in *Something about the Author Autobiography Series (SAAS):* "We lived on a farm a mile and a half outside the village of Norwich on the Connecticut River. In my heart, in my memory, every inch of that countryside is a paradise. It has become the country of my dreams, the world at the core of all my stories." One of four children, Lunn grew up in a close–knit family environment in which stories and storytelling were daily events. Inspired by the stories read to her by her older sister, Lunn soon began making up her own.

Reading on her own opened new horizons for her: "Once I mastered it, I never stopped reading," Lunn wrote in *SAAS.* Favorite childhood books included *Blue Willow, The Secret Garden,* and *The Good Master,* among many others. Lunn invented a rich dream world for herself, populated by Heidi, the March girls of *Little Women,* and Anne of Green Gables. "They were all part of my neighborhood," Lunn recalled. Fantasies and romances that take the reader back in time became special favorites of Lunn, a foreshadowing of her own writing preferences.

"Most of my stories are set in—or partly in—historical times. I like how events in one time are connected to events in other times and I sometimes wonder if time mightn't flow in more than one direction—like a reversing falls. So I write about that.... I can't leave history alone."

—Janet Lunn

At age ten, Lunn and her family moved to Rye, a suburb of New York City. "I have never quite gotten over my homesickness for the Vermont countryside," Lunn noted in *SAAS.* "It was my strength and my joy." In Rye, Lunn's second home was the library; shyness kept her at arm's length from boys. She graduated from high school in Montclair, New Jersey, to which the family had moved two years earlier. Plans for attending Bryn Mawr in Pennsylvania fell through when Lunn failed the chemistry section on her college entrance exams. Instead, on the advice of neighbors, she attended school in Ottawa, Canada, for a year to qualify for Queen's University in Kingston, Ontario.

Becoming a Writer

Here, for the first time, Lunn developed a rich social life. Married to a fellow English student, she stayed on in Canada after graduation. Her husband wrote for a newspaper in Toronto during the first years of their marriage, and then came five children. Lunn's first steps toward professional writing were doing the children's book reviews at her husband's paper. Soon she was reviewing children's books for magazines and radio stations. Not long thereafter, Lunn sold a children's story about gardening for twenty–five dollars. It was the beginning of Lunn's career as a writer of children's books.

Her first novel, *Double Spell,* was many years in the writing, however. A story about twins, old dolls, old houses, and a ghost, the novel was published in the United States as *Twin Spell.* Twelve–year–old identical twins Elizabeth and Jane buy a doll that powerfully attracts them, only to discover that strange powers cause them to be haunted by memories of another girl who once owned the same doll. The past and present begin to merge for the two girls, who live in an old house in Toronto, much like the Lunn family at the time. "The action of the novel," observed Gwyneth Evans in *Canadian Children's Literature,* "is a process of discovery whereby

the protagonists gradually learn to understand the connection between their present lives and the uncanny experiences they have of flashing back into nineteenth century Toronto." Writing in *The School Librarian,* Jane Woodley noted that the "build–up of tension and unease is steady and becomes gripping with a climax of real dramatic quality." Woodley also wrote, "Period detail is well worked in and heightens the colour."

Publication of this first children's book was followed by a decade–long hiatus for Lunn, as she took a job as a children's editor and struggled with what ultimately became *The Root Cellar.* This novel was inspired in part by an old house the Lunn family bought and restored in the Ontario countryside—one they apparently shared with a ghost. Finally leaving her editorial duties behind, she published in quick succession the retelling of a children's tale, *The Twelve Dancing Princesses,* and a compilation of Canadian hero tales, *Larger Than Life.* Reviewing the latter title in *Canadian Children's Literature,* Eleanor Swainson remarked that the "author's heroes are all appealing, but they aren't perfect and they are never ponderous.... Ms. Lunn has a good ear for the way real people talk." Swainson also had high praise for the book in general, asserting that *Larger Than Life* is "beautifully written by a woman who clearly loves words and is extraordinarily skillful using them to portray children's perceptions."

Acclaim for *The Root Cellar*

When Lunn finally returned to her ghost story manuscript, she found that it had metamorphosed in her subconscious. It had become a time–travel story about a young orphan girl who comes to live with an aunt, uncle, and four cousins in an old house after the death of her grandmother. Rose discovers that she can time travel by visits to the house's root cellar. Back in the 1860s she meets Will and Susan. When Will fails to return from the Civil War, Rose and Susan head off to Virginia in search of him. "It's a story of friendship across and through time," Lunn explained at the presentation ceremony of the Canadian Library Association Children's Book of the Year Award, an honor that *The Root Cellar* garnered. Lunn went on to note that the book was a story "of civil war, of here and there, of then and now and young and old, of one reality and another...."

Reviewing the award–winning novel in *Canadian Children's Literature,* Jean Little observed that "Rose Larkin ... is the best kind of heroine. She is old enough to think and feel, grieve, rejoice and grow." Little concluded that, while in earlier books Lunn had written "history, mystery, fantasy and fairytales," in *The Root Cellar* "she has combined her

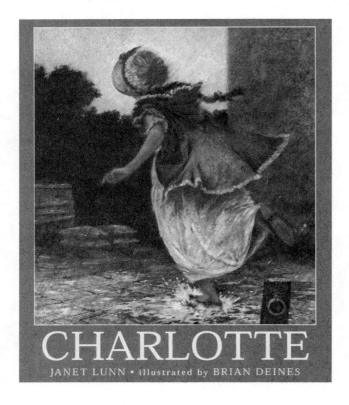

CHARLOTTE

JANET LUNN • illustrated by BRIAN DEINES

Lunn's 1998 picture book opens a window to 1783, as a ten–year–old girl must chose between her desire to be loyal to her family in their support of the new American republic and her affection for her cousins, who are shunned because of their wish to return to British rule.

previous genres and discovered an even more exciting writing experience. Those children who travel with Rose from today to yesterday and back again are grateful. It is a wonderfully rich reading experience." Raymond E. Jones noted in *Children's Literature Association Quarterly* that sections of the book "are as good historical children's fiction as one will find anywhere," while *Growing Point's* Margery Fisher concluded, "It is in the quiet accumulation of detail that this story makes its strong appeal...."

Lunn returned to the same locale of *The Root Cellar*—Prince Edward County, Ontario, and Hawthorn Bay—for her 1986 *Shadow in Hawthorn Bay*. History is again at play, for the book is set in 1815 when fifteen–year–old Mary Urquhart leaves her native Scotland, following the telepathic pleas of her cousin Duncan. But Mary, after a harrowing journey, arrives too late: Duncan is already dead and his family has returned to Scotland. Mary must stay on in the inclement new land until she earns enough for her passage home. In time, Mary adjusts to what

becomes her new home and neighbors, even coming to terms with her extrasensory powers. Reviewing the novel in *Books for Young People,* Sandra Martin observed that the quality of Lunn's novels which readers appreciated most were their "completeness." Martin went on to list the qualities of such completeness: "The facts are accurate, the setting authentic, and the characters so plausible that one slides effortlessly into her world." D. A. Young noted in *The Junior Bookshelf* that *Shadow in Hawthorn Bay* "is a wonderful book of great power...."

Yet another powerful book of historical fiction by Lunn is *The Hollow Tree,* set during the American Revolution and featuring another young orphan girl. Phoebe's father has been killed fighting on the side of the revolution and the motherless child goes to live with cousins still loyal to the king. When Gideon, her beloved cousin, is hanged as a Loyalist spy, Phoebe feels in part responsible for his death. She decides to deliver a secret message to the British at Fort Ticonderoga, a mission Gideon himself had been sent to accomplish. After an arduous journey, Phoebe discovers the fort has been abandoned, but is reunited with her Loyalist relatives. When they in turn capture a young man whom they believe to be a rebel spy, Phoebe releases him, and flees herself. Praising the novel in *Quill and Quire,* Sarah Ellis noted Lunn's gifts as a writer in her "artful orchestration" of events, in her "control of her historical material," and in her recreation of "a time that was genuinely different." Ellis also pointed out that Lunn "proves herself the best young adult romance writer we've got."

Examines Canadian History

Lunn has also written historical nonfiction, teaming up with Christopher Moore on *The Story of Canada,* a heavily illustrated children's book. Many reviewers noted that the work does not treat history in the standard wars–and–famous–men format. Instead, Lunn and Moore focused on the native peoples as much as on the European settlers, and also on the achievements of women. Elizabeth Abbott observed in *Quill and Quire* that in this book history is not "an exclusively white, male–oriented concern," and went on to note that "history is personalized through individuals." Abbott concluded that *The Story of Canada* is a work young readers "will love, treasure, remember." John Bemrose remarked in *Maclean's* that the history is "excitingly written and superbly illustrated," concluding that it provides "one of the finest tools that young Canadians have ever received to help them claim their country's past for themselves."

Lunn has also produced several picture books for younger and older readers, many of them dealing with historical themes, as well. In *One Hundred Shin-*

ing Candles, the children of a poor family in the Canadian wilderness in 1800 secretly make gifts to celebrate Christmas. Joan Arndt noted in *The Five Owls* that the book is a "good read–aloud," with "just the right amount of suspense to keep listeners' attention to the end." Zena Sutherland remarked in *Bulletin of the Center for Children's Books* that *One Hundred Shining Candles* is a "pleasant holiday story ... told in a style that is fluent and direct." *Come to the Fair* is set a couple of generations ago, and takes a look at a day at the fair from the point of view of the Martin family. Lee Block remarked in *School Library Journal*, "Readers will enjoy identifying with the fair–goers' dozens of activities," noting also that "the story is gentle and comforting." *Charlotte* is a picture book that takes the reader farther back in time, to 1783, and once again investigates divided loyalties brought on by the American Revolution. "Intriguing and emotionally wrenching, this [book] provides clear–cut depictions of good and evil," according to *Booklist*'s Carolyn Phelan.

If you enjoy the works of Janet Lunn, you might want to check out the following books:

Jennifer Armstrong, *The Dreams of Mairhe Mehan*, 1996.
Margaret Buffie, *The Dark Garden*, 1997.
Pete Hautman, *Mr. Was*, 1996.
Jean Little, *The Belonging Place*, 1997.

"Most of my stories are set in—or partly in—historical times," Lunn once told *St. James Guide to Children's Writers*. "I like how events in one time are connected to events in other times and I sometimes wonder if time mightn't flow in more than one direction—like a reversing falls. So I write about that.... I can't leave history alone."

■ Biographical and Critical Sources

BOOKS

Children's Literature Review, Volume 18, Gale, 1989.
Sixth Book of Junior Authors & Illustrators, edited by Sally Holmes Holtze, Wilson, 1989.
Something about the Author Autobiography Series, Volume 12, Gale, 1991, pp. 233–47.

St. James Guide to Children's Writers, edited by Sara and Tom Pendergast, St. James Press, 1999, pp. 675–77.

PERIODICALS

Booklist, November 15, 1990; November 1, 1991, p. 533; August 19, 1998, Carolyn Phelan, review of *Charlotte*, p. 1994.
Books for Young People, February, 1987, Sandra Martin, review of *Shadow in Hawthorn Bay*, p. 5.
Bulletin of the Center for Children's Books, October, 1991, Zena Sutherland, review of *One Hundred Shining Candles*, p. 43.
Canadian Children's Literature, numbers 15–16, 1980, Gwyneth Evans, "Nothing Odd Ever Happens Here: Landscape in Canadian Fantasy," pp. 15–30; number 20, 1980, Eleanor Swainson, "Quality and Quantity in Canadian History," pp. 76–79; numbers 35–36, 1984, Jean Little, "The Magic of Another Day," pp. 153–55; number 57, 1990; number 63, 1991, pp. 53–60.
Canadian Library Journal, October, 1982, Janet Lunn, "Acceptance Speech for Book of the Year for Children Award," pp. 329–30.
Children's Literature Association Quarterly, spring, 1985, Raymond E. Jones, "'Border Crossing': Janet Lunn's *The Root Cellar*," pp. 43–44.
Five Owls, November–December, 1991, Joan Arndt, review of *One Hundred Shining Candles*, p. 45.
Growing Point, May, 1985, Margery Fisher, review of *The Root Cellar*, pp. 4432–33.
Junior Bookshelf, February, 1987, D. A. Young, review of *Shadow in Hawthorn Bay*, p. 159.
Maclean's, December 14, 1992, John Bemrose, "Adventures in History," p. 58.
Publishers Weekly, May 8, 1987, p. 73; November 10, 1997, p. 74.
Quill and Quire, November, 1992, Elizabeth Abbott, review of *The Story of Canada*, p. 35; May, 1996, p. 13; January, 1998, Sarah Ellis, review of *The Hollow Tree*, p. 36; February, 1998, p. 42; March, 1998, p. 71.
School Librarian, June, 1986, Jane Woodley, review of *Double Spell*, p. 170.
School Library Journal, September, 1987, p. 197; October, 1991, p. 31; February, 1998, Lee Block, review of *Come to the Fair*, p. 88; September, 1998, p. 194; June, 2000, Robin L. Gilson, review of *The Hollow Tree*, p. 150.
Voice of Youth Advocates, August–September, 1987, p. 122.

ON–LINE

Janet Lunn's Web site, located at http://www.keithn.com/jlunn.

—*Sketch by J. Sydney Jones*

Lurlene McDaniel

■ Personal

Born Lurlene Nora Gallagher, April 5, 1944, in Philadelphia, PA; daughter of James (a chief petty officer in the U.S. Navy) and Bebe (a homemaker; maiden name, Donaldson) Gallagher; married Joe McDaniel, March 12, 1966 (divorced, 1987); children: Sean Clifford, Erik James. *Education:* University of South Florida, B.A., 1965. *Politics:* Republican. *Religion:* Conservative Presbyterian.

■ Addresses

Home—Chattanooga, TN. *Agent*—Meg Ruley/Jane Rotrosen, 318 East 51st St., New York, NY 10022.

■ Career

Novelist and freelance writer, including radio and television scripts, and promotional and advertising copy. Frequent speaker and lecturer at writers' conferences and teacher's conventions.

■ Member

Novelists, Inc.

■ Awards, Honors

Six Months to Live was placed in a literary time capsule in the Library of Congress, November, 1990; RITA Award, 1991; *Somewhere between Life and Death, Too Young to Die,* and *Goodbye Doesn't Mean Forever* were selected as Children's Choice books, International Reader's Association; *A Season for Goodbye, Till Death Do Us Part,* and *The Girl Death Left Behind* were selected as Books for the Reluctant Reader, American Library Association.

■ Writings

YOUNG ADULT NOVELS

What's It Like to Be a Star?, Willowisp Press/School Book Fairs, 1982.
I'm a Cover Girl Now, Willowisp Press/School Book Fairs, 1982.
Will I Ever Dance Again?, Willowisp Press/School Book Fairs, 1982.
Head Over Heels, Willowisp Press/School Book Fairs, 1983.

If I Should Die Before I Wake, Willowisp Press/School Book Fairs, 1983.

Sometimes Love Just Isn't Enough, Willowisp Press/School Book Fairs, 1984.

Three's a Crowd, Willowisp Press/School Book Fairs, 1984.

The Secret Life of Steffie Martin, Willowisp Press/School Book Fairs, 1985.

Why Did She Have to Die?, Willowisp Press/School Book Fairs, 1986.

More Than Just a Smart Girl, Willowisp Press/School Book Fairs, 1987.

Mother, Please Don't Die, Willowisp Press/School Book Fairs, 1988.

My Secret Boyfriend, Willowisp Press/School Book Fairs, 1988.

Too Young to Die, Bantam, 1989.

Goodbye Doesn't Mean Forever, Bantam, 1989.

Somewhere between Life and Death, Bantam, 1991.

Time to Let Go, Bantam, 1991.

Now I Lay Me Down to Sleep, Bantam, 1991.

When Happily Ever After Ends, Bantam, 1992.

Baby Alicia Is Dying, Bantam, 1993.

Don't Die, My Love, Bantam, 1995.

Saving Jessica, Bantam, 1995.

I'll Be Seeing You, Bantam, 1996.

Angels Watching over Me, Bantam, 1996.

Lifted up by Angels, Bantam, 1997.

Till Death Do Us Part, Bantam, 1997.

For Better, For Worse, Forever, Bantam, 1997.

Until Angels Close My Eyes, Bantam, 1998.

The Girl Death Left Behind, Bantam, 1999.

Angel of Mercy, Bantam, 1999.

Angel of Hope, Bantam, 2000.

"DAWN ROCHELLE" SERIES

Six Months to Live, Willowisp Press/School Book Fairs, 1985.

I Want to Live, Willowisp Press/School Book Fairs, 1987.

So Much to Live For, Willowisp Press/School Book Fairs, 1991.

No Time to Cry, Willowisp Press/School Book Fairs, 1993.

Dawn Rochelle: Four Novels, Bantam, 2000.

To Live Again, Bantam, 2001.

"ONE LAST WISH" YOUNG ADULT SERIES

A Time to Die, Bantam, 1992.

Mourning Song, Bantam, 1992.

Mother, Help Me Live, Bantam, 1992.

Someone Dies, Someone Lives, Bantam, 1992.

Sixteen and Dying, Bantam, 1992.

Let Him Live, Bantam, 1992.

The Legacy: Making Wishes Come True, Bantam, 1993.

Please Don't Die, Bantam, 1993.

She Died Too Young, Bantam, 1994.

All the Days of Her Life, Bantam, 1994.

A Season for Goodbye, Bantam, 1995.

One Last Wish: Three Novels, Bantam, 1998.

Please Don't Die, Bantam, 1998.

Reach for Tomorrow, Bantam, 1999.

JUVENILE NOVELS

A Horse for Mandy, Willowisp Press/School Book Fairs, 1981.

The Pony Nobody Wanted, Willowisp Press/School Book Fairs, 1982.

The Battle of Zorn, Willowisp Press/School Book Fairs, 1983.

Peanut Butter for Supper Again, Willowisp Press/School Book Fairs, 1985.

OTHER

Starry, Starry Night: Three Holiday Stories, Bantam, 1998.

How Do I Love Thee?, Bantam, 2001.

Served as fiction editor for the children's magazine *Faith 'n' Stuff* and as editor for *Guideposts for Kids*. McDaniel's books have been translated into German, Norwegian, Slovak, Hebrew, and Dutch.

■ Adaptations

Angels Watching over Me, Lifted Up by Angels, Until Angels Close My Eyes, and *Don't Die, My Love* have been recorded on audio tape by Recorded Books. *Don't Die, My Love* was made into a television film under the title *A Champion's Fight*, NBC, 1999.

■ Sidelights

Talking to Lurlene McDaniel about her work is similar to reading a book of inspirational sayings; her conversation is sprinkled with such phrases as "life works out if you give it a chance," and "all things work to the good of those who love God." She is unflaggingly upbeat and cheerful—traits that seem surprising in the author of dozens of novels that portray teenagers faced with terminal illnesses and their own mortality. More often than not, some form of the word "death" finds its way into the titles of McDaniel's novels, as it does in the following: *A Time to Die, Sixteen and Dying,* and *She Died Too Young.*

As the titles suggest, McDaniel's specialty is dealing with some of life's most difficult blows. In *Somewhere between Life and Death,* Erin's younger sister is severely injured in a car accident. When the doctors declare her brain dead, Erin and her family must decide whether or not to turn off life–support systems and donate her organs to be transplanted. In *Please Don't Die,* heart transplant recipient Katie O'Roark spends the summer at "Jenny House," a retreat for critically ill adolescents. She befriends three girls: Chelsea, a candidate for a heart transplant; Amanda, a victim of leukemia; and Lacey, a diabetic. Not everyone makes it through the summer. Desi, the protagonist of *Baby Alicia Is Dying,* is a teenage volunteer at a home for babies with AIDS. She becomes very attached to a baby who seems healthy but then suddenly succumbs to the disease.

"Adults Are Often Prejudiced"

It's not exactly the stuff of young adult romances, or even the horror novels that currently fill the shelves in teen sections of bookstores. Nevertheless, McDaniel has carved out a niche in the young adult publishing world—one that some people never dreamed existed. "Adults are often prejudiced against my books," McDaniel said in 1995 interview with Sarah Verney for *Authors and Artists for Young Adults* (*AAYA*). "They don't understand why kids would want to read them." The problem, McDaniel speculated, may be that the adults haven't read the books themselves. "They look at the titles and erroneously assume that the books are morbid. They aren't."

"Fiction is about feelings, and empathy is the name of the game."

—Lurlene McDaniel

Illness, death and dying may be at the core of McDaniel's novels, but the stories themselves are really about life, and getting beyond the grieving process. While some people have referred to her books as "ten–hankie novels," McDaniel prefers to think of them as "bibliotherapy"—a means of working out one's grief in a book. To do that, her readers need to get a glimpse of the big picture—"the totality of life, not just the individual moments," as McDaniel told Verney.

Most importantly, though, McDaniel's readers also need to feel hope. "I end all my stories on a note of hope," she pointed out in her *AAYA* interview. Hope is the one thing McDaniel most wants to give her readers, whether they are kids like her characters, facing extraordinary challenges, or ordinary teens with ordinary problems. McDaniel recognizes that many teens face difficulties that those of her own generation never even imagined. "We worried about someone cutting in line," she explained in her interview with Verney. "They worry about getting shot." When terrible things do happen in their lives, teens may have nowhere to turn.

"No one is talking to teenagers about the grieving process," asserted McDaniel in an interview with Mark Curnutte for the *News & Observer* (Raleigh, NC). So she does by offering them a look into the lives of characters who have been through the process and emerged on the other side. As she attests, positive messages abound in her books, as they do in the following passage from *Somewhere between Life and Death:* "The flowers, the butterflies, the greening of the grass, told her that life was cyclic, season after season. It came, it went. It came again. . . . Erin gazed at Amy's coffin . . . and knew with certainty that Amy wasn't in it. Maybe her body would be buried, but the person of Amy, her spirit, would not. For Amy was with Erin still and would live in her heart for all the days of her life." And a similar theme of hope and peace is found in the following excerpt from *All the Days of Her Life:* "As she turned to go inside, she saw a shooting star arc through the darkness. . . . Was it an answer sent to her from a world beyond the rainbows? Lacey found renewed hope within her heart. She'd been given a second chance for all the days of her life. Beginning now, she'd make the most of it."

A Christian Perspective

The hope reaching out to young adults in McDaniel's novels springs from the author's own personal well, which is fed by her faith. She is a devout Christian and is certain her books reflect the inspiration she receives from her religion. But while McDaniel strives to maintain "a biblical perspective" and "a sense of eternal purpose" in her novels, she makes a point of not being dogmatic. "I don't push a Christian agenda on my readers," McDaniel maintained in her *AAYA* interview, pointing out that they come from a variety of religious backgrounds. "I don't preach to them—if someone wants a sermon, they can go to church."

One obvious way McDaniel's Christian perspective comes through is in her treatment of death. "I never send a character to the grave without the hope of eternal life," she explained to Verney. And although her doomed characters suffer plenty, in the end they generally make their peace with God. As Melissa, a high school junior dying of leukemia writes to her best friend in *Goodbye Doesn't Mean Forever*, "I'm not mad at God anymore. . . . I've had some heart–to–heart talks with Him and I've come to believe that He loves me enough to want me with Him in heaven. And that once I'm in heaven, I'll never have to die again." In coming to terms with her own death, Melissa also seems confident that she is going on to an afterlife. She finishes her letter with, "I'll be watching you. And when you least expect it, you'll hear me call you in the wind. I promise."

Saw Infant Son Near Death

McDaniel's faith, in addition to inspiring her young protagonists, helps her through the tough times in her own life. The most difficult of these resulted from her older son's diabetes. Sean, who is now an athletic, healthy (though still diabetic) adult, was only three when diagnosed with the disease. At the time, he was losing weight and was constantly fatigued—all classic signs of diabetes; McDaniel consulted a doctor, but he failed to recognize Sean's illness. "I was getting him undressed that night," McDaniel remembered in her *AAYA* interview, "and I could count every rib on his little body. It was as if there was a voice in my head—I just knew he wasn't going to make it through the night." McDaniel, who was then in the early stages of her second pregnancy, took her son to an emergency room, and the doctors there immediately recognized his condition. Still, it took a tremendous medical effort for Sean to stabilize, and he came perilously close to dying in McDaniel's arms.

When Sean's crisis was over, McDaniel turned to the business of learning everything she could about diabetes management, a process that includes monitoring blood sugar levels and being extremely careful about diet and exercise. She quickly saw how *chronic illness* takes over one's life, and how it affects the dynamics of a family. Nevertheless, she feels her own experiences with Sean's illness support two of the hopeful messages she tries to convey in her novels: "Good can come from bad" and "life works out if you give it a chance." "What possible good could come of my beautiful little red–haired boy having diabetes?" she asked in her interview with Verney, then answered her own question: "If it weren't for Sean's illness, I don't know that I would ever have written my first novel. Would I go back and give up writing if it meant Sean wouldn't have diabetes? Absolutely. But you don't get to pick what happens to you. You do get to pick how you respond to it, however."

"I end all my stories on a note of hope."

—Lurlene McDaniel

One way McDaniel responded to Sean's illness was to choose to work at home as a freelance writer, so that she would be available to care for him. She had previously worked as a promotion copywriter for television stations in Florida and Michigan, and so was able to write advertising and promotional copy at home for a number of different sources. Among the things McDaniel wrote were commercials for local companies, public service announcements, and promotional materials for real estate agencies. Writing had always come naturally to her, as she once recalled, coupled with a love of storytelling. "My earliest childhood memories were of crawling up on my favorite uncle's lap and demanding that he 'read the book,'" she once said. "I started writing poems and stories in the first grade and by third grade had written a play that was performed by my classmates. By high school I was editor of the school newspaper and yearbook, and in college I was co-editor of the yearbook." She has said that her work in advertising and public relations taught her to apply a certain brevity to her writing, one of the most difficult aspects for any writer to master.

Discovering a Talent for Fiction

The beginning of McDaniel's following career as a novelist can be traced back to when Sean was ten or eleven and was asked to model in a poster for the Diabetes Research Institute. As McDaniel waited for Sean, she happened to strike up a conversation with a woman whose father had founded a company, School Book Fairs, that sold remainders of already published books to schools. The company was just starting to branch out into publishing their own titles, and the woman suggested that McDaniel write one. "I think they were just looking for someone who could meet a deadline, and I was used to that," McDaniel related to Verney.

McDaniel wrote several children's books for School Book Fairs, including picture books, before publishing *Will I Ever Dance Again?* This book, which is the story of how diabetes changes the life of a teenage ballet student, did very well for Willowisp, School Book Fairs' imprint. Asked to do more titles that featured teenage characters overcoming physical adversity, McDaniel followed up with *If I Should Die before I Wake,* and later, *Six Months to Live,* which eventually sold more than a million copies and was placed in a literary capsule at the Library of Congress.

McDaniel had found her voice and her subject matter, but it wasn't until she ended her relationship with Willowisp that she really hit her stride as a writer. She and her husband of twenty–one years divorced in 1987, and McDaniel suddenly needed to earn more money. She felt she had stayed at home too long to go back out into the work force, so instead, she concentrated on making her career as a novelist more lucrative. She found a literary agent and within weeks had a contract with Bantam Books. In addition to increasing her financial security, the move to Bantam gave McDaniel an opportunity to work with an editor in a way she hadn't previously experienced. Her books for Willowisp were edited and then sent to press without McDaniel participating in the process. Looking back, she says she realizes that, due to lack of constructive feedback, she wrote "a lot of bad books" before signing on with Bantam. She now works more closely with her editor and feels that the editorial give–and–take has helped her to grow artistically. Nevertheless, McDaniel is grateful to her two editors at Willowisp for their instrumental role in establishing her as an author, and they remain friends to this day.

Endured Other Grieving Experiences

In spite of her feeling that some of her earlier books were not as well-crafted as they might have been, McDaniel comments that "I did have an ability to tap into the reader's emotions," and credits that ability with much of her success. "Fiction is about feelings," she says, "and empathy is the name of the game." Without that empathy, McDaniel might never be able to get her message of hope across. Luckily, empathy comes easily to McDaniel, perhaps because—even though she has not experienced the diseases that her characters endure—serious illness has often touched her life. In addition to Sean's diabetes, her father–in–law had multiple sclerosis, a progressive nerve disease, and her mother–in–law died of liver cancer while still relatively young. "I felt like I was always standing at a hospital bedside," McDaniel remembered in her Verney interview.

From this vantage point, she had the opportunity to observe both the emotional effects of illness and the high–tech world of medicine. "I was always fascinated by things medical," McDaniel explained in her *AAYA* interview. "Maybe I'm really a frustrated doctor." This fascination led to another hallmark of McDaniel's novels, perhaps the flip side to her inspirational themes: realistically stark portrayals of illness and medical procedures. This is another aspect of her books that parents sometimes don't understand, but judging by the comments in her fan mail, McDaniel's readers are as interested in the details as she is. One girl, a pre–med student, wrote that she had become so interested in medicine while reading McDaniel's novels that she intended to become a pediatric oncologist.

In order to keep the medical information as up–to–date and accurate as possible, McDaniel sometimes employs the services of a librarian, who faxes her information from medical journals, and interviews scores of medical experts. She also works with cancer societies, hospice organizations, the Tennessee Organ Donor Services, and an AIDS agency in Atlanta. All of this research, coupled with McDaniel's graphic descriptions, leads to passages that should put to rest anyone's fears that McDaniel somehow romanticizes illness or dying. "I have a responsibility to my readers to be accurate," McDaniel related in her interview with Curnutte. "I call a spade a spade. If somebody vomits, they vomit." Her dedication to realism results in passages like the following, which appears in *She Died Too Young:* "Jillian was on the bed, lead wires from monitors snaking to her chest. Two tubes protruded from her groin area, from the femoral arteries, and led to the ECMO machine. One tube carried her oxygen–poor blood into the machine, where it was oxygenated by a special membrane, and the other tube carried the blood into her body to her oxygen–starved system. The machine was eerily quiet."

Personal Illness Brings New Insight

Ironically, McDaniel got her own glimpse of what it feels like to be on the receiving end of all the medical care she describes in her novels. In August of 1993 the author was diagnosed with breast cancer. Although the diagnosis was frightening, McDaniel considers herself lucky: the disease was caught early enough that she was able to have a lumpectomy (removal of just the cancerous lump, not the entire breast) plus radiation treatment, and she is considered to have made a full recovery. Still, the act itself of facing the cancer gave her a slightly different outlook. And McDaniel believes this comes through in one of her recent novels, *Don't Die, My Love*, in which a high school football star fights Hodgkin's disease, a form of cancer that affects the lymphatic system.

"I remind my readers that good things can come out of bad things. To wit—my entire novel-writing career came out of my son's diagnosis of diabetes. The doors of life are always opening and presenting challenges."

—Lurlene McDaniel

Perhaps her readers will notice the difference in McDaniel's outlook, but perhaps not, since in the past the author had no difficulty convincing her audience that she knows precisely how her characters feel. It is this realistic portrayal of teen crisis that is praised by McDaniel's critics. In a review of *Now I Lay Me Down to Sleep*, a *Booklist* contributor asserted that "McDaniel deals honestly and directly with the emotional and physical challenges of her characters." And Barbara Flottmeier, writing in *Voice of Youth Advocates*, pointed out in a review of *Somewhere between Life and Death* and *Time to Let Go*: "The issues of healing after a loved one dies, sustaining or ending life support systems, and organ donation are handled with care and thoughtfulness."

On the other hand, those who disparage McDaniel's work describe her novels as being too contrived and predictable. "The plot is trite and overly sentimental, with obvious twists and a predictable ending," said Tina Smith Entwistle in a review of *Mourning Song* for *School Library Journal*. *Somewhere between Life and Death* and its sequel, *Time to Let Go*,

were similarly criticized by a *Publishers Weekly* contributor: "These forgettable, lightweight novels have no place among the many wonderful books that offer young readers an authentic vision of what it means to love and lose."

McDaniel is characteristically upbeat about any negative reviews. "I'm a mass market writer, a commercial writer," she explained to Verney. "I'll never win a Newbery Award." And as long as she continues receiving letters at the rate of 200 to 300 a month from her readers, McDaniel will feel confident she's touching their hearts. One reader, Elizabeth, wrote, "In August of 1993, I had a double lung transplant. . . . Your books are so touching and realistic, and I am so thankful for them."

The "Angels" Series

McDaniel's spiritual beliefs found new literary expression with her "Angels" books, which began with *Angels Watching over Me* in 1996. Its protagonist, Leah, has been diagnosed with cancer; she and Rebekah, an Amish child who is her hospital roommate, come to believe they were visited by an angel, Gabriella. Leah recovers from her illness and takes a summer job not far from Rebekah's Amish community. A budding romance develops with Rebekah's brother, Ethan, but both teens are confronted by issues stemming from their religious differences. Holly Ward Lamb, writing about *Angels Watching over Me* in *Voice of Youth Advocates*, granted that while it was not a weighty look at interfaith dating, "this wonderful, escapist romance makes readers care about the young lovers."

Other works from McDaniel in the late 1990s continue to present teens who find spiritual energy from an unexpected sources in their lives. These include *Angels Watching Center*, *Lifted up by Angels*, *Angel Dance*, and *Angel of Mercy*. In this last work, Heather, 18, travels to impoverished East Africa to work as a volunteer at a clinic there. Infused with a desire to help humanity, she finds conditions and suffering far worse than she ever imagined. She also finds romance with another volunteer, a boy from Scotland, but tragedy befalls them as a result of Ian's own commitment to better the world. In *Angel of Hope*, the next work, Heather's younger sister, Amber, feels slighted by the attention Heather receives when she comes back from Uganda, until she decides to make the same journey herself.

Though McDaniel's protagonists have a tenuous hold on life, they also possess a firm sense of purpose. April Lancaster, featured in *Till Death Do*

Us Part, is just such a character. April is a senior in high school when she is suddenly troubled by headaches. A brain tumor she was assumed to have conquered as a kindergartner has returned, and during her course of treatment she meets a cystic fibrosis sufferer, Mark, with whom she falls in love. The next work, *For Better, For Worse, Forever,* finds April and her family vacationing in the Caribbean. She still suffers from the tumor, but has made the St. Croix trip to help her recover from Mark's tragic death in a car wreck. On the island, April meets Brandon, a local teen, who is also dealing with a recent loss. Initially, she refuses to tell him about her illness, but then her condition worsens, and she realizes that life is too short to hide behind unrealistic premises.

Trio of Christmas Tales

In *Starry, Starry Night: Three Holiday Stories,* McDaniel presents three Christmastime tales of teens in difficult situations. In "Christmas Child," Melanie comes to terms with a new sibling born with a birth defect. The hero of "Last Dance," Doug, suffers from leukemia, but the true hero of the story is a girl he has developed a crush upon, Brenda. She agrees to date him initially out of kindness, but finds they have much in common. Doug emerges as a distinct contrast to Brenda's other paramour, a football star named Matt, and she is forced to make a hard decision when both invite her to separate holiday events on the same night. "Kathy's Life," the last tale of the trio, features an unusual premise: Ellie, a poor teenager and daughter of a single mother, envies her classmate Kathy, who works as a nanny for a wealthy family. Kathy drives her own car and has nice clothes, but Ellie's desire to wear Kathy's shoes changes when she learns that the couple is actually planning to adopt the infant, and Kathy is actually the mother. "Once again, this prolific author has written a book that is compelling, sensitive, and insightful," wrote Kathleen Hutchins in her *Voice of Youth Advocates* review of *Starry, Starry Night.*

McDaniel continues to write poignant teen novels for Bantam, such as her 1999 work *The Girl Death Left Behind.* Beth is 14 when her parents and two younger siblings are killed in an automobile accident. She is taken in by her aunt and uncle, and her grief–stricken attempts to deal with the terrible loss, while adjusting to an entirely new home and school, form the basis of the plot. Lisa Denton, reviewing it for *School Library Journal,* found the heart–tugging plot was balanced by McDaniel's prose, which she termed "infused with imagery and nuance."

If you enjoy the works of Lurlene McDaniel, you might want to check out the following books:

Cynthia D. Grant, *Phoenix Rising: Or How to Survive Your Life,* 1989.
Sheila Solomon Klass, *Rhino,* 1993.
Elizabeth Laird, *Loving Ben,* 1989.
Norma Fox Mazer, *Heartbeat,* 1989.

With over fifty books to her credit, McDaniel has become one of the most successful writers in her field. Both of her sons are now adults, and grew into such robust teens that they earned soccer scholarships for their college education. She receives such large amounts of fan mail that she employs an assistant just to help her answer it. "I wouldn't trade my lifestyle for anything," McDaniel once said. "Mail from my readers brightens my days as each letter reminds me that a real live kid is reading and being affected by my work . . . . I remind my readers that good things can come out of bad things. To wit—my entire novel–writing career came out of my son's diagnosis of diabetes. The doors of life are always opening and presenting challenges."

■ Biographical and Critical Sources

BOOKS

McDaniel, Lurlene, *Goodbye Doesn't Mean Forever,* Bantam, 1989.
McDaniel, Lurlene, *Somewhere between Life and Death,* Bantam, 1991.
McDaniel, Lurlene, *She Died Too Young,* Bantam, 1994.
McDaniel, Lurlene, *All the Days of Her Life,* Bantam, 1994.

PERIODICALS

Booklist, March 15, 1991, p. 1506; June 15, 1991, review of *Now I Lay Me Down to Sleep,* p. 1977; January 1, 2000, Shelley Townsend–Hudson, review of *Angel of Mercy,* p. 906
Kliatt, November, 1997, review of *For Better, For Worse,* and *Till Death Do Us Part,* p. 9.
News & Observer (Raleigh, NC), April 10, 1992, Mark Curnutte, "Teen Tear–Jerkers," pp. 1D, 6D.

Publishers Weekly, June 9, 1989, pp. 70–71; review of *Somewhere between Life and Death* and *Time to Let Go,* November 23, 1990, p. 66; April 6, 1992, pp. 23–24; June 7, 1993, p. 71.

School Library Journal, August, 1989, pp. 152–54; June, 1993, Tina Smith Entwistle, review of *Mourning Song,* pp. 130, 132; July, 1993, pp. 101–102; October, 1998, Mary M. Hopf, review of *Starry, Starry Night,* pp. 138–139; March, 1999, Lisa Denton, review of *The Girl Death Left Behind,* p. 211.

Voice of Youth Advocates, April, 1991, Barbara Flottmeier, review of *Somewhere between Life and Death* and *Time to Let Go,* pp. 32–33; June, 1991, p. 98; August, 1992, p. 169; December, 1992, pp. 283–84; August, 1993, p. 154; August, 1998, Holly Ward Lamb, review of *Lifted Up by Angels,* p. 193; December, 1998, Kathleen Hutchins, review of *Starry, Starry Night,* pp. 356–357; April, 1999, Bette Ammon, review of *The Girl Death Left Behind,* p. 38.

OTHER

Lurlene McDaniel Web site, located at http://eclectics.com/lurlenemcdaniel (May 7, 2000).

A videotape interview with McDaniel is available through Tim Podell Productions, New York City.

Patricia C. McKissack

■ Personal

Born August 9, 1944, in Nashville, TN; daughter of Robert (a civil servant) and Erma (a civil servant) Carwell; married Fredrick L. McKissack (a writer), December 12, 1964; children: Fredrick Lemuel Jr., Robert and John (twins). *Education:* Tennessee Agricultural and Industrial State University (now Tennessee State University), B.A., 1964; Webster University, M.A., 1975. *Politics:* Independent. *Religion:* Methodist. *Hobbies and other interests:* Gardening.

■ Addresses

Home—14629 Timberlake Manor Ct., Chesterfield, MO 63017. *Office*—All–Writing Services, P.O. Box 967, Chesterfield, MO 63006-0967.

■ Career

Junior high school English teacher in Kirkwood, MO, 1968–75; Forest Park College, St. Louis, MO, part–time instructor in English, 1975—. Children's book editor at Concordia Publishing House, 1976–81, and Institute of Children's Literature, 1984—; University of Missouri—St. Louis, instructor, 1978—; co–owner with Fredrick L. McKissack of All–Writing Services. Educational consultant on minority literature.

■ Member

Society of Children's Book Writers and Illustrators.

■ Awards, Honors

Helen Keating Ott Award, National Church and Synagogue Librarians Association, 1980, for editorial work at Concordia Publishing House; C. S. Lewis Silver Medal awards, Christian Educators Association, 1984, for *It's the Truth, Christopher,* and 1985, for *Abram, Abram, Where Are We Going?;* Parents' Choice Award, 1989, for *Nettie Jo's Friends;* Jane Addams Children's Book Award, Women's International League for Peace and Freedom, and Coretta Scott King Award, both 1990, both for *A Long Hard Journey: The Story of the Pullman Porter;* Woodson Merit award, 1991, for *W. E. B. DuBois;* Hungry Mind Award, 1993, for *The World in 1492;* Newbery Honor Award and Coretta Scott King Author Award, both 1993, both for *The Dark–Thirty: Southern Tales of the Supernatural;* Coretta Scott King

Honor Award and *Boston Globe–Horn Book* Award, both 1993, both for *Sojourner Truth: Ain't I a Woman?*; Image Award for Outstanding Literary Work for Children, National Association for the Advancement of Colored People, 1999, for *Let My People Go.*

■ **Writings**

FOR CHILDREN

(Under name L'Ann Carwell) *Good Shepherd Prayer,* Concordia, 1978.

(Under name L'Ann Carwell) *God Gives New Life,* Concordia, 1979.

Ask the Kids, Concordia, 1979.

Who Is Who?, Children's Press, 1983.

Martin Luther King, Jr.: A Man to Remember, Children's Press, 1984.

Paul Laurence Dunbar: A Poet to Remember, Children's Press, 1984.

Michael Jackson, Superstar, Children's Press, 1984.

Lights Out, Christopher, illustrated by Bartholomew, Augsburg, 1984.

It's the Truth, Christopher, illustrated by Bartholomew, Augsburg, 1984.

The Apache, Children's Press, 1984.

Mary McLeod Bethune: A Great American Educator, Children's Press, 1985.

Aztec Indians, Children's Press, 1985.

The Inca, Children's Press, 1985.

The Maya, Children's Press, 1985.

Flossie and the Fox, illustrated by Rachel Isadora, Dial, 1986.

Our Martin Luther King Book, illustrated by Rachel Isadora, Child's World, 1986.

Who Is Coming?, illustrated by Clovis Martin, Children's Press, 1986.

Give It with Love, Christopher: Christopher Learns about Gifts and Giving, illustrated by Bartholomew, Augsburg, 1988.

Speak Up, Christopher: Christopher Learns the Difference between Right and Wrong, illustrated by Bartholomew, Augsburg, 1988.

A Troll in a Hole, Milliken, 1988.

Nettie Jo's Friends, illustrated by Scott Cook, Knopf, 1988.

Mirandy and Brother Wind, illustrated by Jerry Pinkney, Knopf, 1988.

Monkey–Monkey's Trick: Based on an African Folk–Tale, illustrated by Paul Meisel, Random House, 1989.

Jesse Jackson: A Biography, Scholastic, 1989.

(With Ruthilde Kronberg) *A Piece of the Wind and Other Stories to Tell,* Harper, 1990.

No Need for Alarm, Milliken, 1990.

A Million Fish—More or Less, illustrated by Dena Schutzer, Knopf, 1992.

The Dark–Thirty: Southern Tales of the Supernatural, illustrated by Brian Pinkney, Knopf, 1992.

History of Haiti, Holt, 1996.

(With Robert L. Duyff) *All Our Fruits and Vegetables,* Many Hands Media, 1996.

(With Robert L. Duyff) *It's a Sandwich!,* Many Hands Media, 1996.

A Picture of Freedom: The Diary of Clotee, a Slave Girl, Scholastic, 1997.

Ma Dear's Aprons, illustrated by Floyd Cooper, Atheneum, 1997.

Run Away Home, Scholastic, 1997.

Color Me Dark: The Diary of Nellie Lee Love, the Great Migration North, Chicago, Illinois, 1919, Scholastic, 2000.

Nzingha, Warrior Queen of Matamba: Angola, Africa, 1595, Scholastic, 2000.

Goin' Someplace Special, illustrated by Jerry Pinkney, Atheneum, 2000.

The Honest–to–God Truth, illustrated by Giselle Potter, Atheneum, 2000.

FOR CHILDREN; WITH HUSBAND, FREDRICK L. MCKISSACK

Look What You've Done Now, Moses, illustrated by Joe Boddy, David Cook, 1984.

Abram, Abram, Where Are We Going?, illustrated by Joe Boddy, David Cook, 1984.

Cinderella, illustrated by Tom Dunnington, Children's Press, 1985.

Country Mouse and City Mouse, illustrated by Anne Sikorski, Children's Press, 1985.

The Little Red Hen, illustrated by Dennis Hockerman, Children's Press, 1985.

The Three Bears, illustrated by Virginia Bala, Children's Press, 1985.

The Ugly Little Duck, illustrated by Peggy Perry Anderson, Children's Press, 1986.

When Do You Talk to God? Prayers for Small Children, illustrated by Gary Gumble, Augsburg, 1986.

King Midas and His Gold, illustrated by Tom Dunnington, Children's Press, 1986.

Frederick Douglass: The Black Lion, Children's Press, 1987.

A Real Winner, illustrated by Quentin Thompson and Ken Jones, Milliken, 1987.

The King's New Clothes, illustrated by Gwen Connelly, Children's Press, 1987.

Tall Phil and Small Bill, illustrated by Kathy Mitter, Milliken, 1987.

Three Billy Goats Gruff, illustrated by Tom Dunnington, Children's Press, 1987.

My Bible ABC Book, illustrated by Reed Merrill, Augsburg, 1987.

The Civil Rights Movement in America from 1865 to the Present, Children's Press, 1987, second edition, 1991.

All Paths Lead to Bethlehem, illustrated by Kathryn E. Shoemaker, Augsburg, 1987.

Messy Bessey, illustrated by Richard Hackney, Children's Press, 1987.

The Big Bug Book of Counting, illustrated by Bartholomew, Milliken, 1987.

The Big Bug Book of Opposites, illustrated by Bartholomew, Milliken, 1987.

The Big Bug Book of Places to Go, illustrated by Bartholomew, Milliken, 1987.

The Big Bug Book of the Alphabet, illustrated by Bartholomew, Milliken, 1987.

The Big Bug Book of Things to Do, illustrated by Bartholomew, Milliken, 1987.

Bugs!, illustrated by Martin, Children's Press, 1988.

The Children's ABC Christmas, illustrated by Kathy Rogers, Augsburg, 1988.

Constance Stumbles, illustrated by Tom Dunnington, Children's Press, 1988.

Oh, Happy, Happy Day! A Child's Easter in Story, Song, and Prayer, illustrated by Elizabeth Swisher, Augsburg, 1989.

God Made Something Wonderful, illustrated by Ching, Augsburg, 1989.

Messy Bessey's Closet, illustrated by Richard Hackney, Children's Press, 1989.

James Weldon Johnson: "Lift Every Voice and Sing," Children's Press, 1990.

A Long Hard Journey: The Story of the Pullman Porter, Walker & Co., 1990.

Taking a Stand against Racism and Racial Discrimination, F. Watts, 1990.

W. E. B. DuBois, F. Watts, 1990.

The Story of Booker T. Washington, Children's Press, 1991.

Messy Bessey's Garden, illustrated by Martin, Children's Press, 1991.

From Heaven Above, Augsburg, 1992.

Sojourner Truth: Ain't I a Woman?, Scholastic, 1992.

God Makes All Things New, illustrated by Ching, Augsburg, 1993.

African–American Inventors, Millbrook Press, 1994.

African–American Scientists, Millbrook Press, 1994.

African Americans, illustrated by Michael McBride, Milliken, 1994.

Sports, Milliken, 1994.

Black Diamond: The Story of the Negro Baseball Leagues, Scholastic, 1994.

The Royal Kingdoms of Ghana, Mali, and Songhay: Life in Medieval Africa, Holt, 1994.

Christmas in the Big House, Christmas in the Quarters, illustrated by John Thompson, Scholastic, 1994.

Red–Tail Angels: The Story of the Tuskegee Airmen of World War II, Walker, 1995.

Rebels against Slavery: American Slave Revolts, Scholastic, 1996.

Let My People Go: Bible Stories of Faith, Hope, and Love, As Told by Price Jefferies, a Free Man of Color, to His Daughter, Charlotte, in Charleston, South Carolina, 1806–1816, illustrated by James Ransome, Atheneum, 1998.

Young, Black, and Determined: A Biography of Lorraine Hansberry, Holiday House, 1998.

Messy Bessey and the Birthday Overnight, illustrated by Dana Regan, Children's Press, 1998.

Messy Bessey's School Desk, illustrated by Dana Regan, Children's Press, 1998.

Black Hands, White Sails: The Story of African–American Whalers, Scholastic, 1999.

Messy Bessey's Holidays, illustrated by Dana Regan, Children's Press, 1999.

Messy Bessey's Family Reunion, illustrated by Dana Regan, Children's Press, 2000.

Miami Gets It Straight, illustrated by Michael Chesworth, Golden Books, 2000.

FOR CHILDREN; *"GREAT AFRICAN AMERICANS" SERIES;* WITH HUSBAND, FREDRICK L. MCKISSACK

Carter G. Woodson: The Father of Black History, illustrated by Ned Ostendorf, Enslow, 1991.

Frederick Douglass: Leader against Slavery, illustrated by Ned Ostendorf, Enslow, 1991.

George Washington Carver: The Peanut Scientist, illustrated by Ned Ostendorf, Enslow, 1991.

Ida B. Wells–Barnett: A Voice against Violence, illustrated by Ned Ostendorf, Enslow, 1991.

Louis Armstrong: Jazz Musician, illustrated by Ned Ostendorf, Enslow, 1991.

Marian Anderson: A Great Singer, illustrated by Ned Ostendorf, Enslow, 1991.

Martin Luther King, Jr.: Man of Peace, illustrated by Ned Ostendorf, Enslow, 1991.

Mary Church Terrell: Leader for Equality, illustrated by Ned Ostendorf, Enslow, 1991.

Mary McLeod Bethune: A Great Teacher, illustrated by Ned Ostendorf, Enslow, 1991.

Ralph J. Bunche: Peacemaker, illustrated by Ned Ostendorf, Enslow, 1991.

Jesse Owens: Olympic Star, illustrated by Michael David Biegel, Enslow, 1992.

Langston Hughes: Great American Poet, illustrated by Michael David Biegel, Enslow, 1992.

Zora Neale Hurston: Writer and Storyteller, illustrated by Michael Bryant, Enslow, 1992.

Satchel Paige: The Best Arm in Baseball, illustrated by Michael David Biegel, Enslow, 1992.

Sojourner Truth: Voice for Freedom, illustrated by Michael Bryant, Enslow, 1992.

Madam C. J. Walker: Self–Made Millionaire, illustrated by Michael Bryant, Enslow, 1992.

Paul Robeson: A Voice to Remember, illustrated by Michael David Biegel, Enslow, 1992.

Booker T. Washington: Leader and Educator, illustrated by Michael Bryant, Enslow, 1992.

OTHER

Also contributor with Fredrick L. McKissack to *The World of 1492,* edited by Jean Fritz, Holt, 1992. Author with F. L. McKissack of "Start Up" series for beginning readers, four volumes, Children's Press, 1985; editor with F. L. McKissack of "Reading Well" series and "Big Bug Books" series, both for Milliken. Writer for preschool series "L Is for Listening," broadcast by KWMU–Radio, 1975–77. Author of radio and television scripts. Contributor of articles and short stories to magazines, including *Friend, Happy Times,* and *Evangelizing Today's Child.* Co–author, with Mavis Jukes, of the short–subject film script, *Who Owns the Sun?,* Disney Educational Productions, 1991.

■ Sidelights

Patricia C. McKissack has written well over one hundred titles under her own name, as well as in collaboration with her husband, Fredrick L. McKissack. The author of historical fiction and biographies for children, McKissack focuses on religious as well as African American themes, and her love of writing is in part inspired by the fact that she has been for many years an English instructor at both the junior high and college levels. The recipient of a 1993 Newbery Honor Award for the short stories gathered in *The Dark–Thirty,* McKissack has also won several Coretta Scott King Awards. Teaming up with her husband, she has contributed numerous titles to Enslow's "Great African Americans" series, as well as many non–series books on little–known aspects of African American history, including *The Red–Tail Angels* and *Black Diamonds.*

The McKissacks' lives were shaped by one of the most optimistic eras in American history—the 1960s. "We're Kennedy products, and we were very idealistic," McKissack once stated. "That was the period in which African Americans were really looking up, coming out of darkness, segregation, and discrimination, and doors were beginning to open—ever so slightly, but still opening." The optimism of those days can be seen in such books as the *Civil Rights Movement in America from 1865 to the Present* and *Martin Luther King, Jr.: Man of Peace.*

Born in 1944 in Nashville, Tennessee, McKissack experienced firsthand many of the injustices about which she and her husband write. These were the days of segregation in which a black person was not allowed to drink from the same public water fountain as a white, nor allowed into the same restaurants as whites. But at home, McKissack's life was rich and filled with the tales that her storytelling grandfather shared. She grew up with a love of narrative and a love of reading.

She also grew up with her future husband, Fred McKissack, "in the same town, where every family knew every other family," McKissack once remarked, "but he was five years older and you just didn't date boys who were five years older than you. When I was fifteen and he was twenty that just would have been forbidden." But then Fred went away to the Marines for several years; later, they both attended college together, graduating in 1964 from Tennessee State University in Nashville, and suddenly the two seemed not so far removed in age. They were married after graduation. "All of our friends said it wouldn't last six months. They said it was ridiculous, and our families were a bit concerned," McKissack recalled. "But we just knew. We talked all the time and we still do. We have always had a very, very close relationship from the first date we had. We just had so much fun together that we knew."

One thing the McKissacks discovered they had in common was a love of literature. Both recalled reading Ayn Rand's *Fountainhead, Atlas Shrugged,* and *Anthem,* as well as Aldous Huxley's *Brave New World* and other novels of similar futuristic themes. "We were talking about the future," McKissack noted. Other influences included Julius Lester, an author known for his historically accurate, heroic depictions of black characters. Lester had graduated in 1960 from Fisk University, also in Nashville.

Troubled Times, Changing Times

While the era was filled with hope and opportunities, it was also a time of violent change. Sit–ins and demonstrations by Southern blacks were finally

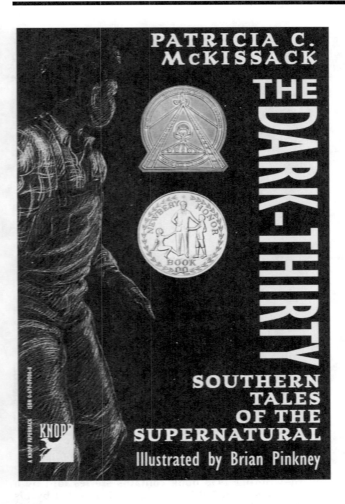

PATRICIA C. McKISSACK

THE DARK-THIRTY

SOUTHERN TALES OF THE SUPERNATURAL

Illustrated by Brian Pinkney

Spooky tales told during the last thirty minutes of daylight are collected in McKissack's 1992 effort, a short story collection that was named a Newbery Honor Book and which received the Coretta Scott King Award.

shaking the segregationist foundations of the region. Schools became desegregated; integration was in the works. "Our generation was the first to do it," McKissack once stated. "I remember when Fred took me to dinner at Morrison's. I was nervous as a flea because a sit–in had occurred only a few years earlier, and there had been people putting shotguns at young people's heads and saying, 'If you sit here we will blow you away.' And that happened to Fred" when he joined a sit–in at a Woolworth department store. The visit to Morrison's was among many firsts for the McKissacks; after years of seeing them only from the outside, the two finally entered a Kentucky Fried Chicken restaurant, a Shoney's, a McDonald's, and a Hardee's. When her younger brother got a job at Shoney's, McKissack realized

that "things were opening up. And we were very proud that we were the first generation to come through that."

Then came the Vietnam War and the "white backlash" to the Civil Rights Movement. McKissack found the television footage at that time, the first ever shown of American soldiers in combat, profoundly disturbing. "That was horrible for us to watch—the body bags coming back in," she related. "I was a young mother—I had three little boys—and I said, 'My God, I hope we never have to go through anything this nonsensical again.'" The assassinations of John F. Kennedy and his brother Robert, Martin Luther King Jr., Medgar Evers, and Malcolm X, along with church bombings and innumerable other violent incidents, all served to temper the McKissacks' positive attitude. "Just as blacks experienced white resistance to equality during Reconstruction, there was another backlash to the Civil Rights Movement of the 1960s," McKissack commented. "By 1980 blacks were once again on the defense, trying to safeguard their and their children's rights."

These experiences have all combined to produce the variety and depth of writing McKissack has produced. One of her goals is to write in such a way that the past comes alive for her young readers. One of her first writing projects was a biography of Paul Lawrence Dunbar, written for her class of eighth–grade English students in Kirkwood, Missouri. "The school was twenty–five percent black and I wanted to teach about an African American writer who I had come to know and appreciate when I was growing up," McKissack recalled. When she began researching Dunbar, "I couldn't find a biography, so I wrote his biography myself for my students." She also sought information on Langston Hughes and James Weldon Johnson, both of whom she and her husband later wrote about. Many more biographies have followed.

James Weldon Johnson: "Lift Every Voice and Sing," co–authored with her husband, "makes Johnson come alive for young readers," Jeanette Lambert commented in *School Library Journal.* Readers learn that Johnson was the author of "Lift Every Voice and Sing," the song recognized as the African American national anthem, and also was the first African American to pass the bar in Florida, was principal of the first black high school in Jacksonville, Florida, and served as executive secretary of the NAACP.

Examining Historical Figures

Together, the McKissacks have penned nearly a score of biographies in Enslow's "Great African Americans" series, short nonfiction titles intended for the primary grades. These books describe the lives of important black leaders, both cultural and political, in brief chapters using a basic, concise style accompanied by photographs and other illustrations. In a review of the McKissacks' *Ida B. Wells–Barnett: A Voice against Violence, Marian Anderson: A Great Singer, Martin Luther King, Jr.: Man of Peace,* and *Ralph J. Bunche: Peacemaker, School Library Journal* contributor Phyllis Stephens noted that the authors present each of the subjects as people with convictions so strong that "not even a racially biased society could provide effective obstacles to deter them" from achieving their dreams. Writing about *Paul Robeson: A Voice to Remember* and *Booker T. Washington: Leader and Educator,* Laura Culberg noted in *School Library Journal* that these brief biographies "fill a need for materials on noted African–Americans for primary–grade readers." Culberg went on to conclude, "the books will find an eager audience among beginning readers." Reviewing a group of five more such biographies on notables, including black historian Carter G. Woodson, anti–slavery leader Frederick Douglass, scientist George Washington Carver, jazz musician Louis Armstrong, and equal rights proponent Mary Church Terrell, Anna DeWind noted in *School Library Journal* that all five books "have simplified vocabularies, large print, and plenty of black–and–white photographs and illustrations." DeWind further commented that in spite of some "flaws . . . these [biographies] are a step in the right direction."

The McKissacks also have several non–series biographies to their credit. "A revealing book," *W. E. B. DuBois* "should entice readers to seek more information about this complex man," Lydia Champlin remarked in *School Library Journal. Voice of Youth Advocates* reviewer Bruce Lee Siebers recommended *W. E. B. DuBois* as "a good addition to African American history and biography collections." With *Sojourner Truth: Ain't I a Woman,* a Coretta Scott King Honor Book from 1993, they tell the story of this nineteenth–century preacher, abolitionist, and activist for the rights of both African Americans and women. They have also told the story of the brilliant black writer Lorraine Hansberry in *Young, Black, and Determined.* The author of the acclaimed play *A Raisin in the Sun,* Hansberry fought prejudice throughout her brief career. "The McKissacks' biography sparkles with the energy and passion that characterize her subject," observed *Booklist* contributor Anne O'Malley. Marilyn Heath, reviewing the same book in *School Library Journal,* called it a "well–written biography" that is "lively and engaging"

Coauthored with her husband, McKissack's NAACP award–winning 1998 book contains stories told by a former slave named Price Jeffries and recorded by his daughter in the years before the Civil War.

and that "brings its subject to life by successfully capturing that unique spark that makes Hansberry noteworthy and interesting."

Other history books of note include *Black Diamond: The Story of the Negro Baseball Leagues, Red Tail Angels: The Story of the Tuskegee Airmen of World War II,* and *Black Hands, White Sails: The Story of African–American Whalers,* all collaborative efforts. Racism in sports is brought into focus in the first of these, "a lucid, comprehensive study of a vital chapter of baseball history," according to Randy M. Brough in a review of *Black Diamond* in *Kliatt.* In *Red–Tail Angels,* the authors tell the little–known story of black pilots who fought in World War II in a special squadron because the regular Air Force was still segregated. Mary M. Burns enthusiastically praised this history in a *Horn Book* review: "Impeccably documented, handsomely designed, thoughtfully executed, this book by two of our most committed and talented writers gives these pioneers' accomplishments meaning for a new generation." David A. Lindsey, reviewing the same title in *School Library Journal,* commented, "The prolific McKissacks have collaborated once again to produce yet another well-crafted, thoroughly researched account of a little-known facet of African American history." Of the McKissacks' 1999 book *Black Hands, White Sails,* a reviewer for *Booklist* felt it was a "fascinating look at the convergent histories of whaling and the abolitionist movement" that "weaves seemingly disparate threads into a detailed tapestry."

Patricia McKissack also has numerous solo books in history and fiction to her credit. Her books for very young readers, such as *Flossie and the Fox* and the Caldecott Honor Book *Mirandy and Brother Wind,* have won critical praise and a wide readership. A contributor for *Kirkus Reviews* called *Flossie and the Fox,* based on a tale McKissack's grandfather once told her, "a perfect picture book." *Mirandy and Brother Wind* was also inspired by McKissack's grandfather, more specifically from a photograph of both her grandfather and grandmother as teenagers after they had won a cakewalk contest in 1906. In the book, Mirandy enlists Brother Wind as her partner in a cakewalk contest in a "delightful book," according to Valerie Wilson Wesley, writing in the *New York Times Book Review.* Wesley concluded, "each page of *Mirandy and Brother Wind* sparkles with life." *Booklist*'s Ilene Cooper called the book "a graceful fantasy." Remembrances of her great-grandmother and her eternal apron inspired McKissack's 1997 work *Ma Dear's Aprons,* a book that a contributor to the *New York Times Book Review* called "[a]ffectionate, appealing and full of information about the routines of domestic life." In her 1999 title *The Honest-to-Goodness Truth,* McKissack tells the story of young Libby, who learns that truth-telling is not always as straightforward as it seems. "The story is very much a lesson," *Booklist*'s Hazel Rochman noted, "but it's a subtle one."

Award-winning Fiction

McKissack became the recipient of a Newbery Honor Award for the stories collected in *The Dark Thirty.* The title comes from that half-hour before dark in which kids were still allowed to play outside when McKissack herself was growing up. The ten original stories in the collection reflect African-American history or culture. "Some are straight ghost stories," commented Kay McPherson in a *School Library Journal* review, "many of which are wonderfully spooky and all of which have well-woven narratives." McPherson concluded, "This is a stellar collection." Other works for older readers

include the fictionalized diaries of African American girls for Scholastic, including *A Picture of Freedom: The Diary of Clotee, a Slave Girl* and *Color Me Dark: The Diary of Nellie Lee Love, the Great Migration North.* The first title is set on a Virginia plantation in 1859, and the second title follows the fortunes of a young girl who migrates to Chicago after World War I. Reviewing *A Picture of Freedom* for *School Library Journal,* Melissa Hudek called the book "an inspiring look at a young girl coming of age in terrible circumstances who manages to live life to the fullest." *Booklist*'s Carolyn Phelan, reviewing *Color Me Dark,* felt "the strong narrative will keep children involved and give them a great deal of social history to absorb along the way." In *Run Away Home* McKissack tells the story of a young Apache who escapes federal custody and is aided by an African American family. Reviewing this historical novel in *Horn Book,* Burns noted, "McKissack knows how to pace a story, create suspense, and interweave period details of the late nineteenth century into a coherent narrative" to produce a book "sophisticated in content yet tuned to the understanding of a middle-school audience—no small accomplishment."

If you enjoy the works of Patricia C. McKissack, you might want to check out the following books:

Virginia Hamilton, *Sweet Whispers, Brother Rush,* 1982.
Angela Johnson, *Toning the Sweep,* 1993.
Julius Lester, *And All Our Wounds Forgiven,* 1994.
Mildred D. Taylor, *Let the Circle Be Unbroken,* 1981.
Rita Williams-Garcia, *Like Sisters on the Homefront,* 1994.

McKissack sees her work as something that can possibly unite disparate communities in this country. "It's a kind of freedom," she once explained. "Writing has allowed us to do something positive with our experiences, although some of our experiences have been very negative. We try to enlighten, to change attitudes, to form new attitudes—to build bridges with books." And for her, reaching the young with her books is vital. "It's quite interesting how your youth shapes how you think in the future," McKissack remarked. "The things that are happening to you now will affect how you parent, how you will function in your work, and how you will treat your neighbors." She stresses that intervention at this crucial time in a young person's development must help to provide a strong foundation for his or her future. "When I do a workshop with teachers, I always say, 'Someone in your class might be the person who has the cure for cancer. The cure for AIDS is sitting in someone's classroom right now. The solution for world hunger can be found by someone sitting in a classroom. You do not know whether you will be the person to touch that person. So, therefore, you have to respect and treat all of these students with an equal measure of concern.'"

■ Biographical and Critical Sources

BOOKS

McKissack, Patricia, *Can You Imagine?*, Richard C. Owen, 1997.

PERIODICALS

Booklist, February 1, 1992, Ilene Cooper, review of *Mirandy and Brother Wind*, p. 1037; March 1, 1992, p. 1270; April 15, 1992, p. 1525; June 19, 1994; February 15, 1997, p. 1027; June 1, 1997, p. 1696; October 1, 1997, p. 329; February 15, 1998, Anne O'Malley, review of *Young, Black, and Determined: A Biography of Lorraine Hansberry*, p. 995; February 15, 1999, p. 1068; September 1, 1999, review of *Black Hands, White Sails*; December 15, 1999, Hazel Rochman, review of *The Honest-to-Goodness Truth*, p. 791; February 15, 2000, Carolyn Phelan, review of *Color Me Dark*, p. 1113.

Bulletin of the Center for Children's Books, June, 1997, p. 367; February, 1998, p. 213; December, 1998, p. 137.

Horn Book, March–April, 1996, Mary M. Burns, review of *Red–Tail Angels*, p. 226; May–June, 1997, p. 310; November–December, 1997, Mary M. Burns, review of *Run Away Home*, p. 681.

Interracial Books for Children Bulletin, Number 8, 1985, p. 5.

Kirkus Reviews, November 1, 1988, review of *Flossie and the Fox*, p. 1607; December 15, 1991; February 15, 1998, p. 271.

Kliatt, November, 1998, Randy M. Brough, review of *Black Diamond*, p. 40; May, 1999, p. 27.

New York Times Book Review, November 20, 1988, Valerie Wilson Wesley, review of *Mirandy and Brother Wind*, p. 48; November 29, 1992, p. 34; August 3, 1997, review of *Ma Dear's Aprons*, p. 14; June 21, 1998, p. 20.

Publishers Weekly, February 9, 1998, p. 98; October 26, 1998, p. 62.

School Library Journal, January, 1991, Lydia Champlin, review of *W. E. B. DuBois*, p. 103; February, 1991, Jeanette Lambert, review of *James Weldon Johnson: "Lift Every Voice and Sing,"* p. 79; November, 1991, Phyllis Stephens, review of *Ida B. Wells–Barnett: A Voice against Violence*, *Marian Anderson: A Great Singer*, *Martin Luther King, Jr.: Man of Peace*, and *Ralph J. Bunche: Peacemaker*, p. 111; February, 1992, Anna DeWind, review of *Carter G. Woodson: The Father of Black History*, p. 83; October, 1992, Laura Culberg, review of *Paul Robeson: A Voice to Remember*, pp. 105–6; December, 1992, Kay McPherson, review of *The Dark Thirty*, p. 113; September, 1994, pp. 251–52; February, 1996, David A. Lindsey, review of *Red–Tail Angels*, p. 119; September, 1997, Melissa Hudek, review of *A Picture of Freedom*, p. 220; April, 1998, Marilyn Heath, review of *Young, Black, and Determined: A Biography of Lorraine Hansberry*, pp. 148–49; August, 1998, p. 144; July, 2000, Jennifer Ralston, review of *Color Me Dark*, p. 107.

Voice of Youth Advocates, October, 1990, Bruce Lee Siebers, review of *W. E. B. DuBois*, p. 248; August, 1998, p. 224.*

Mike Resnick

■ Personal

Born March 5, 1942, in Chicago, IL; son of William (a salesman) and Gertrude (a writer; maiden name, Diamond) Resnick; married Carol L. Cain (a writer and kennel owner), October 2, 1961; children: Laura L. *Education:* Attended University of Chicago, 1959–61, and Roosevelt University, 1962–63. *Politics:* Independent. *Hobbies and other interests:* Travel, reading, Africana, breeding and exhibiting purebred collies.

■ Addresses

Home and office—10547 Tanager Hills Dr., Cincinnati, OH 45249. *E–mail*—Resnick@delphi.com. *Agent*—Spectrum Literary Agency, 111 East 8th Ave., Suite 1501, New York, NY 10011.

■ Career

Full–time freelance writer, 1966—. Santa Fe Railroad, Chicago, IL, file clerk, 1962–65; National Features Syndicate, Chicago, editor of *National Tattler,* 1965–66, and *National Insider,* 1966–69; Oligarch Publishing, Libertyville, IL, editor and publisher, 1969–70; *Collie Cues Magazine,* Hayward, CA, columnist, 1969–80; Briarwood Pet Motel, Cincinnati, OH, co–owner with wife, 1976—. *Speculations,* columnist, 1975—; *Magazine of Fantasy and Science Fiction,* columnist, 1997–98, Science Fiction and Fantasy Writers of America (SFWA) *Bulletin,* columnist, 1998—.

■ Member

Science Fiction Writers of America.

■ Awards, Honors

Best Short Fiction award, American Dog Writers Association, 1978, for "The Last Dog," and 1979, for "Blue"; Browning Award finalist for Best SF Humorist, 1993 and 1994; Hugo Award nominations for best editor, 1994 and 1995; Hugo Awards for best short story, for "Kirinyaga," "The Manamouki," "Seven Views of Olduvai Gorge," and "The 43 Antarean Dynasties"; Hugo Award nominations for "For I Have Touched the Sky," *Bully!,* "Winter Solstice," "One Perfect Morning, with Jackals," "The Lotus and the Spear," "Mwalimu in the Squared Circle," "Barnaby in Exile," "A Little Knowledge," "Bibi," "When the Old Gods Die," and "The Land of Nod"; Nebula Award for "Seven Views of Olduvai Gorge"; Nebula nominations for "Kirinyaga," "For I Have Touched the Sky," *Ivory*, "The Manamouki," *Bully!*, "Bibi," and "When the Old Gods Die"; Skylark Award for Lifetime Achievement in Science Fiction; HOMer Awards for "The Manamouki," "Song of a Dry River," "Mwalimu in the Squared Circle," "Seven Views of Olduvai Gorge," "Bibi" and "When the Old Gods Die"; HOMer nominations for *Bully!*, "Bwana," "How I Wrote the New Testament, Brought Forth the Renaissance, and Birdied the 17th Hole at Pebble Beach," *Oracle*, "The Lotus and the Spear," *Purgatory*, "The Pale Thin God," "Birdie," "Barnaby in Exile," *A Miracle of Rare Design*, and "A Little Knowledge"; *SF Chronicle* Poll awards for "Kirinyaga," "For I Have Touched the Sky," *Bully!*, "The Manamouki," "Seven Views of Olduvai Gorge," and "Bibi"; Universitat Politecnica de Catalunya Novella Contest winner for "Seven Views of Olduvai Gorge"; Hayakawa SF award (Japan), for "For I Have Touched the Sky"; Hayakawa SF award finalist for "Song of a Dry River," "Posttime in Pink," and "Kirinyaga"; Alexander Award, AT&T, for "Winter Solstice"; Golden Pagoda Award for "The Manamouki"; Clarke nomination (England) for *Ivory*; Ignotus Award (Spain) for "Seven Views of Olduvai Gorge"; Futura Poll Winner (Croatia), for "Seven Views of Olduvai Gorge"; Nowa Fantastyka Poll Winner (Poland) for "Kirinyaga"; SFinks Award (Poland) for "For I Have Touched the Sky" and "When the Old Gods Die"; Seiun–Sho nomination (Japan) for "For I Have Touched the Sky," "Bwana," *Ivory*, "Posttime in Pink," and *Santiago*; *Locus* Poll Winner for "When the Old Gods Die"; Science Fiction Weekly Poll Winner for "When the Old Gods Die" and "The 43 Antarean Dynasties"; Asimov's Readers Poll Winner for "The 43 Antarean Dynasties"; Year's Best SF Anthology awards for "Kirinyaga," "For I Have Touched the Sky," "Mwalimu in the Squared Circle," "Seven Views of Olduvai Gorge," "The Land of Nod," and "One Perfect Morning, with Jackals."

■ **Writings**

SCIENCE FICTION

The Forgotten Sea of Mars (novella), Camille E. Cazedessus, Jr. (Baton Rouge, LA), 1965.
The Goddess of Ganymede, illustrated by Neal MacDonald, Jr., Grant (West Kingston, RI), 1967.
Pursuit of Ganymede, Paperback Library (New York City), 1968.
Redbeard, Lancer (New York City), 1969.
(With Glen A. Larson) *Battlestar Galactica Number Five: Galactica Discovers Earth*, Berkley, 1980.

The Soul Eater, Signet, 1981.
Birthright: The Book of Man, Signet, 1982, Alexander Books, 1997.
Walpurgis III, Signet, 1982.
The Branch, Signet, 1984.
Adventures, Signet, 1985.
Santiago: A Myth of the Far Future, Tor, 1986.
Stalking the Unicorn: A Fable of Tonight, Tor, 1987.
The Dark Lady: A Romance of the Far Future, Tor, 1987.
Ivory: A Legend of Past and Future, Tor, 1988.
Paradise: A Chronicle of a Distant World, Tor, 1989.
Second Contact, Tor, 1990.
Through Darkest Resnick with Gun and Camera, Washington Science Fiction Association, 1990.
Bully!, illustration by George Barr, Axolotl Press, 1990.
(With Jack L. Chalker and George Alec Effinger) *The Red Tape War*, Tor, 1991.
Bwana [and] *Bully!* (two novellas), Tor, 1991.
Stalking the Wild Resnick, NESFA, 1991.
Will the Last Person to Leave the Planet Please Shut Off the Sun?, Tor, 1992.
Lucifer Jones, Warner/Questar, 1992.
Purgatory: A Chronicle of a Distant World, Tor, 1993.
Inferno: A Chronicle of a Distant World, Tor, 1993.
A Miracle of Rare Design: A Tragedy of Transcendence, Tor, 1994.
Return of the Dinosaurs, DAW, 1997.
A Hunger in the Soul, Tor, 1998.
Kirinyaga: A Fable of Utopia, Del Rey, 1998.
A Safari of the Mind (short stories), Wildside Press, 1999.

Also author of *An Alien Land*, Dark Regions; "Seven Views of Olduvai Gorge," Axolotl Press; *Solo Flights through Shared Worlds*, Dark Regions; *Exploits*, Wildside Press; *Encounters*, Wildside Press; *The Alien Heart*, Pulphouse; *Pink Elephants and Hairy Toads*, Wildside Press; and *The Outpost*.

"TALES OF THE VELVET COMET" SCIENCE FICTION SERIES

Eros Ascending, Phantasia Press, 1984.
Eros at Zenith, Phantasia Press, 1984.
Eros Descending, Signet, 1985.
Eros at Nadir, Signet, 1986.

"THE ORACLE" TRILOGY

Soothsayer, Ace, 1991.
Oracle, Ace, 1992.
Prophet, Ace, 1993.

"THE WIDOWMAKER" TRILOGY

The Widowmaker, Bantam, 1996.
The Widowmaker Reborn, Bantam, 1997.
The Widowmaker Unleashed, Bantam, 1998.

MYSTERIES

Dog in the Manger, Alexander Books, 1995.

Also editor of mystery *The Compleat Chance Perdue*, by Ross Spencer, Alexander Books.

EDITOR

Shaggy B.E.M. Stories, Nolacon Press (New Orleans, LA), 1988.
Alternate Kennedys, Tor, 1992.
Whatdunnits, DAW, 1992.
Aladdin: Master of the Lamp, DAW, 1992.
Alternate Presidents, Tor, 1992.
More Whatdunnits, DAW, 1993.
Alternate Warriors, Tor, 1993.
(With Martin H. Greenberg) *Christmas Ghosts*, DAW, 1993.
(With Gardner Dozois) *Future Earths: Under African Skies*, DAW, 1993.
(With Gardner Dozois) *Future Earths: Under South American Skies*, DAW, 1993.
(With Martin H. Greenberg) *By Any Other Fame*, DAW, 1994.
(With Loren D. Estleman and Martin H. Greenberg) *Deals with the Devil*, DAW, 1994.
Alternate Outlaws, Tor, 1994.
Arthur H. Neumann, *Elephant Hunting in East Equatorial Africa*, St. Martin's, 1994.
(With Anthony R. Lewis) *The Passage of the Light: The Recursive Science Fiction of Barry N. Malzberg*, NESFA, 1994.
Witch Fantastic, DAW, 1995.
(With Martin H. Greenberg) *Sherlock Holmes in Orbit*, DAW, 1995.
Alternate Tyrants, Tor, 1997.
Girls for the Slime God, Obscura Press, 1997.

Also editor of *Inside the Funhouse*, Avon; *Alternate Worldcons*, Axolotl Press; *Again, Alternate Worldcons*, WC Press; (with Patrick Nielsen Hayden) *Alternate Skiffy*, Wildside; (with Martin H. Greenberg) *Dinosaur Fantastic*, Daw; (with Greenberg) *Return of the Dinosaurs*, DAW. Series editor for "The Library of African Adventure," St. Martin's Press; "The Resnick Library of African Adventure," Alexander Books, "The Resnick Library of Worldwide Adventure," Alexander Books, and (co–editor with Carol Resnick) "The Resnick Library of Travelers' Tales," Alexander Books.

OTHER

Official Guide to Fantastic Literature, photographs by Larry Reynolds, House of Collectibles (Florence, AL), 1976.
Official Guide to Comic Books and Big Little Books, House of Collectibles, 1977.
Gymnastics and You: The Whole Story of the Sport, Rand McNally, 1977.
Official Guide to Comic and Science Fiction Books, House of Collectibles, 1979.
Unauthorized Autobiographies and Other Curiosities (collection of short fiction), Misfit Press (Detroit, MI), 1984.
The Inn of the Hairy Toad (short stories), Delta Con (New Orleans, LA), 1985.
(Contributor) *The Gods of War*, Baen, 1992.

Also author of *Putting It Together: Turning Sow's Ear Drafts into Silk Purse Stories*, 2000, and with Nick DiChario, of *Magic Feathers: The Mike & Nick Show*, 2000. Author of screenplay adaptations, with wife, Carol, of *Santiago* and *The Widowmaker*. Author of introduction to Edgar Rice Burrough's *The Land that Time Forgot*, University of Nebraska Press, 1999, and Tom Easton's *The Electric Gene Machine*, Wildside Press, 2000. Also author of many other novels and stories under various pseudonyms; contributor of reviews to periodicals. Resnick's works have been published in Germany, Japan, Italy, Poland, Bulgaria, Russia, Czech Republic, Spain, Holland, England, Sweden, France, Hungary, Romania, and Lithuania.

■ Adaptations

Several of Resnick's books have been optioned for movies, including *Eros Ascending, Santiago, Stalking the Unicorn, Ivory, Second Contact, Soothsayer, Oracle, Prophet, The Widowmaker, The Widowmaker Reborn, The Widowmaker Unleashed, The Outpost*, and *Dog in the Manger*. A number of his stories have been recorded on audiocassette. Gaming rights to *Santiago* have also been sold to Editions De Noel in France.

■ Work in Progress

The Mike and Nick Show, for Old Earth Books; *An Ambiguous Clay*, for Tor.

■ Sidelights

Michael D. Resnick has had a long and prolific career as an author—mostly of science fiction—that dates back to the 1960s. However, it was not until the 1980s that he began to come into his own as a writer. His science–fiction stories since then have varied from comical adventures to tales of alternate universes to Westernesque sagas of rough and rugged gunslingers. But Resnick has become most noted for setting stories in the future that have themes relevant to the continent and people of Africa. Of these, his utopian short story "Kirinyaga" has become one of the most awarded works in science fiction history. "I've been writing science fiction most of my life," Resnick once stated. "The short story is still very much alive and well in science fiction, and I like writing short stories. Humor is still marketable in science fiction, and I write a lot of humor. Twice–told tales are frowned upon at the highest levels of science fiction, and creativity and imagination are rewarded. I find that artistically both challenging and satisfying."

Resnick earned a comfortable living early on with his writing. He worked for newspapers and periodicals, as well as churning out literally hundreds of books under a variety of pseudonyms. He wrote so quickly that his output was not of the highest quality, the author confesses. "For dozens of years, from 1964 until 1976, I was—I freely admit—a pseudonymous hack writer ...," he once said. "I wrote every word of seven monthly newspapers— that's about 175,000 words a month—in addition to the never–ending stream of more than two hundred junk books. Finally, the stream did end.... In late 1976 I took my ill–gotten literary gains (and they were munificent) and invested them in the largest and most luxurious boarding and grooming kennel then extant. I stopped writing almost completely for about four years while turning the business around, and then, totally secure financially for the rest of my life, I returned to my typewriter, albeit at a far slower pace, to see what I could do now that my writing didn't have to put bread on the table.

"All those books which have appeared since mid–1981 have been written during this period, and it is on these that I would like to be judged. I am still getting used to the luxury of rewriting and polishing, of not having to churn out fifty pages a day, of occasionally not completing even one page a day. I feel guilty about it—old habits die hard—but I suspect my books are about three thousand percent better for it, and for their author being completely free from the demands of the marketplace.

"Most of my recent output has been labelled science fiction, though I sometimes wonder if 'moral parable' isn't a more proper category. I am not con-

First published in 1982 and reissued in 1997, Resnick's "Birthright Universe"—a detailed outline of seventeen millenniums of future social, political, religious, and scientific "history"—has served as the backdrop for each of his science–fiction novels.

cerned with aliens (I have never met one), telepaths (ditto), invading extra–terrestrial armadas (still ditto). I am concerned, to borrow from Mr. Faulkner, with the human heart in conflict with itself—and far from proving a hindrance to such a quest, science fiction, with all of time and space to draw from, seems especially fitting for it."

Science Fiction with a Purpose

Resnick's early 1980s SF works are adventure tales that nevertheless often have serious undertones. A number of these works have a distinctive Western

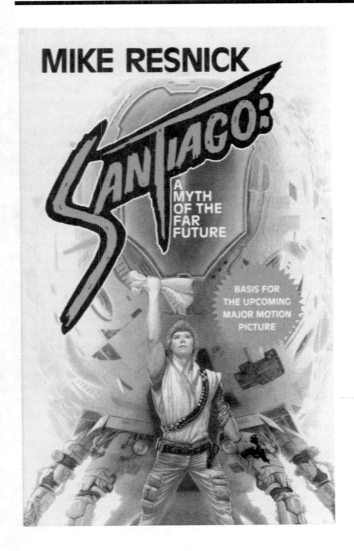

MIKE RESNICK

SANTIAGO:
A MYTH OF THE FAR FUTURE

BASIS FOR THE UPCOMING MAJOR MOTION PICTURE

With an ending sure to surprise readers, Resnick's 1986 futuristic Western pits a lawless gunslinger against a succession of heartless bounty hunters whose motives for hunting down the wanted man range from wealth to fame.

flavor, including *Santiago: A Myth of the Far Future* and his "Tales of the Galactic Midway" series, which includes *Sideshow, The Three–Legged Hootch Dancer, The Wild Alien Tamer,* and *The Best Rootin' Tootin' Shootin' Gunslinger in the Whole Damned Galaxy.* The "Galactic Midway" stories all involve characters who work at a circus called the Ahasuerus and Flint Traveling Carnival and Sideshow. The books can be quite violent, as in *The Wild Alien Tamer,* in which an animal tamer named Jupiter Monk takes turns playing a wild beast with a batlike alien, depending on which world the circus is performing. But the

pact between human and alien deteriorates into a contest of who can stand being tortured the most without giving in.

In *The Best Rootin' Tootin' Shootin' Gunslinger in the Whole Damned Galaxy,* Billybuck Dancer proves himself to be an unbeatable shot, facing down and beating any opponent—human or alien—that challenges him at the circus. While his performances are extremely profitable, Billybuck is depressed because he has met no one who poses a true challenge to his skills. But the circus boss, Thaddeus Flint, comes up with a brainstorm: he gets an android to play Doc Holliday, Billybuck's idol, thus managing to satisfy both the gunslinger and his entertainment–hungry audiences.

In what a *Publishers Weekly* critic called a "pleasing adaptation of the Wild West to outer space," *Santiago: A Myth of the Far Future* pits a legendary criminal named Santiago against several colorful bounty hunters who are out to get him for reasons ranging from money to fame to art to personal redemption. Critics applauded Resnick's ending, calling it both surprising and satisfying. "Highly recommended for all readers," concluded David Snider in a *Voice of Youth Advocates* review.

Resnick's *Prophet*—part of the "Oracle" trilogy—is also replete with Westernesque elements. It's the story of a hired gun called "Gravedancer" who is after the dangerous Penelope Bailey, known as "the Prophet." The Prophet has the ability to change the future just by moving her body in certain ways. The Prophet is also being hunted, however, by a cult leader with designs on ruling the universe. Despite the laser weapons and spaceships, the feel of the novel is highly reminiscent of classic Westerns, with gunfighters pacing down dusty streets toward frontier saloons, and other similar scenes. "If you [librarians] ... have patrons who enjoy both science fiction and westerns," wrote Vicky Burkholder in *Voice of Youth Advocates,* "this is definitely the book for them."

What distinguishes these novels from other similar adventure tales, according to Don D'Ammassa in *Twentieth–Century Science Fiction Writers,* is that Resnick pays more attention to characterization than many other authors in the genre, thus "providing a greater depth to the stories." D'Ammassa made a similar observation about other Resnick books, such as *The Branch, Birthright,* and *Walpurgis III.* "Although primarily adventure stories," remarked the critic, "there was an underlying seriousness missing in many similar books, concerns about the future of humanity, and the nature of power and government."

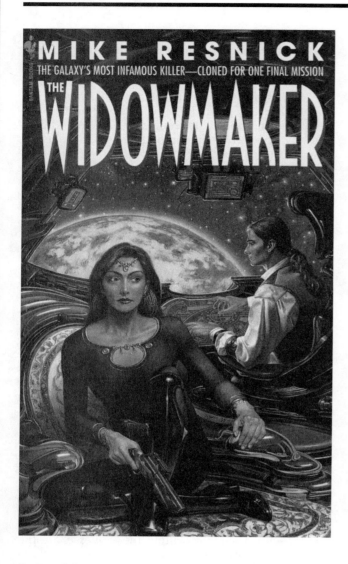

In Resnick's 1996 novel, readers meet talented mercenary Jefferson Nighthawk who, after a century on ice, is cloned and put on the trail of an assassin—with the assassin's beautiful wife destined to be Nighthawk's ultimate prize.

Walpurgis III portrays a battle between Conrad Bland, a mass murderer who has literally destroyed the populations of entire planets, and Jericho, an assassin hired by the government to kill him once and for all. But because Jericho is given license to do anything he needs to to execute Bland, including killing anyone in his way, the question becomes who is the worse monster, Bland or the unscrupulous government bent on his destruction. "Violent SF, this is graphic but well-written, with an unexpected ending," attested Barb Kerns in *Voice of Youth Advocates.*

Resnick tackles religious themes with his 1984 work, *The Branch,* but he does so with a definite twist. The book, set in the year 2047 in Chicago, is about the Second Coming of the Messiah, who takes on the very unexpected form of a gangster. When "Jeremiah the B" starts horning in on crime boss Solomon Moody Moore's territory, Moore tries to off the new competition. This proves impossible when "J the B" shows himself to be impervious even to bullets. Taking a growing crowd of followers with him to Jerusalem, Jeremiah writes a new gospel and thwarts his attackers. *The Branch* received some mixed reviews. A *Publishers Weekly* critic felt that Resnick wrote "himself into a dead end about halfway through the book," finding only the first half of interest. However, John M. Landsberg, a reviewer for *Kliatt,* was impressed that the author had "done his religious homework," creating a believable scenario that "makes the reader think more than the average SF adventure."

What would become a major concern in Resnick's more recent writing begins to reveal itself as early as his 1982 book, *Birthright: The Book of Man. Birthright* is an ambitious collection of stories that traces the story of human civilization over a 17,000 year period. The stories follow humanity's progression from planet colonizer, to empire builder, to decline, and finally destruction. While obviously admiring humanity's ingenuity and determination, Resnick also clearly illuminates mankind's many flaws as humans establish brutal and destructive reigns over the various alien races they conquer. In the end, it is these same alien races that eventually unite to destroy the last of the humans. *Voice of Youth Advocates* contributor Pat Pearl called *Birthright* a "cold-eyed, cleverly-conceived, wry view of our potential future," and Dennis A. Hinrichs, writing in *Kliatt,* described the novel as "an impressive work that will have strong appeal to the mainline SF fan."

Examines Effects of Colonization

The concern Resnick shows for man's cruelty when it comes to colonizing lands already inhabited by other people stems from his interest in Africa, a continent he has visited several times. "It has been noted that almost all of my more famous and popular science fiction deals with Africa," Resnick once remarked, "or at least with African themes transferred to other times and worlds. The answer to that is really quite simple: I think just about everyone believes that if we can ever reach the stars, we're going to colonize them ... and that if we colonize enough of them, sooner or later we're going to come into contact with a sentient alien race. Africa offers fifty-one separate, distinct, and devastating

HUGO AND NEBULA AWARD–WINNING AUTHOR

MIKE RESNICK

KIRINYAGA

"Ambitious...Well-written...A novel of ideas."
—*The New York Times Book Review*

A FABLE OF UTOPIA

A people's attempt to eschew modern civilization and return to a state of nature is the basis for the collection of award–winning stories in Resnick's 1998 collection, which focuses on an African settlement led by a visionary leader named Koriba.

examples of the effects of colonization on both the colonized and the colonizers. And if fiction holds a mirror up to life, then science fiction holds a funhouse mirror up to it. My mirror just happens to be set in Africa more often than not."

Resnick stories with themes relating to Africa and colonialism include *Paradise: A Chronicle of a Distant World, A Hunger in the Soul*, the novella *Bully!*, and his award–winning short story "Kirinyaga." While books such as *Paradise* illustrate the adverse effects of colonization on native peoples, Resnick shows that the converse is also true in *Bully!* and *A Hunger in the Soul*. "*Paradise* is a barely concealed portrayal

of the pillage of the African wilderness by outside powers," wrote D'Ammassa. As the story begins, Planet Peponi is a beautiful paradise, but when human colonists arrive, the land is soon raped of its natural resources and its people oppressed. Eventually, after years of struggle, the native people manage to force the humans to give them back their world, but Peponi's inhabitants have already had their way of life destroyed. "Resnick avoids stock solutions; there is no magical reconciliation in the final chapter," commented D'Ammassa. "Beautifully handled, engrossing, and thought provoking ... [this is] top–notch science fiction," declared a *Kirkus Reviews* critic. Resnick repeated this performance with *Purgatory: A Chronicle of a Distant World*, in which the natives of the planet Karimon experience the same fate as those on Peponi.

In works such as *A Hunger in the Soul, Bully!*, and *A Miracle of Rare Design*, the author shows the negative effects of colonialism on the colonizers themselves. Adapting the well–known historical tale of H. M. Stanley's search for Dr. David Livingstone after he has disappeared into the jungles of Africa, Resnick reconfigures the story in *A Hunger in the Soul* as journalist Robert Markham's search for Dr. Michael Drake, who had gone missing on another planet. Markham gathers together a team of humans and a group of aliens—called "Orange–Eyes"—to serve as porters. Markham brutalizes the aliens—both on the planet and on his own team—and leads most of his team's members to their deaths in his single–minded pursuit of the doctor. Finding Drake, he learns the doctor has discovered a cure for a horrible plague, but Drake is unwilling to give it to Markham. Markham decides to kill Drake and returns home triumphant. Markham's descent into his own brutal nature clearly shows the "civilized" actions of colonialists in a grim light. "With finesse, discernment, and splashes of vitriol," as a *Kirkus Reviews* contributor put it, "Resnick continues to expose colonialism and its vicious attitudes."

Resnick accomplishes this with more subtlety in his novella *Bully!*, whose main character is President Theodore Roosevelt. Set in an alternate history, the story follows Roosevelt, after he has left office, and his efforts to create a democratic nation in Africa. "Roosevelt is Resnick's most fully realized character," observed D'Ammassa, "earnest and sincere on one hand, flawed by egotism and an inability to recognize the reality of his situation on the other. Although he makes great strides toward his goal, it is ultimately doomed to failure because the historical basis for such a rapid alteration of the social climate doesn't exist."

A Miracle of Rare Design offers a more bizarre twist on colonization's effects on the colonizers. Xavier

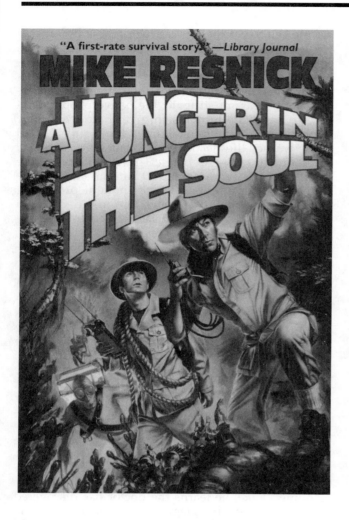

"A first-rate survival story." —*Library Journal*

MIKE RESNICK

A HUNGER IN THE SOUL

Paralleling the search for nineteenth–century African explorer David Livingstone by fellow explorer Henry Morton Stanley, Resnick's 1998 novel transfers the search to a futuristic planet, as a ruthless journalist exacts a high toll of otherworldly life in tracking down a missing scientist.

William Lennox accepts the opportunity to have his body surgically manipulated to resemble that of various aliens, whereupon he is sent to other worlds to persuade the natives to allow various human businesses and other interests to infiltrate their worlds. After a number of these procedures, Xavier begins to lose track of his human identity, and eventually decides to never go back to his original human form. In this way, Resnick uses the overt alteration of the physical appearance of his main character to illustrate the loss of people's humanity through the exploitation of others. A *Kirkus Reviews* critic called this entry into Resnick's ongoing explo-

ration of a theme "low–key, thoughtful, [and] absorbing," and *Booklist* reviewer Carl Hays described the novel as "insightful as well as entertaining."

"Kirinyaga"

Among all his stories and novels with African themes, Resnick's "Kirinyaga" stories have garnered the most awards and acclaim, including two Hugo Awards for "Kirinyaga" and "The Manamouki." Originally published separately in various science fiction magazines, the stories were collected in 1998's *Kirinyaga: A Fable of Utopia.* Resnick got his idea of African people settling a terraformed world from fellow novelist Orson Scott Card. The central figure of these stories is the witch doctor—or *mundumugu*—named Koriba. Koriba is the spiritual leader of the people who settle Kirinyaga. He is a wise but very strict leader, forbidding his people from emulating European culture in any way and forcing them to live a primitive, traditional lifestyle. While there are many positive sides to this way of life, there are also drawbacks. For example, in one story a young girl with a fervent desire to learn how to read commits suicide after Koriba forbids this education because it is a Western practice. "Koriba is in fact a fanatic ...," remarked a *Publishers Weekly* critic. "Yet throughout, as Resnick's superb use of first–person narration makes clear, Koriba remains a man of integrity and vision, and a gifted storyteller." *Booklist* reviewer John Mort felt that the stories were more effective before they were published in a collection, where they get a bit repetitive, but, overall, Mort proclaimed the book an "extraordinary work."

If you enjoy the works of Michael D. Resnick, you might want to check out the following books:

Philip K. Dick, *The Man in the High Castle,* 1962.
Frank Herbert, *Dune,* 1965.
Kim Stanley Robinson, *Red Mars,* 1993.
Robert Silverberg, *Lion Time in Timbuctoo,* 1986.
Connie Willis, *Impossible Things,* 1994.

With numerous awards to his credit for both his short and long fiction, Resnick has contributed much to his chosen genre by providing his readers with both entertaining and thought–provoking stories. The author once stated, "For years science fiction has been sneered at by the 'literary establishment' as being nothing but trashy pulp literature, teenaged power fantasies in clumsy disguise. But while the litcrits were busy sneering, the science fiction writers were busy working at their craft, to the point where not only isn't science fiction the mainstream's poor relation any longer, but the very best writing around can actually be found in science fiction." Resnick is likely to continue contributing to the growing respectability of science fiction, too. "Many of the writers I know hate writing, but love having written," he said. "Not me. I love the act of writing, of pushing nouns up against verbs, of looking at the day's output and deciding that it was pretty much what I intended to say when I sat down to work."

■ **Biographical and Critical Sources**

BOOKS

Twentieth–Century Science Fiction Writers, St. James Press, 1991, pp. 660–61.

PERIODICALS

Booklist, April 1, 1990, p. 1532; November 1, 1991, p. 496; July, 1992, p. 1925; February 1, 1993, p. 972; November 1, 1994, Carl Hays, review of *A Miracle of Rare Design*, p. 482; February 15, 1998, John Mort, review of *Kirinyaga: A Fable of Utopia*, p. 990.

Kirkus Reviews, April 15, 1989, review of *Paradise: A Chronicle of a Distant World*, p. 592; June 15, 1992, p. 753; January 1, 1993, p. 29; October 1, 1994, review of *A Miracle of Rare Design*, p. 1318; January 15, 1998, p. 88; April 15, 1998, review of *A Hunger in the Soul*, p. 538.

Kliatt, spring, 1982, Dennis A. Hinrichs, review of *Birthright: The Book of Man*, p. 20; spring, 1984, John M. Landsberg, review of *The Branch*, p. 12; September, 1990, p. 22; April, 1991, p. 21; March, 1993, p. 18; July, 1993, pp. 18, 20; September, 1993, p. 22; January, 1995, p. 19.

Library Journal, February 15, 1998, p. 173.

Publishers Weekly, December 23, 1983, review of *The Branch*, pp. 55–56; January 10, 1986, review of *Santiago: A Myth of the Far Future*, p. 83; July 27, 1992, pp. 52–53; January 18, 1993, p. 465; January 26, 1998, review of *Kirinyaga: A Fable of Utopia*, p. 73.

School Library Journal, August, 1990, p. 177; March, 1993, pp. 234, 236; March, 1999, p. 231.

Voice of Youth Advocates, August, 1982, Pat Pearl, review of *Birthright: The Book of Man*, p. 40; April, 1983, Barb Kerns, review of *Walpurgis III*, p. 46; June, 1986, David Snider, review of *Santiago: A Myth of the Far Future*, p. 90; February, 1993, p. 357; October, 1993, Vicky Burkholder, review of *Prophet*, pp. 232, 234; February, 1995, p. 346.

—Sketch by Kevin S. Hile

Diego Rivera

■ Personal

Born Jose Diego Rivera, December 13, 1886, in Gua-najuato, Mexico; died November 24, 1957, in Mexico City, Mexico; son of Don Diego Rivera (a schoolteacher) and Maria del Pilar (a schoolteacher); married Angelina Beloff, 1914 (marriage ended); married Guadalupe Marin, 1932 (marriage ended); married Frida Kahlo (a painter), 1929, divorced 1939, remarried 1940 (died 1954); married Emma Hurtado, 1955; children: one son, Diego (first marriage); two daughters, Chap (Ruth) and Pico (second marriage); one daughter, Marika, with Marevna Vorobev–Stebelska. *Education:* San Carlos National Academy of Fine Arts, Mexico City, 1898–1905; also studied in Spain, 1907–08, and Munich, Germany.

■ Career

Painter and muralist. Administrator, Bureau of Plastic Arts, commissioned to decorate National Preparatory School and Courtyard of New Ministry, Mexico City, 1921; director of Academy of San Carlos, Mexico City, 1929–30; worked on murals for Detroit Institute of Arts, 1933. *Exhibitions:* Rivera's work was exhibited in solo shows, including Galerie Berthe Weill, Paris, 1914, Museum of Modern Art, New York City, 1931, Museo Nacional de Bellas Artes, Mexico City, 1949 and 1977, and Galeria Diego Rivera, Mexico City, 1955; and in group exhibitions, including *Salon des Independants,* Paris, 1910, *Exhibition of Modern Art,* Madrid, Spain, 1914, *Pan American Exhibition,* Los Angeles, CA, 1925, and *Golden Gate International Exhibition,* San Francisco, CA, 1946. Collections of Rivera's work are housed at Palacio de Bellas Artes and San Carlos Academy of Fine Arts, Mexico City; Museum of Art, Guadalajara, Mexico; Metropolitan Museum of Art and Museum of Modern Art, New York City; Detroit Institute of Arts, Detroit, MI; Fine Arts Museum, San Francisco, CA; and other locations worldwide.

■ Awards, Honors

Purchase Prize, Pan American Exhibition, Los Angeles, 1925.

■ Writings

La accion de los ricos yanquis y la servidumbre del obrero mexicano, [Mexico City], 1923.
Abraham Angel, [Mexico City], 1924.
Genius of America, [New York], 1931.

(With Bertram D. Wolfe) *Portrait of America*, [New York], 1934.

(With Bertram D. Wolfe) *Portrait of Mexico*, [New York], 1938.

Memoria y Razon de Diego Rivera, [Mexico City], 1959.

(With Gladys March) *My Art, My Life: An Autobiography*, Citadel Press (New York), 1960, Dover, 1992.

Confesiones, edited by Luis Suarez, [Mexico City], 1962.

Contributor of articles to periodicals, including *Arts Magazine, Mexican Life, Workers' Age, Partisan Review*, and *Espacios*.

■ Sidelights

Diego Rivera, Mexico's most revered painter before his 1957 death, also came to be considered one of the most noteworthy artists of the twentieth century. In a visual sense, Rivera's imagery blended Central American folk traditions with European styles, but on a deeper level his works were extensive allegorical portraits of Mexican history, the colonization of the hemisphere, and the development of the modern industrial age. Rivera was able to incorporate such large themes into his work because of the medium with which he is indelibly associated: the wall fresco. After studying the most impressive examples of this method from the Italian Renaissance, Rivera abandoned the small canvas and painted nearly two dozen such extensive murals across North America, some as long as entire city blocks.

Though Rivera is credited with reviving the fresco form in the modern era, at times his art was derided by critics as too political in spirit. Furthermore, a series of well–publicized controversies plagued his career. He was an avowed Communist, but was criticized by the left for accepting commissions from some of the most powerful tycoons of the modern capitalist age. Conservatives called his work either obscene or sacrilegious. Biographies offer varied accounts of events in Rivera's life, for he liked to embellish. He was married several times, and even the longest and most compatible match, to artist Frida Kahlo, was troubled at times by his infidelities. Above all, however, Rivera has been credited with giving modern Mexico its national identity. He celebrated its traditions, the spirit of its people, and tried, through his art, to portray a future in which the country's generations–long suffering at the hands of its own environment, and then a string of conquerors, would have come to an end. "In the awkward grace of his Mexican children and the simple, elegant, abstracted curve of the back of one of his burden–bearers, it is not poverty we see but the tenderness of the vision of a painter who loved his country and his people," remarked one of his biographers, Bertram D. Wolfe, in *The Fabulous Life of Diego Rivera*.

An Educated Family

Rivera was born in December of 1886 in Guanajuato, a large city in the Guanajuato province of central Mexico. His family's ancestry was mixed and possessed Mexican, Spanish, Indian, African, and Italian blood; allegedly there were some Jewish, Russian, and Portuguese ancestors as well. Rivera was the first twin in a difficult birth that nearly killed his mother, Maria del Pilar. Both parents were schoolteachers; Don Diego Rivera had met his wife when he was hired to teach at the school founded by her mother in Guanajuato. Don Diego, who had a background in industrial chemistry and had prospected for silver for a time, also held local government office and edited a liberal newspaper in Guanajuato, *El Democrata*. Maria, by contrast, was a devout Roman Catholic. When the twin, Carlos, died before his second birthday, she was so devastated that she slept in the local cemetery for a time at the caretaker's lodge. The local physician suggested that she attend university to assuage her grief, and she studied obstetrics with the aim of becoming a midwife.

"Art has always been employed by the different social classes who hold the balance of power as one instrument of domination—hence, as a political instrument. One can analyze epoch after epoch—from the stone age to our own day—and see that there is no form of art which does not also play an essential political role. For that reason, whenever a people have revolted in search of their fundamental rights, they have always produced revolutionary artists."

—Diego Rivera

For a time—perhaps because of his mother's studies, or to cure him of a case of rickets—a very young Rivera was sent with his nurse, a Tarascan Indian, to her rural mountain village. Allegedly, he returned speaking their language, not Spanish, but the sojourn likely seeded in him an appreciation for such cultures, whose people did not abide by the same constraining rules that governed Mexico's European–descended population. In his own household, Rivera grew up in relative affluence: the family owned a grand piano and an impressive library, and he was read to often by his schoolteacher grandmother. His artistic talents became evident at an early age, for he began drawing on nearly every surface in the house. In response, his parents stretched a large canvas against one wall and allowed him to draw freely there. He displayed a fascination for drawing machines and trains from these years as well. A great–aunt introduced him to the folk art of Mexico through her collection, which also intrigued him.

Sailed for Spain

In 1892, when Rivera was six, the family moved to Mexico City. Two years later, he began attending school. He eventually enrolled in art classes at night, and as an adolescent even lied about his age to gain admission to one school. He applied for and won a scholarship to the San Carlos National Academy of Fine Arts in Mexico City, where he studied the European canon of art. At the age of sixteen, he abandoned his formal studies and began traveling around Mexico, attempting to earn money to move to Spain. With the help of a local politician, he won a study grant from the government and arrived in Spain in January of 1907. For the next year, Rivera studied with a well–known realist painter in Madrid, Eduardo Chicharro. He also studied the works of Diego Velasquez, El Greco, and Francisco Goya, Spain's more revolutionary–spirited artists of centuries past.

Rivera traveled to Paris in 1909, and to Munich, Germany as well. In 1911, he moved permanently to the French capital, where he first lived at 26 rue de Depart. Initially, he painted in a postimpressionist style, similar to works by Paul Cezanne, Paul Gauguin, Vincent Van Gogh, and Henri Matisse. Rivera also became friends with Pablo Picasso, whose name and work were already well known. For a time, beginning around 1913, Rivera painted in the Cubist style of Picasso and Georges Braque; he was also heavily influenced by the work of contemporaries Juan Gris and Fernand Leger.

The Revolutionary Mood

In 1914, Rivera and a Russian painter, Angelina Beloff, entered into a common–law marriage. An emigre six years his senior, Beloff intrigued her husband with tales of imperial Russia and its dire political fortunes; both were stunned and jubilant when the Bolshevik Revolution occurred in 1917. It was a cataclysmic event in international politics, for it brought about the world's first ever Communist state. By now Rivera had enjoyed some modest success as a painter, with exhibitions in Madrid and inclusion in a group gallery show in New York City. During the years of World War I, he was painting in a style similar to Cezanne. But in 1918, he traveled to Italy and encountered the famed frescoes in Rome's Sistine Chapel. He spent the next year and a half in Italy sketching and making notes on several other stunning examples of this art form, traveling from Pompeii to Ravenna, and even visited the celebrated Byzantine–era works in Constantinople.

The art of fresco—the application of pigment to wet plaster, which yields a particularly rich hue—dates back to ancient Greek culture. From there it spread to other Mediterranean cultures, and had been practiced in Italy since the waning days of the Roman Empire. Some of the earliest paintings of Christian religious art were frescoes executed in the famed Catacombs beneath Rome. A thirteenth–century Florentine artist, Giotto, took the method to a new level, and with his skilled use of perspective, helped usher in the Italian Renaissance. Rivera was tremendously impressed by the work of a later artist, Masaccio, who died in 1428. Masaccio executed several famed frescoes for churches in Florence, including the Brancacci Chapel and Santa Maria Novella.

Emerged as Important Artist

Rivera tired of Europe after over a decade there, and began to long for his native Mexico. He was also intrigued by the political developments that had occurred in his absence. Several years of uprisings had helped install a reformist government with a constitution in 1917. A seditious mood still remained, however, and shortly after Rivera returned to Mexico City in 1921, he joined the country's Communist Party. He served on its Central Committee, headed the Workers' and Peasants' Bloc for a time, and edited *El Machete,* the party organ. He also began working to create a syndicate of artists in Mexico, or an official union; he had found that many of the younger generation of painters in Mexico were quite radical in their political beliefs.

Rivera was determined to use his artistic talents in the service of a greater good. He believed that art was revolutionary in itself, and that powerful images could inspire people more than the most elo-

Rivera at work on a mural in the Hotel Reforma in Mexico in 1936.

quent speech or editorial. Moreover, he had grown dissatisfied with the business of art and wanted to create works that would be available for all to enjoy, not just those who could afford to buy paintings, or pay the admission price to a museum. Frescoes, he believed, were the solution: epic, allegorical stories could be presented in large spaces that were accessible to everyone. Finally, he also believed that frescoes were an art form that looked aesthetically fitting in both classical and modern architecture.

First Important Murals

Mexico's new Minister for Education, Jose Vasconcelos, agreed with Rivera about mural painting and its role as a revolutionary art form. Vasconcelos would become one of the Rivera's most important patrons, though he would later suffer his own political traumas. A young attorney and philosopher, Vasconcelos had been politically active for years, and had even been forced to spend time in exile—much of which he passed at the New York Public Library. When he assumed the ministry post, he announced ambitious plans: new schools were to be built, editions of literary classics would be free of charge, new libraries created in every community, and the entire country to be adorned with impressive murals. Like Rivera, Vasconcelos believed that educational opportunity and appreciation for Mexican culture and heritage would foster stability and prosperity in the nation.

> "For the first time in the history of art, Mexican mural painting made the masses the hero of monumental art . . ., the man of the fields, of the factories, of the cities, and towns."
>
> —Diego Rivera

In the new mural program, Vasconcelos offered Rivera his first commission: *The Creation*, finished in 1922, though it was technically not a fresco. It was executed in encaustic, a method in which a wax or resin is used to bind the pigment to the surface. The work, a thousand square feet, decorated the Bolivar Amphitheater in the preparatory school of the National University in Mexico City. It has been described as the first important mural of the twentieth century. His next major work also originated with Vasconcelos's office: a massive work at the Ministry of Education Building in Mexico City, which took him three years to complete. Helped by a team of assistants, he worked long days to create the 124 panels across 17,000 square feet. The assistants would prepare the walls during the night, and he arrived at dawn to paint, since the actual painting had to be done while the surface was still wet. Here, the Mexican labor movement and its traditional festivals are the work's twin themes. The first panels he painted, depicting some of the history and culture of the Tehuantepec region of Mexico, were done in tribute to Vasconcelos, who hailed from this area.

A Storied Personal Life

Around this time Rivera met and married Guadalupe Marin, with whom he had two daughters. His marriages suffered, however, because he conducted numerous extramarital affairs. Rivera was already the father of two children—one with Beloff, and another with Marievna Vorobiev–Stebelska, another Russian emigre—from his years in Paris. During the 1920s, as his career advanced, he formed Mexico's Union of Technical Workers with two other artists who would also become well–known muralists: David Alfaro Siqueiros and Jose Clemente Orozco. But as Rivera's reputation grew, so did attacks from enemies. He won another large commission to embellish the Auditorium of the National School of Agriculture at Chapingo (1927), which chronicled the biological and social progress of humankind together in panels such as "Good Government" and "Dividing the Land." Rumors arose that Rivera, Siqueiros and Orozco were being paid exorbitant sums by the government. Others objected to such murals because of their stark populist imagery—showing workers and peasants as the strength of the nation. "Academic painters and professors of art were enraged," the artist himself recalled in a 1924 interview with Katherine Anne Porter for *Survey,* "at what they termed our cult ugliness. This because we neglected to paint beautiful young ladies with white useless hands, or to compose pretty studies of water reflecting trees and castles."

Rivera traveled to the Soviet Union at the invitation of its government in 1927 for the tenth anniversary of the revolution. He was slated to create a mural for the Red Army headquarters in Moscow, but in the contentious leadership struggle within the country, Rivera sided with Leon Trotsky, who was bested by his rival, Josef Stalin. When Rivera returned to Mexico, his marriage to Marin dissolved, in part over a romance he had conducted with her younger sister; he also became involved with a photogra-

Rivera, seen here at work in 1945, painted murals that addressed social themes, particularly the plight of Mexican peasants and laborers.

pher named Tina Modotti, who had modeled for him. Marin became enraged when she learned of this affair and destroyed many of Rivera's paintings—she even threatened to maim him so that he might never paint again.

Met Frida Kahlo

In 1928, at a party thrown by Modotti, Rivera met Frida Kahlo, who had been a teenager and student at the preparatory school of the National University when he created the mural for the Bolivar Amphitheater earlier in the decade. Kahlo was one of the students who liked to heckle the scaffold–bound artist. An opinionated, daring sort who had taken up painting as well, Kahlo was enamored with Rivera, and the two were wed in 1929. But Kahlo was also a near–invalid, after a bus accident a few years before had permanently damaged her spine, fractured her pelvis, and left her with chronic pain. They had no children, but Kahlo enjoyed a successful career as an artist in her own right. Like her husband, she was fascinated by Mexico's folk art and traditional culture.

Rivera was appointed director of his alma mater, the Academy of San Carlos, for a year in 1929, which brought his expulsion from the Communist Party on charges that he was far too involved in a bourgeois government. Moreover, he also ran afoul of his more ideological–minded colleagues that year when he began work on a mural for the Palace of Cortes, in Cuernavaca, at the invitation of the American ambassador to Mexico. Rivera's images depicted the history of the region, and sympathetically chronicled the suffering inflicted upon the Indians in the area during Mexico's battle against the Spanish conquistadors. Nevertheless, he was criticized for taking the Cuernavaca job—and its $12,000 fee, his largest to date—for a restored historical building located in a city that was primarily a resort town for Mexico's wealthy.

American Patrons Take Notice

Because it had been commissioned by the American diplomat Dwight Morrow, the Cuernavaca mural generated interest in Rivera's work north of the border. He traveled to the United States in 1930, and created a work for the interior of a private dining club inside San Francisco's Stock Exchange. After a successful 1932 show at New York City's Museum of Modern Art, Rivera accepted a commission from the son of Detroit auto magnate Henry Ford. Edsel Ford, an art lover who was involved in the establishment of the city's Museum of Fine Arts (later renamed the Detroit Institute of Arts), offered Rivera the Italianate interior courtyard of the museum for a work that would celebrate the city's emergence as the center of industry in the world.

Accepting such commissions—from the tycoons and captains of industry who, according to Communist theory, became rich from the physical labor and insufferable living conditions of the masses—would become one of the more unusual hallmarks of Rivera's career. His more ideologically–bound colleagues castigated him for taking money from such sources, despite the fact that his work still retained its forthright social criticism, and he was sometimes called an opportunist.

Rivera accepted the Detroit offer without hesitation, for he recognized that what had been happening in the city was possibly the portent of a more equitable future for workers everywhere. Before the Depression, thousands of automobiles were being pro-

duced daily in factories that were models of scientific efficiency and modernity; the elder Ford had built the world's largest industrial complex, the Rouge Plant, in the 1920s as well. Ships unloaded iron ore at the mouth of the Rouge River, a few miles south of downtown, which was then refined and shaped into cars, which emerged several miles later at the other end of the plant.

The *Detroit Industry* Murals

Rivera and Kahlo visited the mighty Rouge complex as well as other parts of the city. He once said he would have liked to have spent eight to ten years in preparation and execution of *Detroit Industry*, as the museum murals were called, but could only afford one year. "The industries of Detroit—metallurgy, industrial and biological chemistry, and the mechanics of the automobile—were precisely those which most suited my taste as subjects for painting," he declared in *Portrait of America*. As with his other works, the mural chronicles the triumph of human endeavor over nature and the progress and prosperity this creates. Yet Rivera also depicts the ways in which technology is used for destructive purposes: he celebrates the birth of biochemistry with the vaccination of a child, but also includes imagery relating to poison gas, a purposefully deadly achievement in this scientific field. In another panel, one of the Ford company's famous trimotor planes cruises the air, but a menacing fighter plane piloted by a masked figure appears in another.

"The industries of Detroit—metallurgy, industrial and biological chemistry, and the mechanics of the automobile—were precisely those which most suited my taste as subjects for painting."

—Diego Rivera

Some workers putting together an engine block have green complexions, Rivera's reminder of the toxicity of the industrial age. "Ford workers as pinched and pallid worms are seen enmeshed in the metallic entrails of conveyors," wrote Edmund Wilson about other elements of the Detroit murals

This photograph of Rivera with his wife, artist Frida Kahlo, was taken during the 1940s.

in a 1933 essay for the *New Republic.* "Creatures like infernal pigs with jointed mosquito proboscides brew poison–gas and manufacture projectiles; a Holy Family consisting of a medical Joseph, a white–halo–capped nurse–Virgin and a dough–faced Infant Jesus, whom Joseph is vaccinating, rise above the manger animals, the horse, the cow and the sheep, which have piously supplied the serum, while, above, a dead–eyed biologist is vivisecting a dog." Above it all, a quartet of female Titans hovers at the upper corners—black, red, white, and· yellow, symbolizing coal, iron ore, limestone and sand, the four primary raw materials for industry. But, as Wilson noted, "in the background, the hands of hidden masses—grasping fingers and menacing fists—reach up, huger still, from behind a wall. Edsel Ford, with popping eyes, looks on scared."

The Holy Family panel ignited the wrath of the local clergy in Detroit, who called it sacrilegious. Moreover, the museum's Art Commission—comprised primarily of the wives of some of the city's leading automotive–industry executives—did not like Rivera's work, either, and the city council, involved in some of the funding for the museum, was also upset. After it was unveiled in March of 1933, the entire work was called obscene, and one of the city's major newspapers suggested that whole thing be destroyed. The international art community sided with Rivera and Edsel Ford, however, and in a move that cheered Rivera immensely, some 12,000 industrial workers sent a letter to Detroit's mayor threatening to defend the murals themselves. The support

he received from such quarters was "for me the clearest demonstration of the worth of the decade of experimentation in art for the masses which I was just completing," he wrote in *Portrait of America.*

The Rockefeller–Lenin Debacle

Rivera's next commission, however, sparked even greater controversy. Nelson Rockefeller, scion of the oil family, contracted with the artist to create a large work for the RCA Building inside the newly–built Rockefeller Center. The work was to be titled *Man at the Crossroads Looking with Hope and High Vision to the Choosing of a New and Better Future.* "Anyone who knew Rivera's work could have predicted that one element would almost certainly be peasants, workers and soldiers marching under a Red flag, and so it was," wrote *Smithsonian* essayist William Weber Johnson. The Rockefeller family approved the sketches before work on the mural was started, but was miffed when the press began commenting on the irony of the commission itself—an avowed Communist painter taking money from one of the most famous names in capitalism, and using it to create a visual criticism of that very system.

Then the Rockefellers asked Rivera to remove a large image of Vladimir Ilych Lenin, leader of the Bolshevik revolution, in the work, and he refused. As the artist explained in *Portrait of America,* Rockefeller Center was not a museum, nor a private dining club, nor any other restricted structure. It was a large building for public use—with offices, stores, radio stations, and even its own subway station. "There I could only paint that which corresponded to and was significant for the entire mass of producing citizens," Rivera wrote, "for the buildings which today have been erected out of the capitalist drive for profits, will tomorrow, because of their public functional utility, be delivered over into the hands of the workers."

Soon, armed guards hired by the Rockefellers were posted around Rivera and his seven assistants as they worked to finish *Man at the Crossroads.* The press coverage fanned the flames, and workers came to picket in support. "Tens of million of people were informed that the nation's richest man had ordered the veiling of the portrait of an individual named Vladimir Ilyitch Lenin," Rivera argued in *Portrait of America,* "because a painter had represented him in a fresco as a Leader, guiding the exploited masses towards a new social order based on the suppression of classes, organization, love and peace among human beings, in contrast to the war, unemployment, starvation, and degeneration of the capitalist disorder." In the end, the murals were never seen by the public. They were covered with canvas, and six months later the plaster was smashed. The work survives only in photographs taken secretly by one of Rivera's assistants with a tiny camera—a daring move that went undetected by the guards. Rivera was still paid in full, and he used the funds to create a more permanent fresco at the New Workers' School in New York City.

Limited Himself to Mexican Themes

His next major work, inside Mexico City's Palace of Fine Arts, replicated some of the images from the doomed *Man at the Crossroads*. The mural, which Rivera began in 1934 and then spent the next two decades augmenting, was an extensive chronicle of Mexican history from the pre–Columbian era to the present. *Mexico: Yesterday, Today and Tomorrow* is said to be the most extensive visual story of a country ever executed anywhere in the world. It glorifies the Aztec, Maya, Toltec, and other pre–Columbian civilizations, illustrates their decimation at the hands of the Spanish, and narrates the struggle for independence from European colonialism. A large image of Karl Marx appears at the end, gesturing to a worker, peasant, and soldier. "The landscape he points to lacks the beauty possessed by so many of the landscapes in the upper reaches of Diego's frescoes," declared Wolfe's *Fabulous Life of Diego Rivera*. Yet the critic, biographer, and friend of the artist noted that the "Yesterday" section fares much better. Wolfe called it "lyrical in organization and in the treatment of its nameless figures, in the poetry of the arts and crafts of that vanished Golden Age, the graceful flowery wars, the idyllic landscape over-hung by a personified and animated sun, presided over by three legendary incarnations of Quetzalcoatl."

Rivera was still active in Communist politics, de-spite the fact that his petitions for readmission to the Mexican Communist Party were continually rejected. The larger movement was enmeshed in an ideological split over the Stalin/Trotsky rift. In 1936, Rivera used his influence to obtain an entry visa for Trotsky to Mexico, personally requesting it from Mexican president Lazaro Cardenas. Trotsky even stayed with Rivera and Kahlo for a time at their home and dismissed Rivera's warnings that his life was imperiled. Siqueiros, Rivera's longtime painter friend with whom he had fallen out, attempted to kill the Russian. A Spaniard eventually succeeded, using an ice pick as a weapon, in 1940.

Productive Later Career

Rivera's personal life remained tumultuous. He and Kahlo were divorced in 1939, but remarried a year later. She joined him in California when he won a commission to create a mural for the Golden Gate International Exposition in 1940. Fairgoers could watch the work, titled *Marriage of the Artistic Express of the North and South on this Continent*, in progress before it was crated and sent to San Francisco's City College at the close of the Exposition. During the next decade, Rivera painted a number of other out-standing murals, including those of the Instituto Nacional de Cardiologia (1943) and *Dream of a Sunday Afternoon in the Alameda* for the Hotel del Prado (1948) in Mexico City. This latter work contained the words "Dios no existe" (God Does Not Exist) in one section, which launched one final controversy for Rivera's career. The work remained hidden from the public for nine years.

Still, Rivera was inarguably Mexico's greatest living painter at the time, and was feted with a retrospec-tive in Mexico City in 1949. Kahlo died in 1954, and in the following year Rivera wed his longtime art dealer, Emma Hurtado, and made an extensive trip into Communist eastern Europe. His health was fail-ing, though, and he had been diagnosed with cancer. On November 24, 1957, he suffered a fatal heart attack in his studio at his San Angel home. He was buried in the Rotonda de los Hombres Ilustres in Mexico City's pantheon of Dolores. In his will, the artist donated his extensive collection—some 40,000 artifacts in all—of pre–Hispanic art and crafts to the Mexican people.

If you enjoy the works of Diego Rivera, you might want to check out the follow-ing:

The frescoes of the Renaissance master Michelangelo, whose work Rivera studied.

The works of Frida Kahlo, a Mexican artist who was married to Rivera.

The works of African American artist Ja-cob Lawrence, a follower of social realism.

Despite the political controversies that encircled his work and reputation during much of his career, Riv-era came to be considered one of the most signifi-cant artists of the twentieth century. He is credited with single–handedly reviving the Renaissance me-dium of fresco painting and creating a place for it in the soaring new forms of modern architecture. The principles of Marx, Lenin, and economic collectivism that he integrated into his imagery—along with a forceful criticism of imperialist politics and the cult of capitalism—are viewed by scholars as one of Rivera's most unique contributions to contemporary art. "Art has always been employed by the different social classes who hold the balance of power as one instrument of domination—hence, as a political instrument," Rivera told the editors of a 1945 tome, *Artists on Art*. "One can analyze epoch after epoch—from the stone age to our own day—and see that there is no form of art which does not also play an essential political role. For that reason, whenever a people have revolted in search of their fundamental rights, they have always produced revolutionary artists."

■ Biographical and Critical Sources

BOOKS

Ergas, G. Aimee, *Artists: From Michelangelo to Maya Lin*, UXL, 1995.

Goldwater, Robert and Marco Treves, editors, *Artists on Art from the XIV to the XX Century*, Pantheon Books, 1945.

Hamill, Pete, *Diego Rivera*, Abrams, 1999.

Helms, Cynthia Newman, editor, *Diego Rivera: A Retrospective*, Norton, 1998.

International Dictionary of Art and Artists, St. James Press, 1990, pp. 709–11.

Lucie–Smith, Edward, *Lives of the Great 20th Century Artists*, Thames and Hudson, 1999.

Marnham, Patrick, *Dreaming with His Eyes Open: A Life of Diego Rivera*, Knopf, 1998.

Modern Arts Criticism, Volume 2, Gale, 1992.

Oxford Dictionary of Twentieth–Century Art, Oxford University Press, 1988, pp. 784–85.

Rivera, Diego, *Portrait of America*, Covici, Friede, 1934.

Wolfe, Bertram D., *The Fabulous Life of Diego Rivera*, Stein and Day, 1963, Scarborough House, 1990.

PERIODICALS

Art in America, November, 1999, Edward J. Sullivan, "From Mexico to Montparnasse—and Back," p. 102.

Lancet, November 20, 1999, Marilynn Larkin, "Pan–American Unity Portrayed on the Web," p. 1831.

New Republic, July 12, 1933, Edmund Wilson, "Detroit Paradoxes," pp. 230–33.

New Statesman, January 22, 1988, John Spurling, "Wall to Wall," pp. 30–31.

Newsweek, July 19, 1999, Guadalupe Rivera Marin, "The Painting on the Wall," p. 50.

Smithsonian, February, 1986, William Weber Johnson, "The Tumultuous Life and Times of the Painter Diego Rivera," p. 36.

Survey, May 1, 1924, Katherine Anne Porter, "The Guild Spirit in Mexican Art" (interview with Diego Rivera), pp. 174–78.

Town and Country, April, 1999, Phyllis Tuchman, "The Great Rivera," p. 54.

ON—LINE

Diego Rivera Web site, located at http://www.diegorivera.com (May 7, 2000).*

—*Sketch by Carol Brennan*

Martin Scorsese

■ Personal

Born November 17, 1942, in Flushing, NY; son of Charles and Catherine (Cappa) Scorsese (garment workers); married Laraine Marie Brennan, May 15, 1965 (divorced); married Julia Cameron (a journalist), 1975 (divorced); married Isabella Rosellini (a model and actress), September 29, 1979 (divorced, 1983); married Barbara DeFina (a film production worker), February 9, 1985 (divorced); married Helen Morris (an editor), July 22, 1999; children: (first marriage) Catherine Terese Glinora Sophia; (second marriage) Dominica Elizabeth. *Education:* New York University, B.S., 1964, M.A., 1966.

■ Addresses

Agent—c/o Creative Artists Agency, 9830 Wilshire Blvd., Los Angeles, CA 90212.

■ Career

Film director, producer, and writer. New York University, film department, faculty assistant and instructor, 1963–66, instructor, 1968–70; director of television commercials in England, 1968; news editor, CBS–TV, 1968. Director of motion pictures *Who's That Knocking at My Door?*, Joseph Brenner Associ-

ates, 1968, *Boxcar Bertha*, American International, 1972, *Mean Streets*, Warner Bros., 1973, *Italianamerican*, Scorsese Productions, 1974, *Alice Doesn't Live Here Anymore*, Warner Bros., 1975, *Taxi Driver*, Columbia, 1976, *New York, New York*, United Artists (UA), 1977, *The Last Waltz*, UA, 1978, *American Boy*, Scorsese Productions, 1979, *Raging Bull*, UA, 1980, *The King of Comedy*, Twentieth Century–Fox, 1983, *After Hours*, Geffen Films, 1985, *The Color of Money*, Buena Vista, 1986, *The Last Temptation of Christ*, Universal, 1988, *New York Stories* (with Woody Allen and Francis Ford Coppola), Buena Vista, 1989, *Good-Fellas*, Warner Bros., 1990, *Cape Fear*, Universal, 1991, *The Age of Innocence*, Columbia, 1993, *Casino*, Universal, 1995, *Kundun*, Buena Vista, 1997, and *Bringing Out the Dead*, Paramount, 1999. Producer of *Mad Dog and Glory*, Universal, 1993; executive producer, *Woodstock: Three Days of Peace and Music*, Warner Bros., 1994; co–producer, *Clockers*, Universal, 1995.

■ Awards, Honors

Edward L. Kingsley Foundation Award, 1963, 1964; First Prize, Rosenthal Foundation Award, Society of Cinemetologists, 1964; Brown University Film Festival Award, 1965; First Prize, Screen Producer's Guild Award, 1965, for *It's Not Just You, Murray!*; Academy Award nomination for best director, Academy of Motion Picture Arts and Sciences, 1981, for *Raging Bull*; Cannes Film Festival Award, best director, 1986, for *The Color of Money*; Academy Award nomination for best director, Academy of Motion

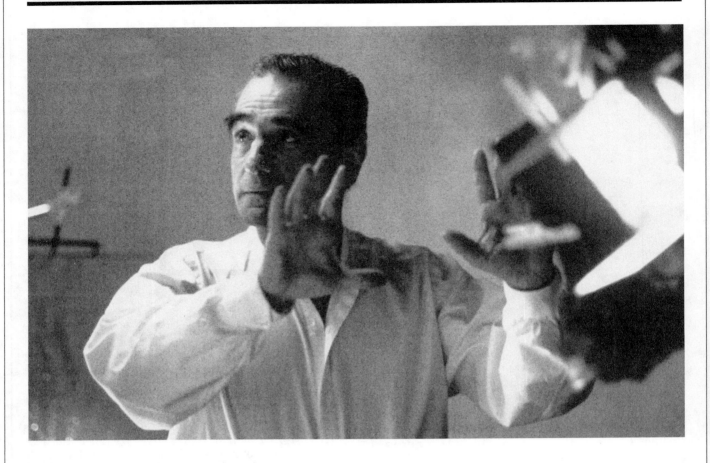

Martin Scorsese

Picture Arts and Sciences, and Orson Award for Freedom of Expression, both 1989, both for *The Last Temptation of Christ;* honored by Florence Film Festival—U.S.A., 1990; Academy Award nominations for best director and for best screenplay (with Nicholas Pileggi), Academy of Motion Picture Arts and Science, 1991, both for *GoodFellas;* Academy Award nomination for best screenplay (with Jay Cocks), Academy of Motion Picture Arts and Sciences, 1994, for *The Age of Innocence;* Life Achievement Award, American Film Institute, 1997.

■ Writings

SCREENPLAYS

The Big Shave, Scorsese Productions, 1967.
(With Betzi Manoogian) *Who's That Knocking at My Door?,* Joseph Brenner Associates, 1968.

(With Mardik Martin) *Mean Streets,* Warner Bros., 1973.
Italianamerican, Scorsese Productions, 1974.
(With Nicholas Pileggi) *GoodFellas* (based on Pileggi's nonfiction book *Wiseguy*), Warner Bros., 1990, published with introduction by David Thompson, Faber, 1990.
(With Jay Cocks) *The Age of Innocence* (based on Edith Wharton's novel of the same title), Columbia, 1993.
(With Nicholas Pileggi) *Casino,* Universal, 1995.

Also author of screenplays *What's a Nice Girl Like You Doing in a Place Like This?,* 1963, *It's Not Just You, Murray!,* 1964, *Bring on the Dancing Girls,* 1965, and *Somewhere Down the Crazy River.*

OTHER

Scorsese on Scorsese, edited by Ian Christie and David Thompson, Faber, 1989.

(With Jay Cocks) *The Age of Innocence: The Illustrated Story of the Film*, Newmarket Press, 1993.

(With Jay Cocks) *The Age of Innocence: The Shooting Script*, Newmarket Press (New York City), 1995.

(With Michael Henry Wilson) *A Personal Journey with Martin Scorsese through American Movies*, Hyperion (New York City), 1997.

■ Sidelights

Martin Scorsese is the director of some of American cinema's most striking works, including the celebrated *Mean Streets, Taxi Driver, Raging Bull*, and *GoodFellas*. He first became interested in movies while growing up in Manhattan's Little Italy. Prohibited by poor health from indulging in neighborhood sports, the asthmatic Scorsese turned to the cinema as a refuge from the hectic ethnic environment. He was especially impressed by Hollywood productions of the 1940s. "There's a great similarity in the way I look at reality and the things I saw in the musicals and the dark 'noir' films," he told a *Christian Science Monitor* interviewer. "My reality and film reality are interchangeable."

By age fourteen Scorsese was planning a career as a Roman Catholic priest, though his expulsion from a junior seminary (the charge was unruly behavior) resulted in his transfer to a Bronx high school. Upon graduation he had hoped to attend divinity school at Fordham College but failed the entrance examination, and so he enrolled instead at New York University (NYU). There Scorsese concentrated on film making courses and earned honors for several short works. After receiving his degree in 1966 he worked as a director and editor in British and American television; at the same time, he wrote and directed the short film *The Big Shave*, a brief, bloody depiction of a Vietnam veteran's suicide.

In 1968 Scorsese returned to NYU as a film instructor, where he quickly became popular as an enthusiastic lecturer on American cinema. While there he co-wrote and directed *Who's That Knocking at My Door?*, a portrait of an unemployed film buff whose rigid Catholic values conflict with his occasionally crazed activities. Vincent Canby, writing in *New York Times*, described the film's protagonist, J. R., as "the sort of young man who . . . can one minute offer to 'forgive' the girl he loves for having been forcibly raped, and the next minute accuse her of being a whore."

Scorsese's directorial method in *Who's That Knocking at My Door?* is largely *cinema verite* (documentary realism), mixing jarring sequences of hand-held camera work with slow panoramas of New York City in order to evoke both the tension and the emptiness that fill J. R.'s life. Critics, while acknowledging the awkward theatricality of *Who's That Knocking at My Door?*, nonetheless found Scorsese's first full-length work commendable. "Working on what must have been a minuscule budget," Canby wrote, "he has composed a fluid, technically proficient movie, more intense and sincere than most commercial releases." In *A Cinema of Loneliness* Robert Phillip Kolker defined Scorsese's early style as "partly neo-realist, partly documentary," and noted that in this work there is already evidence of the "camera strategies, the restless, foreboding movement" that would permeate *Mean Streets*.

Scorsese followed *Who's That Knocking at My Door?* with *Boxcar Bertha*, an often violent depiction of a union organizer's adventures with a female hobo during the Depression. Scorsese directed the film for cost-cutting producer Roger Corman, who released it in drive-ins with *1000 Convicts and a Woman*. Fellow filmmaker John Cassavetes reportedly scolded Scorsese for squandering his time and ability on Corman's production and urged him to develop his own projects.

Impressive Big-Screen Debut

Perhaps prompted by Cassavetes, Scorsese wrote and directed *Mean Streets*, an unnerving film about life in New York City's Little Italy. The film's protagonist is Charlie, a modest mob employee torn between loyalty to his uncle, a sympathetic mobster, and his deranged friend Johnny Boy. It is the latter friendship that jeopardizes Charlie's standing in the mob. In debt to loan sharks everywhere, the crazed Johnny Boy taunts his lenders, shoots casually at his neighbors, and assaults both friends and strangers. When Charlie and his epileptic lover Theresa, Johnny Boy's cousin, try to escort Johnny Boy away from vengeful loan sharks, all three are shot.

Although *Mean Streets* was not a box-office success, it did impress several critics. Jon Landau, writing in *Rolling Stone*, hailed *Mean Streets* as "the most original American movie" of 1973. He praised the improvisatory tone of the dialogue—a technique pioneered by Cassavetes—as "a perfect aural equivalent" to Scorsese's unsettling use of Italian arias and cameras that prowl and lurk as they capture the action. *New York*'s David Denby was similarly impressed with Scorsese's technique, calling the young director "a master of film texture and expressive atmosphere" and praising *Mean Streets* as "remarkable . . . for its moral realism—realism without cynicism."

Robert De Niro and Jodie Foster starred in Scorsese's 1976 film *Taxi Driver*, in which De Niro stars as an antisocial Vietnam veteran whose violent and twisted crusade against the filth of New York City culminates ironically in his public commendation as a hero.

After completing *Mean Streets*, Scorsese accepted a more commercial project as director of *Alice Doesn't Live Here Anymore*, Robert Getchell's story about a suddenly widowed singer/waitress and her struggles and romances while supporting herself and an unruly son. Although *Alice* resulted in Scorsese's first box–office success, some critics complained that, as with *Boxcar Bertha*, he had compromised his abilities in directing it. Writing in *Hudson Review*, Stephen Farber called *Alice*'s screenplay "artificial" and attributed the film's success solely to Scorsese's "raw energy."

Explores Alienation and Anxiety

In 1976 Scorsese directed his next major film, *Taxi Driver*. Working from a screenplay by Paul Schrader, Scorsese fashioned a disturbing portrait of an unbalanced loner in New York City. The taxi driver is Travis Bickle, a Vietnam veteran (played by Robert De Niro, who had portrayed the twisted Johnny Boy in *Mean Streets*) who works midnights chauffeuring a seemingly endless clientele of sleazy characters and psychotics. Alone and unwanted, Travis creates a fantasy life for himself: he writes to his parents of a secret assignment for the CIA and arms himself in preparation for his hallucinatory conflict with the "scum and filth" of the city.

Like *Mean Streets*, *Taxi Driver* culminates in violence. After abandoning an assassination attempt on a politician, Travis decides to rescue an adolescent prostitute from her smug pimp. Armed with two pistols and a long knife, he drives to the pimp's hotel and blasts his way into the girl's room, killing three people—including the girl's pimp and her customer—before attempting suicide. But his pistols are empty, and in a perverse epilogue it is revealed that Travis has become a media hero for rescuing the girl.

In *Taxi Driver* Scorsese modified the unsettling technique of *Mean Streets* to merge realism and expressionism. The jerky camera work of the earlier film is replaced by eerie sweeps and intruding shots—including an acclaimed sequence in which Travis addresses the camera, asking, "Are you talkin' to *me?*" The soundtrack accentuates the expressionistic tone, with Bernard Herrmann's ominous score coming out of the silence as Travis's cab emerges in slow motion from the manhole steam.

The popular and critical success of *Taxi Driver* established Scorsese as one of the industry's leading film makers, earning him his first Academy Award nomination for best director. Robert E. Lauder, reviewing the film in *Christian Century*, called *Taxi Driver* "one of the most disturbing films ever made" and wrote that "the extraordinary talent of Scorsese is evident again and again," while in *Take One* George Mortis lauded *Taxi Driver* as "a remarkable achievement, a crazy, excessive, erratic masterpiece." Specifically, Mortis praised Scorsese's skill in pacing, noting that Scorsese "builds the film slowly, quietly, creating a mood of anxiety and imminent violence."

Scorsese next directed *New York, New York,* an ambitious, big–budget tribute to 1940s musicals in which he sought to recreate the artificiality of the genre while depicting a detailed and sometimes disturbing romance between two musicians. To realize this goal, Scorsese shot the film almost entirely in studios, using props such as cut–out trees and an obviously cardboard train to duplicate the distinctly fake and campy look of those old musicals. For the love story, however, Scorsese relied heavily on actors' improvisations—a technique he had used in *Mean Streets* and *Taxi Driver* to create a feeling of intensity. In *New York, New York,* however, the realistic confrontations between the lovers clashed with the stylized sets, and some critics complained that Scorsese had either undermined an homage to old musicals with a depressing love story or had corrupted a vivid portrait of romance among musicians with anachronistic musical numbers. Kolker complained of the "uncomfortable mixture of styles" in *New York, New York,* and contended that Scorsese "denies the tradition he apparently wants to celebrate." Canby was less gracious in his review, calling the film "painful . . . nervy and smug."

Scorsese followed the failure of *New York, New York* with two modest projects. In 1978 he directed *The Last Waltz,* a documentary about the rock group The Band and their last concert. Working closely with members of the group, Scorsese fashioned a film that reveals both the gloom of touring and the exhilaration of performing. Terry Curtis Fox, re-

In 1980's Academy Award–nominated *Raging Bull*, Scorsese profiles middleweight boxer Jake LaMotta (played by De Niro), utilizing black–and–white film and other stylistic elements to capture his subject's violent, claustrophobic world.

viewing *The Last Waltz* in *Village Voice*, called it "the best rock concert movie ever made." During this period Scorsese also directed *Italianamerican*, a forty–five–minute film about his parents that J. Hoberman, also in *Village Voice*, described as "funny and touching."

An Award–winning Classic

Scorsese's next major film was 1980's *Raging Bull*, considered by many to be the finest motion picture of that decade. A biographical film (or biopic), it details the career of Jake LaMotta, the boxer who held the middleweight championship during the 1950s. Working again with De Niro, Scorsese created an often gruesome portrait of an insecure bully who abuses and cheats on his two wives, alienates his brother, hocks the gems he has pried from his heavyweight belt in order to pay his debts, is thrown in jail for employing a fourteen–year–old as a cocktail waitress, and eventually embarks on a "comeback" career as a verse–spouting comedian in a dark, empty club.

Scorsese knew that, after the tremendous success of *Rocky* a few years earlier, the very down–beat *Raging Bull*, shot entirely in black and white, was a risky move. "I had decided that *Raging Bull* would be pretty much the end of my working in America," he told *American Film.* "I thought it was a swan song for Hollywood . . . that I was going to be living in New York and Rome, and I was going to make documentaries and educational films on the saints. I was going to make films for television, that sort of thing." Anticipating the end of his tenure as a Hollywood director, Scorsese approached *Raging Bull* with a style he described in *Rolling Stone* as "kamikaze film making": "I threw everything I knew into it, and if it meant the end of my career, then it would have to be the end of my career."

Stanley Kauffmann wrote in *New Republic* that watching *Raging Bull* "is like visiting a human zoo." He described Scorsese's direction—rife with camera work that is alternately gliding and lurching—as "imaginative but controlled" and added that his "mannerisms have coalesced and evolved into a strong style." *New Yorker*'s Pauline Kael, however, claimed that Scorsese's skillful direction was undermined by his apparent willingness to condone LaMotta's often brutal behavior, observing that "the picture seems to be saying that in order to become champ, Jake LaMotta had to be mean, obsessive, crazy." But most critics deemed *Raging Bull* an exciting and stylish work. The film earned Scorsese another Academy Award nomination for best director.

After completing *Raging Bull* Scorsese directed *The King of Comedy,* an off–beat film about Rupert Pupkin, a boorish comedian who kidnaps talk–show host Jerry Langford and demands a guest spot on Langford's show. Though its conservative camera work and amusing (if appalling) action marked a departure from Scorsese's trademark flashiness and intensity, *The King of Comedy* nonetheless earned acclaim as quintessential Scorsese from many critics. "It's very funny," noted Canby. "Yet it's also bristly, sometimes manic to the edge of lunacy and . . . terrifying." *Newsweek*'s Jack Kroll concurred, calling *The King of Comedy* a "scarifying anatomy of modern mania."

Directs Challenging Film about Christ

In 1983, Scorsese began what would eventually become his most controversial project to date: the adaptation of Nikos Kazantzakis's 1955 novel *The Last*

Temptation of Christ. Itself the subject of controversy, the novel details Jesus' gradual and reluctant acceptance that he is, indeed, the son of God. In the final scene, the dying Christ dreams of the life of humanity he was denied—a "normal" life in which he would have married and raised children with Mary Magdalene. Scorsese had planned for nearly a decade to film Kazantzakis's novel, and had worked for more than a year writing and casting the picture; a few weeks before shooting was scheduled to begin, however, Paramount studios halted production, fearing the wrath of conservative religious groups who had mistakenly heard the film portrayed Jesus as a homosexual.

Frustrated by Paramount's lack of support, Scorsese went on to make 1985's *After Hours,* a film about an office worker who, through a series of coincidences, finds himself trapped in the seedy underworld of New York City at night. "I read the script and I said, 'I know just how this guy feels,'" Scorsese told the *New York Times.* "This poor guy was being put through his paces by something other than his own actions. What *After Hours* really is, is a reaction against my year and a half in Hollywood trying to get *The Last Temptation of Christ* made." He continued: "There were all these people talking about something they'd never even read, saying things which weren't even true and no one would listen to me. . . . I thought I was stuck in one long nightmare, going from person to person, from one studio executive to the next. It was like Kafka."

In 1986 Scorsese made one of his most commercially successful films, *The Color of Money,* starring Tom Cruise and Paul Newman. A sequel to Robert Rossen's 1961 classic *The Hustler* (which also starred Newman in the title role), *The Color of Money* was also a critical success, garnering Newman an Oscar and Scorsese best director honors from the Cannes film festival. Armed with a little more clout, Scorsese found a new studio, Universal, to lend him enough money to finally make *The Last Temptation of Christ.*

Before the film was even released in 1988, a furor unlike any seen in years had begun to form. Conservative religious organizations called for the boycotting of Universal and its parent company, MCA; one group offered to purchase all copies of the film from Universal, so that they could be destroyed before release; an ugly demonstration was staged in front of the home of MCA chairman Lew Wasserman, reviling him as a "Jesus–hating Jew." Scorsese—who was dubbed "the greatest blasphemer in 2,000 years" by one organization's leader—pointed out in *Time* that "ninety–nine percent of the people who are complaining have not seen the picture," and were basing their complaints upon a bootlegged

A cast portrait from 1990's *Goodfellas:* from left to right, Ray Liotta, Robert De Niro, Paul Sorvino, and Joe Pesci as high–ranking members of a New York Mafia organization.

copy of an outdated script. When Universal invited groups to attend a special advance screening, many chose to picket the theater rather than view the film.

"More than any other film of its type," Michael Morris praised in *American Film,* "Scorsese's *Last Tempta-*

tion measures the magnanimity of Christ's sacrifice in terms of moral choices. This above all is the value of the film." Though Morris pointed out that the story contains a number of theological flaws, "the film is nevertheless significant as an earnest effort to present Christ in a different way." By depicting

Jesus as a man who must surrender his humanity in order to accept his divinity, Scorsese explained, his death on the cross is more meaningful. "It was never my intention to set out and shake anyone's faith," the director told *American Film*, "but rather to ignite it."

Independent of the theological controversy surrounding the film, some critics found *The Last Temptation of Christ* lacking. "Individual sequences are brilliantly conceived," Terrence Rafferty began in *New Yorker*, "but the movie's intensity, over a span of two hours and forty minutes, is sputtering, fitful. . . . This movie isn't a sacrilege; it's just an honorable mistake." Richard A. Blake, writing in *America*, expressed a similar opinion: "*The Last Temptation of Christ* is not a blasphemous film at all. In fact, Martin Scorsese is probably sincere in his belief that he has made an important religious film. The sad fact is that he has made neither." *Time* movie reviewer Richard Corliss, however, found the film "severe, coherent, passionate, and beautifully made." He concluded: "Those willing to accompany Scorsese on his dangerous ride through the Gospels may believe he has created his masterpiece." In the midst of the critical and theological controversy the film earned Scorsese a 1989 Academy Award nomination for best director. A number of interviews and essays defending *The Last Temptation of Christ*—as well as articles predating the film—are collected in the director's 1989 book, *Scorsese on Scorsese*.

Captures "The Mob" on Film

In 1990, Scorsese directed *GoodFellas*, based on Nicholas Pileggi's book *Wiseguy*. A gangster film based on the true story of New York mobster Henry Hill's rise through the ranks of the Family, *Good-Fellas* shows Scorsese once again in top form. *Film Comment* contributor Kathleen Murphy called the movie "so surefooted, so teeming with authentic action, color, character, and risk, it literally takes your breath away," while a *New Statesman* reviewer noted that, with *GoodFellas*, Scorsese "has been elevated to the ranks of the untouchables. The failure of any single film would no longer prevent him from getting others off the ground." Though *Commonweal*'s Richard Alleva expressed some displeasure with the film's protagonist, he asserted that "after seeing *GoodFellas*, you will understand why a young man would want to be a gangster."

Scorsese followed *GoodFellas* with 1991's *Cape Fear*, a thriller and remake of J. Lee Thompson's 1962 picture of the same title. Though stylishly filmed, several critics felt its characters were too one–dimensional to support Scorsese's themes of guilt, obsession, and retribution. "*Cape Fear* is one of the costliest and most elaborate duds to come out of Hollywood," wrote John Simon in *National Review*, "which, given the state of our culture, need not prevent it from becoming an enormous hit." In 1993 Scorsese directed an adaptation of Edith Wharton's *The Age of Innocence*, which is about a romantic gentleman who, though pledged to one young woman, dreams of a life with her cousin. Set in New York in the 1870s, *The Age of Innocence* was described by Corliss as "a gravely beautiful fairy tale of longing and loss" that demonstrates Scorsese "can be as attentive to the tiniest twinges of the heart as he has been to the gunfire of taxi drivers and goodfellas."

In 1995 Scorsese directed *Casino*, a film that revisits many of his trademark themes: violence, criminal life, and greed. Robert De Niro works with Scorsese again, this time portraying a Las Vegas gangster married to a woman (played by Sharon Stone) who only loves his money. Stuart Klawans, in his review for *Nation*, expressed disappointment, commenting that "there's something pre–fab about his [Scorsese's] direction this time around. . . . It's all dauntingly skillful, but empty." Gavin Smith, on the other hand, was enthusiastic in his review for *Film Comment*: "Like the modestly scaled, personally expressed, and psychologically observed *Mean Streets*, *Casino* is a fundamentally introspective film that embroiders a classic tragic narrative of hubris and retribution with an episodic surfeit of incidentals, anecdotes, and asides." Smith added, "Scorsese's genius, here as ever, is his insistence on depicting the interior emotional, psychological, and spiritual landscapes of his characters in startlingly heightened terms. With his busiest and most tawdry visuals and most relentlessly assaultive style to date, Scorsese is grimly intent on materializing in sensory and dramatic form the spiritual economy of materialism—its emptiness, its sound and fury signifying nihilism. . . . Critics have interpreted *Casino*'s wanton disregard for cinematic decorum and classic screen writing values, and its pushing of formal control beyond the breaking point, as symptoms of a great director going through the motions. On the contrary, they express Scorsese's if anything too–intense engagement with and abstraction of his material."

For his next film, *Kundun*, Scorsese again turned his attention to matters of faith, this time Buddhism instead of Christianity. Released in 1997, *Kundun* details the first twenty–four years of the life of the fourteenth Dalai Lama, the spiritual leader of Tibet. Working from a screenplay by Melissa Mathison and casting only Tibetan actors, Scorsese produced a film that met with a complicated critical response. While critics praised Scorsese for the beauty and

Starring Daniel Day–Lewis and Michelle Pfeiffer, Scorsese's 1993 adaptation of Edith Wharton's *The Age of Innocence* marked a change of pace for the director, as it focuses on one man's conflicting emotions concerning the cousin of his betrothed.

imagery of the film, many also found it lacking in both plot and character development. Roger Ebert of the *Chicago Sun–Times* wrote: "Once we understand that *Kundun* will not be a drama involving a plausible human character, we are freed to see the film as it is: an act of devotion, an act even of spiritual desperation, flung into the eyes of 20th century materialism. The film's visuals and music are rich and inspiring, and like a mass by Bach or a Renaissance church painting, it exists as an aid to worship: it wants to enhance, not question." Ebert also commented on the episodic plot structure, likening it to "illustrations bound into the book of life," a technique not well suited to cinema, "which hungers for story and character." Corliss described *Kundun* as Scorsese's "simplest and most experimental film." In spite of its flaws, Corliss concluded: "Scorsese devises a poem of textures and silences. Visions, nightmares, and history blend in a tapestry as subtle

as the Tibetans' gorgeous mandalas of sand. For some, *Kundun* will be a slog. For the open mind and eye, though, it is rapture in pictures."

In 1999 Scorsese directed *Bringing Out the Dead*, his long–anticipated return to the streets of New York. Based on a semi–autobiographical novel of the same name by Joe Connelly, *Bringing Out the Dead* is the story of fifty–six hours in the life of Frank Pierce (played by Nicholas Cage), an emergency medical services paramedic working the graveyard shift in Hell's Kitchen, haunted by the ghost of a young woman whose life he failed to save. *Detroit News* critic Tom Long wrote of the film: "It careens around corners at blinding speed, stops and starts with shrieks, and dances with the dead on every street corner . . . It all adds up to the awful and giddy feeling an ambulance driver in hell likely has, knowing at every turn you too may burst into flames.

Bringing Out the Dead stands along with Scorsese's best work—which stands alongside anyone's best work."

If you enjoy the works of Martin Scorsese, you might want to check out the following:

Donnie Brasco, a film starring Johnny Depp, 1996.
Serpico, a film starring Al Pacino, 1973.
Somebody Up There Likes Me, a film starring Paul Newman, 1956.

Scorsese's penchant for remakes, sequels, and adaptations is perhaps a reflection of his avid interest in film history—a subject upon which he has lectured extensively at NYU. Indeed, this interest informs all of his works. "He is constantly adding to his own videotape collection of old films, which he studies and reviews as fervently as a medieval monk poring over sacred manuscripts," wrote David Ansen in *Interview.* "Scorsese eats, sleeps and breathes movies, and his obsession has made him one of a handful of American movie directors whose movies really matter." Ansen is not alone in praising the importance of Scorsese's long career. Ebert wrote: "Scorsese is never on autopilot, never panders, never sells out, always goes for broke; to watch his films is to see a man risking his talent, not simply exercising it. He makes movies as well as they can be made."

■ **Biographical and Critical Sources**

BOOKS

Arnold, Frank, and others, *Martin Scorsese,* [Munich], 1986.
Bliss, Michael, *Martin Scorsese and Michael Cimino,* Metuchen, 1986.
Bliss, Michael, *The Word Made Flesh: Catholicism and Conflict in the Films of Martin Scorsese,* Scarecrow Press (Lanham, MD), 1995.
Brunette, Peter, editor, *Martin Scorsese: Interviews,* University Press of Mississippi, 1999.

Connelly, Marie Katheryn, *Martin Scorsese: An Analysis of His Feature Films, with a Filmography of His Entire Directorial Career,* McFarland (Jefferson, NC), 1993.
Contemporary Literary Criticism, Volume 20, Gale, 1982.
Contemporary Newsmakers 89, Volume 1, Gale, 1989.
Ebert, Roger, *The Future of the Movies: Interviews with Martin Scorsese, George Lucas, and Steven Spielberg,* Andrews and McMeel, 1991.
Ehrenstein, David, *The Scorsese Picture: The Art and Life of Martin Scorsese,* Carol Publishing Group, 1992.
Friedman, Lawrence S., *The Cinema of Martin Scorsese,* Continuum (New York City), 1997.
Hollywood Renaissance, A. S. Barnes, 1977.
Kelly, Mary Pat, *Martin Scorsese: The First Decade,* Redgrave Publishing, 1980.
Kelly, Mary Pat, *Martin Scorsese: A Journey,* Thunder's Mouth Press, 1992.
Kolker, Robert Phillip, *A Cinema of Loneliness: Penn, Kubrick, Coppola, Scorsese, Altman,* Oxford University Press, 1980, revised edition, 1988.
Lourdeaux, Lee, *Italian and Irish Filmmakers in America: Ford, Capra, Coppola, and Scorsese,* Temple University Press, 1993.
Pirie, David, editor, *Anatomy of the Movies,* Macmillan, 1981.
Scorsese, Martin, *Scorsese on Scorsese,* edited by Ian Christie and David Thompson, Faber, 1989.
Scorsese, Martin, and Michael Henry Wilson, *A Personal Journey with Martin Scorsese through American Movies,* Hyperion, 1997.
Stern, Lesley, *The Scorsese Connection,* Indiana University Press (Bloomington), 1995.
Weiss, Marian, *Martin Scorsese: A Guide to References and Resources,* [Boston], 1987.
Wood, Robin, *Hollywood from Vietnam to Reagan,* [New York], 1986.

PERIODICALS

Action, May–June, 1975.
America, November 17, 1979; August 20, 1988, p. 99.
American Film, November, 1982; November, 1986, p. 30; October, 1988, p. 44; March, 1989, p. 46.
Chicago Sun–Times, January 16, 1998; October 22, 1999.
Christian Century, May 12, 1976; September 14, 1988, p. 799.
Christian Science Monitor, February 19, 1976; May 1, 1978.
Commonweal, September 9, 1988, p. 467; December 7, 1990, p. 720; December 20, 1991, p. 748.
Cue, August 19, 1972; March 3, 1975.

Detroit News, October 22, 1999.

Economist, January 6, 1990, p. 87.

Esquire, February, 1975.

Film Comment, December, 1973; September–October, 1988, p. 32; January–February, 1996, p. 59; May–June, 1996, p. 4; May–June, 1998, pp. 16, 24, 29, 30, 46, 64, 68.

Film Heritage, spring, 1975.

Film Quarterly, spring, 1975; spring, 1986, p. 17; spring, 1996, p. 43.

Guardian Weekly, January 28, 1990, p. 87.

Horizon, January, 1981.

Hudson Review, autumn, 1975.

Interview, January, 1987, p. 49; November, 1991, p.16.

Los Angeles Times Book Review, November 26, 1989, p.29.

Maclean's, January 19, 1998, p. 66.

Monthly Film Bulletin, September, 1976; September, 1977.

Nation, November 5, 1990, p. 537; December 23, 1991, p. 826; December 18, 1995, p. 803.

National Review, January 28, 1991, p. 63; December 16, 1991, p. 56; January 26, 1998, p. 52.

New Republic, October 27, 1973; December 6, 1980; September 12, 1988, p. 28; December 25, 1995, p. 26.

Newsday, August 11, 1988.

New Statesman, November 24, 1989, p. 43; November 9, 1990, p. 12; March 6, 1992, p. 42.

Newsweek, May 16, 1977; February 21, 1983.

New York, September 15, 1986, p. 56; August 29, 1988, p. 50; September 24, 1990, p. 78; December 24, 1990, p. 69; November 27, 1995, p. 78; March 4, 1996, p. 32; January 5, 1998, p. 51.

New Yorker, October 8, 1973; February 9, 1976; July 4, 1977; December 8, 1980; September 5, 1988, p. 78; September 24, 1990, p. 98; September 13, 1993, p. 121; November 27, 1995, p. 46; December 8, 1997, p. 111.

New York Review of Books, October 13, 1988, p. 8; November 4, 1993, p. 3; January 11, 1996, p. 15.

New York Times, September 9, 1969; September 15, 1970; July 18, 1972; December 16, 1973; March 30, 1975; February 8, 1976; June 23, 1977; February 18, 1983; February 20, 1983; September 29, 1985; October 26, 1986.

New York Times Magazine, February 8, 1976.

People, August 9, 1988, p. 40; October 23, 1989, p. 12; December 4, 1995, p. 19.

Premiere, November, 1991, p. 60.

Rolling Stone, November 8, 1973; June 16, 1977; June 1, 1978; April 14, 1983; November 1, 1990, p. 58.

Sight and Sound, winter, 1973–74; autumn, 1977; summer, 1983.

Take One, December 30, 1969; May 21, 1976.

Time, August 15, 1988, p. 34; November 11, 1991, p. 84; September 20, 1993, p. 82; December 22, 1997.

Times Literary Supplement, January 12, 1990, p. 33.

Variety, June 17, 1987, p. 80.

Village Voice, April 24, 1978; May 29, 1978.

Washington Post Book World, November 19, 1989, p. 13.*

Charles Sheffield

Personal

Born June 25, 1935, in Hull, England; immigrated to the United States, 1971. *Education:* St. John's College, Cambridge, B.A., 1957, M.A., 1961, Ph.D., 1965.

Addresses

Home—2833 Gunarette Way, Silver Springs, MD 20906. *Agent*—Eleanor Wood, Spectrum Literary Agency, 111 Eighth Ave., Room 1501, New York, NY 10011.

Career

Earth Satellite Corp., chief scientist and board member, 1971—; freelance writer, c. 1978—.

Member

American Astronomical Society (former president), Science Fiction Writers of America (former president).

Awards, Honors

Sei–un Award, 1991, for *The McAndrew Chronicles;* John W. Campbell Award, 1992, for *Brother to Dragons;* Hugo Award and Nebula Award, both 1994, both for *Georgia on My Mind and Other Places.*

Writings

YOUNG ADULT FICTION

(With Jerry Pournelle) *Higher Education: A Jupiter Novel,* Tor, 1996.
The Billion Dollar Boy: A Jupiter Novel, Tor, 1997.
Putting Up Roots: A Jupiter Novel, Tor, 1997.
The Cyborg from Earth: A Jupiter Novel, Tor, 1998.

NOVELS

Sight of Proteus, Ace (New York City), 1978.
The Web Between the Worlds, Ace, 1979.
(With David F. Bischoff) *The Selkie,* Macmillan (New York City), 1982.
Erasmus Magister, Ace, 1982.
My Brother's Keeper, Ace, 1982.
Between the Strokes of Night, Baen (New York City), 1985.
The Nimrod Hunt, Baen, 1986, expanded version published as *The Mind Pool,* 1993.

Trader's World, Ballantine (New York City), 1988.

Proteus Unbound, Ballantine, 1989.

Proteus Manifest, Guild America (New York City), 1989.

Summertide, Ballantine, 1990.

Divergence, Easton Press (Norwalk, CT), 1991.

Transcendence, Ballantine, 1992.

Brother to Dragons, Easton Press, 1992.

Cold as Ice, Tor (New York City), 1992.

The Heritage Universe, Guild America, 1992.

Godspeed, Tor, 1993.

(With David F. Bischoff) *The Judas Cross,* Blue Moon (Eugene, OR), 1994.

Proteus Combined, Baen, 1994.

Proteus in the Underworld, Baen, 1995.

The Ganymede Club, Tor, 1995.

Convergence, Baen, 1997.

Tomorrow and Tomorrow, Bantam Spectra (New York City), 1998.

Aftermath, Bantam Spectra, 1998.

Transvergence, Pocket Books, 1999.

Starfire, Bantam Spectra, 1999.

Convergent Series, Baen, 2000.

The Spheres of Heaven, Baen, 2001.

SHORT STORY COLLECTIONS

Vectors, Ace, 1979.

Hidden Variables, Ace, 1981.

The McAndrew Chronicles, Tor, 1983, expanded version published as *One Man's Universe: The Continuing Chronicles of Arthur Morton McAndrew,* Tor, 1993.

Dancing with Myself, Baen, 1993.

Georgia on My Mind and Other Places, Tor, 1995.

(Editor) *How to Save the World,* Tor, 1995.

NONFICTION

Earthwatch: A Survey of the World from Space, Macmillan, 1981.

(Editor with John L. McLucas) *Commercial Operations in Space 1980–2000,* American Astronautical Society (San Diego, CA), 1981.

Man on Earth: How Civilization and Technology Changed the Face of the World, Macmillan, 1983.

(With Carol Rosin) *Space Careers,* Morrow (New York City), 1984.

(Editor with Marcello Alonso and Morton A. Kaplan) *The World of 2044: Technological Development and the Future of Society,* Paragon House (St. Paul, MN), 1994.

The Borderlands of Science, Baen, 1999.

OTHER

Also author of more than one hundred technical papers since 1965; contributor of stories and articles to periodicals, including *Analog.*

■ **Sidelights**

Charles Sheffield is one of the premiere voices in contemporary hard science fiction. A native of Great Britain, he earned his doctorate in physics from Cambridge University before coming to the United States to work in the space industry. He has worked on projects connected with the National Aeronautics and Space Administration (NASA) and is the chief scientist and board member of the Earth Satellite Corporation. Sheffield has also served in the past as president of the American Astronautical Society.

Sheffield took up writing science fiction somewhat late in his career, with his first novel in the genre, *Sight of Proteus,* seeing print in 1978. He has since become prolific in the field, and continues to produce stories and novels as well as nonfiction books and articles about space. Many critics agree that the scientific ideas explored in Sheffield's fiction are often spectacular, and his works have garnered him science fiction's most prestigious honors, including the Hugo and Nebula Awards. His novels often revolve around interplanetary or interspecies conflict. Sheffield has often been compared to fellow science fiction great Arthur C. Clarke.

Varied Output

Examining the morality of science, the novel *Sight of Proteus* introduces a future Earth where mankind has perfected the ability to change the shape of the human body through the trials of genetic research and plastic surgery. Most people utilize the technique solely for cosmetic reasons, but some abuse it. It is the task of Behrooz Wolf of the Biological Equipment Corporation to track down this abuse and put an end to it. In addition, Wolf must match wits with a man who is using the new technology to adapt the human body for life on other planets. Dan Miller in *Booklist* called *Sight of Proteus* an "intelligent and sophisticated" effort, and Carolanne Isola in the *Library Journal* hailed the book as "a compelling story and fascinating reading." *Publishers Weekly* contributor Barbara A. Bannon discussed Sheffield's debut, asserting that it proved him "one of the most imaginative, exciting talents" to break into science fiction during the 1970s.

Sheffield's 1995 novel takes readers to the twenty–second century, as humans have evolved into a myriad of forms, some so unrecognizable as to be confused with vicious beasts preying on outlying space outposts.

Sheffield worked in the genre of historical fantasy for 1982's *Erasmus Magister*. The book's hero is the grandfather of famed evolutionary theorist Charles Darwin who was also a well–respected scientist in his time. The novel shows the elder Darwin solving mysteries using scientific principles and deductive reasoning in much the same way as Sir Arthur Conan Doyle's Sherlock Holmes. Don Strachan in the *Los Angeles Times Book Review* recommended *Erasmus Magister* for adolescent readers, while Roland Green in *Booklist* praised the novel as having been "researched thoroughly" and "written well."

With David F. Bischoff, Sheffield collaborated on the 1982 horror novel *The Selkie*. Based on the Scottish

In his first "Jupiter" novel, Sheffield and collaborator Jerry Pournelle send young Rick Luban out of the failing public school classroom and into an asteroid mining colony in a novel designed for teen readers.

In 1979's *The Web Between the Worlds*, Sheffield explores the idea of a "space elevator"—a huge, strong cable that is grounded at the earth's equator and extends into space—a creation that Sheffield labels a "beanstalk." As Tom Easton of *Analog* reported, Clarke proposed a similar creation in his science fiction. "What is surprising," announced Easton, "is that someone should do a job that is in ways better than Clarke's, and that he should correct Clarke's physics in a way that makes the story's accomplishment even more spectacular." A reviewer for *Publishers Weekly* remarked that "the author manages to invoke ... the sense of wonder."

legend of wereseals who must mate with human females in order to reproduce, *The Selkie* follows the troubled marriage of Don and Mary Willis. While on an expedition at the Scottish coast, Mary is seduced by a man named Jamie McPherson, who is not exactly what he seems. A *Kirkus Reviews* contributor asserted: "Steady writing and rich backgrounds give a touch of class" to *The Selkie*. James McPeak, writing in *Voice of Youth Advocates* (*VOYA*), proclaimed it "one of the better supernatural novels to come down the pike." A *Publishers Weekly* reviewer found *The Selkie* "very readable." Sheffield teamed with Bischoff again for 1994's *The Judas Cross,* a tale which concerns an artifact supposedly containing the trapped soul of Judas Iscariot, betrayer of Jesus Christ.

Between the Strokes of Night, published in 1985, portrays a future in which the only humans to survive a worldwide nuclear holocaust were those traveling in space when it occurred. They have colonized other planets and have developed over time into two separate races—one that lives almost forever but has trouble reproducing, and one which is fertile, but has a relatively brief lifespan. Critics varied in their opinion of *Between the Strokes of Night.* *Publishers Weekly* contributor Sally A. Lodge called it a "tantalizing but less than satisfying novel." Gene Deweese in the *Science Fiction Review,* however, declared that *Between the Strokes of Night* "has more than enough sense of wonder" and is "one of the best of its kind for 1985."

In 1986, Sheffield published a novel entitled *The Nimrod Hunt,* which he later revised as *The Mind Pool.* This tale features a universe where there are four known races of sentient beings, of which humans are the only ones who are able to kill. Thus a human is needed for each team in search of rogue intelligent machines originally intended to patrol the far reaches of the universe, but which are now turning upon their creators. The second version of the story drew a positive response from critics. Thomas Pearson in *VOYA* affirmed that "the aliens [in *The Mind Pool*] are as well–realized and seem as interesting as the human characters," and summed up the book as "an entertaining and thought–provoking novel." Howard G. Zaharoff announced in *Kliatt* that "Sheffield speculates about the future with the best of them," then concluded that *The Mind Pool* "is hard SF at its best."

Sheffield again used a post–nuclear setting for *Trader's World.* In this novel, however, people have survived on Earth, but they exist in many splintered nations that are suspicious of one another. One society, the Traders, attempts to restore the world to what it once was. In the course of the novel, they

Spoiled teen Shelby Cheever finds his family's megabucks of no use when he is sent several light years away from earth and is rescued by a mining family that expects him to work for his keep in Sheffield's 1997 YA offering.

recruit an orphan named Mike and utilize a master computer named Daddy O. Penny Kaganoff, a contributor reviewing *Trader's World* for *Publishers Weekly* conceded that "each segment of the book is clever and colorful in itself," and Peter L. Robertson in *Booklist* asserted that Sheffield "has a pleasing way with his characters."

Resurrects "Proteus" Series

Sheffield returned to the world of Behrooz Wolf with 1989's *Proteus Unbound.* In this sequel to *Sight of Proteus,* Wolf's investigative work sends him on

CHARLES SHEFFIELD

TRANSVERGENCE

"The new Arthur C. Clarke. . . ."
—*The Washington Post*

Containing both 1992's *Transference* and 1997's *Convergence*, Sheffield's 1999 novel brings readers to the Heritage Universe, where humans share their planet with a group of large, insect–like creatures and the vicious, rapacious Zardalu, as well as what seems to be an ancient race of builders.

travels to the Outer System, which is a rival to his own Earth and its allies. War threatens the two systems, but the odd phenomena Wolf is tracking turns out to be the work of a space pirate named Black Ransome. A *Publishers Weekly* contributor praised *Proteus Unbound* as "a fine sequel." Sheffield penned another book about Wolf, 1995's *Proteus in the Underworld*. This title sees Wolf drawn from retirement by a young woman named Sondra Dearborn employed by the Office of Form Control. Dearborn enlists Wolf's aid to solve yet another form–change

mystery. Mary K. Chelton in *VOYA* hailed *Proteus in the Underworld* as "interesting, accessible hard science fiction."

In 1990, Sheffield began another fiction series, set in the Heritage Universe. In *Summertide,* the known universe is thought to be populated by only two races of sentient beings—humans and Cecropians, a race of large, bug–like creatures. A third race, the deadly and vicious Zardalu, is known to have existed, but is believed to be extinct until the heroes and heroines of *Summertide* encounter them in *Divergence,* the second novel in the series. In all of the books of the "Heritage Universe" series, including the third, *Transcendence,* the characters find huge artifacts strewn about the universe—the products of what turns out to be a fourth race, the unknown Builders. In 1997 Sheffield added a fourth novel to the series, *Convergence.*

Critical reaction to the "Heritage Universe" series has been varied. "I found myself gripped," reported Gerald Jonas in the *New York Times Book Review,* speaking of his experience reading *Summertide.* He also observed that Sheffield was obviously "concerned with the inner life of his characters." *Publishers Weekly* reviewer Sybil Steinberg hailed *Summertide* as a "promising first installment." *Divergence,* according to Jackie Cassada in the *Library Journal,* proves to be a "fast–paced sequel," though a *Kirkus Reviews* contributor judged that it contained "no real surprises, but no disappointments either." Roland Green in *Booklist* labeled *Divergence* "the liveliest sort of hard–science sf." Of *Transcendence,* the third installment of the series, *Publishers Weekly* critic Sybil Steinberg concluded that the "narrative is smooth, and the joys, pitfalls and dangers of exploration are conveyed well."

In 1992, fans of Sheffield's work were treated to *Cold as Ice.* This novel is set after a bloody interplanetary war in which characters hunt for a lost secret weapon. The weapon turns out to be a new species scientifically created by humans. *Booklist's* Roland Green felt it was quite possibly "Sheffield's best book yet." David E. Jones in the Chicago *Tribune Books* was similarly complimentary, putting forth the opinion that the characters' struggle against each other "is ... unlike any conflict that has invaded your imagination in novels past."

Brother to Dragons, which also saw print in 1992, drew comparisons of Sheffield with famed nineteenth–century British novelist Charles Dickens. Dickens's heroes were often poor, handicapped, or otherwise disadvantaged. In *Brother to Dragons* Sheffield's story hinges upon Job, born with birth defects to a crack–addicted mother, abandoned, and

A JUPITER™ NOVEL

PUTTING UP ROOTS

Charles Sheffield

The promise of a new life in a farming paradise is quickly dashed when Josh Kerrigen, his autistic cousin Dawn, and several other homeless teens find themselves instead sent to a planet being torn apart by competing mining interests.

not expected to live beyond infancy. Job not only survives, but after being virtually drafted into the underworld of crime, leads a revolution against the privileged classes. *Brother to Dragons* prompted Dennis A. Hinrichs in *Kliatt* to remark that "Sheffield is a witty and clever writer," while Green predicted in another *Booklist* review that this novel "will ... attract the broader range of readers that Sheffield is coming to deserve." Penny Kaganoff summed up the book for *Publishers Weekly* as "a highly readable, entertaining novel by one of science fiction's brightest lights."

Godspeed features another young protagonist, Jay Hara. He is stuck on the isolated planet Erin, which, like many other colonized outposts, is suffering a

slow decline because of the mysterious malfunction of the Godspeed drive that in the past had allowed faster–than–light space travel. But Hara and his family take in a fugitive, who, before he dies, presents Hara with what might be the key to another Godspeed drive. *Godspeed* prompted Cassada in *Library Journal* to state that "Sheffield never slights his characters or his science," while Karen Jay Fowler, critiquing the novel in the *Washington Post Book World*, assured readers that its "pace never flags, until we reach a satisfyingly smart and exciting climax."

SF for Teens

Sheffield, in collaboration with fellow famed science–fiction author Jerry Pournelle, began his "Jupiter" series—books aimed at more adolescent fans of science fiction—with 1996's *Higher Education*. This novel has the premise that the public school systems have deteriorated to such a degree that students are unable to receive a suitable education—until they are taken under the wing of private corporations and strictly trained for their jobs. Such is the case with protagonist Rick Luban, who is sent to work mining asteroids. A *Kirkus Reviews* contributor announced that "the novel opens as a dead–on satire on public education," and *Publishers Weekly* reviewer Steinberg lauded it as a "high–spirited exemplar" of the "SF coming–of–age novel." Sheffield continued the "Jupiter" series without Pournelle, producing titles such as *The Billion Dollar Boy, Putting Up Roots,* and *The Cyborg from Earth.*

The Billon Dollar Boy takes place one–and–a–half centuries later than *Higher Education,* and much farther from Earth. Spoiled rich kid Shelby Cheever starts out on a space cruise and ends up being hurtled twenty–seven light years out, where he is rescued by a family that mines interstellar dust clouds. Shelby learns to adapt and become a useful member of the crew. Susan Hamburger of *Library Journal* called the book "well–written," and *Booklist's* Green asserted that Sheffield puts his own brand on the familiar coming–of–age theme, "providing first–rate scientific and technical extrapolation, brisk pacing and a more plausible depiction of his young hero's maturation."

Putting Up Roots, the third novel in the "Jupiter" series, finds Josh Kerrigen and other abandoned teenagers shipped off to a distant farming planet. Instead of a benign agrarian paradise unpopulated by intelligent life, the ragtag teens meet a native species called ruperts and end up in the middle of a war between two giant corporations over the rights

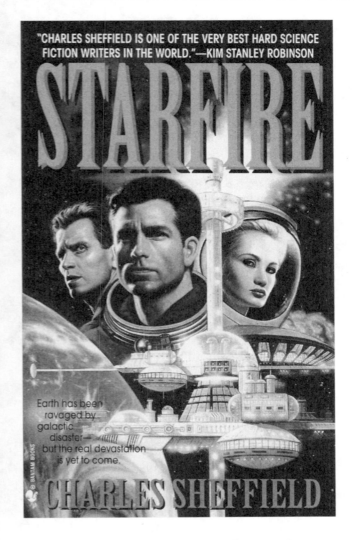

"CHARLES SHEFFIELD IS ONE OF THE VERY BEST HARD SCIENCE FICTION WRITERS IN THE WORLD."—KIM STANLEY ROBINSON

STARFIRE

Earth has been ravaged by galactic disaster— but the real devastation is yet to come.

CHARLES SHEFFIELD

Sheffield's 1999 sci–fi offering takes place in the near future, as the aftereffects of a supernova promise to destroy what is left of Planet Earth unless an international space colony can shield the embattled planet.

plausible and imaginative." *Hidden Variables*, another Sheffield collection, was printed in 1981. Its stories, according to Valentin R. Zivada in *Kliatt*, are "all stimulating and worth reading at any level." *Dancing with Myself*, which also included scientific articles along with the stories, became available in 1993; this collection brought rave reviews from Easton in *Analog*. "Sheffield," Easton stated, "is one of the few who can do it all—both the science and the fiction—himself." Sheffield also penned the *McAndrew Chronicles, Georgia on My Mind and Other Places*, and edited a collection of short fiction by other authors entitled *How to Save the World*.

Sheffield has also made his mark with nonfiction books about space. *Earthwatch: A Survey of the World from Space* and *Man on Earth: How Civilization and Technology Changed the Face of the World* both feature photographs taken from space and computer–processed by Sheffield's Earth Satellite Corporation. When *Earthwatch* first saw print in 1981, a *Choice* reviewer pointed out that its photographs are "far superior to those in any previous book of its kind." Laurie Tynan in *Library Journal* hailed *Earthwatch* as a "very attractive collection of previously unpublished pictures." William Bradley Hooper in *Booklist* appreciated *Man on Earth* as a "fascinating, large–format book."

If you enjoy the works of Charles Sheffield, you might want to check out the following books and films:

David Brin, *Earth,* 1990.
Lois McMaster Bujold, *Brothers in Arms,* 1988.
Dan Simmons, *Hyperion,* 1989.
2001: A Space Odyssey, a film directed by Stanley Kubrick, 1968.

---

to mine hidden mineral wealth. A *Publishers Weekly* reviewer praised the novel's characterization, calling it "the richest of the Jupiter series so far," and *Booklist's* Green echoed that sentiment, saying "Josh and his autistic cousin, Dawn, are the best drawn of any in the series so far."

Throughout the years he was penning novels, Sheffield was also crafting short stories, and he has put out several collections of shorter fiction. The first of these is 1979's *Vectors*, which Spider Robinson, another well–known science fiction author, reviewed in *Analog*. He remarked that "Sheffield's scientific speculations are fascinating indeed, informed and

Sheffield teamed with Carol Rosin to create 1984's *Space Careers*, a volume aimed at helping adolescents find the proper educational facilities and opportunities to prepare them for careers related to all aspects of the space program. Denise P. Donovin in *Booklist* applauded it as "a valuable resource," while Pat Royal praised it in *School Library Journal* as "a clear, concise, readable, well thought–out book." Ten years later, he helped to edit *The World of 2044: Technological Development and the Future of Society*, which includes speculative ideas such as nasal spray birth control and underwater amusement parks. According to a critic for the *Futurist,* the volume "portrays futures worth getting excited about—and working for."

■ Biographical and Critical Sources

PERIODICALS

Analog, January, 1980, Tom Easton, review of *The Web Between the Worlds,* pp. 167–68; May, 1980, Spider Robinson, review of *Vectors,* pp. 165, 173; May, 1994, Tom Easton, review of *Dancing with Myself,* p. 166.

Booklist, January 1, 1979, Dan Miller, review of *Sight of Proteus,* p. 740; September 15, 1982, Roland Green, review of *Erasmus Magister,* p. 95; September 15, 1983, William Bradley Hooper, review of *Man on Earth: How Civilization and Technology Changed the Face of the World—A Survey from Space,* p. 122; May 1, 1984, Denise P. Donovin, review of *Space Careers,* p. 1215; November 15, 1988, Peter L. Robertson, review of *Trader's World,* p. 544; February 1, 1991, Roland Green, review of *Divergence,* p. 1115; June 15, 1992, Roland Green, review of *Cold as Ice,* p. 1811; October 15, 1992, Roland Green, review of *Brother to Dragons,* p. 407; September 1, 1995, p. 48; January 1, 1997, p. 826; April 1, 1997, Roland Green, review of *The Billion Dollar Boy,* p. 1283; August, 1997, Roland Green, review of *Putting Up Roots,* p. 1887.

Choice, February, 1982, review of *Earthwatch: A Survey of the World from Space,* pp. 785–86.

Futurist, January–February, 1995, review of *The World of 2044: Technological Development and the Future of Society,* p. 62.

Kirkus Reviews, February 15, 1982, review of *The Selkie,* pp. 229–30; January 1, 1991, review of *Divergence,* p. 24; May 1, 1992, p. 578; April 15, 1996, review of *Higher Education,* p. 607; November 1, 1996.

Kliatt, winter, 1982, Valentin R. Zivada, review of *Hidden Variables,* p. 23; March, 1993, Dennis A. Hinrichs, review of *Brother to Dragons,* p. 20; July, 1993, Howard G. Zaharoff, review of *The Mind Pool,* p. 20.

Library Journal, January 1, 1979, Carolanne Isola, review of *Sight of Proteus,* p. 130; October 1, 1981, Laurie Tynan, review of *Earthwatch: A Survey of the World from Space,* p. 1936; February 15, 1991, Jackie Cassada, review of *Divergence,* p. 224; November 15, 1993, Jackie Cassada, review of *Godspeed,* p. 102; December, 1996, Susan Hamburger, review of *The Billion Dollar Boy,* p. 152; August, 1997, p. 141; January, 1998, p. 149.

Los Angeles Times Book Review, August 1, 1982, Don Strachan, review of *Erasmus Magister,* p. 8.

New York Times Book Review, March 25, 1990, Gerald Jonas, review of *Summertide,* p. 30.

Publishers Weekly, July 31, 1978, Barbara A. Bannon, review of *Sight of Proteus,* p. 95; June 25, 1979, Barbara A. Bannon, review of *The Web Between the Worlds,* pp. 114, 116; March 12, 1982, Barbara A. Bannon, review of *The Selkie,* p. 77; June 14, 1985, Sally A. Lodge, review of *Between the Strokes of Night,* p. 70; October 14, 1988, Penny Kaganoff, review of *Trader's World,* p. 69; February 10, 1989, Penny Kaganoff, review of *Proteus Unbound,* p. 65; December 15, 1989, Sybil Steinberg, review of *Summertide,* p. 60; May 4, 1992, Sybil Steinberg, review of *Transcendence,* p. 45; January 16, 1995, pp. 442–43; October 19, 1992, Penny Kaganoff, review of *Brother to Dragons,* p. 74; May 27, 1996, Sybil Steinberg, review of *Higher Education,* p. 70; November 4, 1996, p. 78; August 11, 1997, review of *Putting Up Roots,* p. 391; February 9, 1998, p. 80.

School Library Journal, April, 1985, Pat Royal, review of *Space Careers,* pp. 108–9.

Science Fiction Review, November, 1985, Gene Deweese, review of *Between the Strokes of Night,* p. 22.

Tribune Books (Chicago), August 30, 1992, David E. Jones, "Williamson, Bova and Pohl Are Turning Their Lights on Mars," p. 7.

Voice of Youth Advocates, October, 1982, James McPeak, review of *The Selkie,* p. 46; December, 1992, p. 295; October, 1993, Thomas Pearson, review of *The Mind Pool,* p. 234; December, 1995, Mary K. Chelton, review of *Proteus in the Underworld,* p. 317; June, 2000, Joyce Yen, review of *Starfire,* p. 128.

Washington Post Book World, January 30, 1994, Karen Jay Fowler, review of *Godspeed,* p. 15.

—Sketch by Elizabeth Wenning

Gloria Skurzynski

■ Personal

Surname pronounced "skur–*zin*–ski"; born July 6, 1930, in Duquesne, PA; daughter of Aylmer Kearney (a steelworker) and Serena (a telegraph operator; maiden name, Decker) Flister; married Edward Joseph Skurzynski (an aerospace engineer), December 1, 1951; children: Serena Rose, Janine, Joan, Alane, Lauren. *Education:* Attended Mount Mercy College (now Carlow College), 1948–50. *Hobbies and other interests:* Science, technology.

■ Addresses

Home—2559 Spring Haven Dr., Salt Lake City, UT 84109. *E–mail*—skurz@ix.netcom.com. *Agent*—Edite Kroll Literary Agency, 12 Grayhurst Pk., Portland, ME 04102.

■ Career

Writer. U.S. Steel Corp., statistical clerk, 1950–52.

■ Member

International Women's Forum, Society of Children's Book Writers and Illustrators, Utah Women's Forum.

■ Awards, Honors

Golden Kite Honor Book Award for nonfiction, Society of Children's Book Writers, 1978, for *Bionic Parts for People: The Real Story of Artificial Organs and Replacement Parts*; *Horn Book* Honor Book, and Booklist Reviewer's Choice Award, American Library Association (ALA), both 1979, and Christopher Award, 1980, all for *What Happened in Hamelin*; Best Books for Young Adults Award, ALA, and Notable Children's Trade Book in the Field of Social Studies, National Council for the Social Studies and the Children's Book Council, both 1981, and *Booklist* Reviewer's Choice Award, ALA, 1982, all for *Manwolf*; Golden Kite Award for fiction, *School Library Journal* Best Books of 1983 Award, and Best Books for Young Adults Award, ALA, all 1983, all for *The Tempering*; Utah Children's Choice Book Award, 1984, for *Lost in the Devil's Desert*; Golden Spur Award, Western Writers of America, 1985, for *Trapped in the Slickrock Canyon*; Science Writing Award, American Institute of Physics, 1992, for *Almost the Real Thing: Simulation in Your High–Tech World*; *School Library Journal* Best Books of 1992 Award, for *Good–bye, Billy Radish*; *Trapped in the Slickrock Canyon* and *Bionic Parts for People* were Junior Literary Guild selections.

■ Writings

The Magic Pumpkin, illustrated by Rocco Negri, Four Winds, 1971.

The Remarkable Journey of Gustavus Bell, illustrated by Tim and Greg Hildebrandt, Abingdon, 1973.

The Poltergeist of Jason Morey, Dodd, 1975.

In a Bottle with a Cork on Top, illustrated by Glo Coalson, Dodd, 1976.

(Adapter) *Two Fools and a Faker: Three Lebanese Folk Tales,* illustrated by William Papas, Lothrop, 1977.

Martin by Himself, illustrated by Lynn Munsinger, Houghton, 1979.

What Happened in Hamelin (novel; also known as *Rattenfanger von Hameln*), Four Winds, 1979.

Honest Andrew, illustrated by David Wiesner, Harcourt, 1980.

Manwolf, Clarion, 1981.

(Contributor) *Three Folktales,* Houghton, 1981.

The Tempering (novel), Clarion, 1983.

The Minstrel in the Tower, illustrated by Julek Heller, Random House, 1988.

Dangerous Ground, Bradbury, 1989.

Good-bye, Billy Radish (novel), Bradbury, 1992.

Here Comes the Mail, Bradbury, 1992.

Caitlin's Big Idea, illustrated by Cathy Diefendorf, Troll, 1995.

Cyberstorm, Macmillan, 1995.

(With Alane Ferguson) *Mystery of the Spooky Shadow,* illustrated by Jeffrey Lindberg, Troll, 1996.

Virtual War, Simon & Schuster, 1997.

Spider's Voice, Atheneum, 1999.

Rockbuster, Atheneum, 2001.

"THE MOUNTAIN WEST ADVENTURE" SERIES

Lost in the Devil's Desert, illustrated by Joseph M. Scrofani, Lothrop, 1982.

Trapped in the Slickrock Canyon, illustrated by Daniel San Souci, Lothrop, 1984.

Caught in the Moving Mountains, illustrated by Ellen Thompson, Lothrop, 1984,

Swept in the Wave of Terror, Lothrop, 1985.

"YOUR HIGH-TECH WORLD" SERIES

Robots: Your High-Tech World, Bradbury, 1990.

Almost the Real Thing: Simulation in Your High-Tech World, Bradbury, 1991.

Get the Message: Telecommunications in Your High-Tech World, Bradbury, 1993.

Know the Score: Video Games in Your High-Tech World, Bradbury, 1994.

"NATIONAL PARKS MYSTERY" SERIES; WITH ALANE FERGUSON

Wolf Stalker, National Geographic Society, 1997.

Rage of Fire, National Geographic Society, 1998.

Cliff Hanger, National Geographic Society, 1999.

Deadly Water, National Geographic Society, 1999.

The Hunted, National Geographic Society, 2000.

Ghost Horses, National Geographic Society, 2000.

NONFICTION

Bionic Parts for People: The Real Story of Artificial Organs and Replacement Parts, illustrated by Frank Schwartz, Four Winds, 1978.

Safeguarding the Land: Women at Work in Parks, Forests, and Rangelands, foreword by Cecil D. Andrus, Harcourt, 1981.

Zero Gravity, Bradbury, 1994.

Waves: The Electromagnetic Universe, National Geographic Society, 1996.

Discover Mars, National Geographic Society, 1998.

On Time: From Seasons to Split Seconds, National Geographic Society, 2000.

OTHER

Contributor of articles and short stories to periodicals, including *Teen* and *School Library Journal.*

■ Adaptations

What Happened in Hamelin was adapted for film and telecast by the Columbia Broadcasting System on "Storybreak" in 1987.

■ Sidelights

"Perhaps if I'd known how long it would take me to acquire satisfactory writing skills," wrote author Gloria Skurzynski in the *Fifth Book of Junior Authors and Illustrators,* "I would have been too intimidated to try. But with the innocence of ignorance, I began putting words on paper." Skurzynski, who had been a busy wife and mother, started writing children's books after the last of her five daughters began school, a time when she realized she would need something other than bringing up her children to fill her life. She was also encouraged by the Pulitzer prize-winning poet Phyllis McGinley, whose verse

Skurzynski had read after seeing McGinley on the cover of *Time*. When Skurzynski posted a fan letter, McGinley replied, and a correspondence began which lasted until the poet died in 1978. Reacting to Skurzynski's observation–filled letters, McGinley told her that she had talent and should consider writing professionally. Now, Skurzynski is the author of more than forty popular and acclaimed books for children and young adults.

Skurzynski was born at the beginning of the Great Depression in Duquesne, Pennsylvania, a small town built around the steel mill in which her father, Aylmer (Al) Flister, worked. Her family was fortunate because her father's job allowed them to weather the Depression with relative ease. Mr. Flister had held dreams of succeeding in Hollywood as a producer or director—he was offered a job in the production department of Metro–Goldwyn–Mayer—but finally decided that he would actually be happier staying in Duquesne and working in the mill. To pursue his interest in acting and theatre on the side, Mr. Flister staged amateur theatrical productions, a total of ninety before he died. Serena Flister, Skurzynski's mother, worked as a telegraph operator at Western Union; of her four children, only Gloria survived infancy.

As a girl, Skurzynski was a devoted library patron and often attended movies. "The books I checked out of the library and the movies I saw each week made me believe in romance," she once said. The glamorous, hero–filled world she was admitted to through movies and books was one unlike her own hometown, which was inhabited by hard–working citizens representing a rich diversity of ethnicities. Skurzynski once described the conversations she would overhear while riding around Duquesne in the daytime: "The bus would buzz with the clicking consonants and sibilant syllables of Polish, Russian, and Slovak words, underscored by liquid Italian vowels."

Part of her "National Parks Mystery" series, Skurzynski's 1997 novel finds young Jack and Ashley Landon and their foster brother Troy camping out at Yellowstone while their veterinarian mom investigates a reported killing by a wolf.

Abandoned College Plans

After graduating first in her high school class, Skurzynski received scholarships from several colleges. She decided to attend Mount Mercy, a Catholic college whose students were exclusively women, because she had been charmed by a group of nuns she had seen playing in the college's yard during her visit. Unfortunately, her delight wouldn't last; the nuns were strict and had little tolerance. This oppressive atmosphere and her own inability to choose a field to major in made Skurzynski quit after her sophomore year and get a job at U.S. Steel Corporation in Pittsburgh. She married Edward Skurzynski on December 1, 1951, as he was finishing his senior year of college. Before the end of the decade, she and her husband were the parents of five children, all daughters, who immediately became the center of their lives. As Skurzynski once wrote: "The playpen became a permanent fixture in the living room and the high chair stood rooted to the dining room floor, cemented in place by spilled baby food. All my tablecloths were plastic. By the time our oldest daughter reached six, she'd become expert at folding diapers. Had I yet thought about being a writer? Ha! I wrote nothing longer than grocery lists."

By the time her youngest daughter was about to enter school, though, Skurzynski had begun to think that she should go back to college and become a history teacher. Her plans were broken when her husband, an aerospace engineer, was transferred to Utah. Once in her new home, Skurzynski postponed her plans for college so she could have time to adjust to her new surroundings. "Then . . . pure chance, the element that controls so much of our lives, took over and changed my direction for good," she later recalled. That was when Skurzynski began to correspond with Phyllis McGinley. The housewife filled her letters with observations such as: "There's something hypnotic about a pot of boiling macaroni." She began to write stories, but for a year and a half she received nothing but rejections from magazines. Finally, on her fifty–eighth submission, Skurzynski sold a short story to 'Teen.

Positive Reception for Grisly Tale

The difficulties Skurzynski had in making her first sale did not disappear once she became a published writer. She struggled, but managed to have several picture books published. She enjoyed writing children's novels more, however, and her interest in history made her lean naturally toward historical fiction. Just as being a mother had absorbed all of Skurzynski's time, now writing was her passion. In the *Fifth Book of Junior Authors and Illustrators*, Skurzynski wrote, "While I write a novel, I'm only half aware of what's happening in my family, my house, and the world." Her ability to immerse herself in her created worlds began to pay off: she received a Christopher Award for her historical novel *What Happened in Hamelin*. Skurzynski's retelling of the Pied Piper story is based on actual documents from the town of Hamelin, Germany, which indicate that, in 1284, a relative stranger led 130 children from the town into the surrounding mountains. Neither the Piper nor the children ever returned. Skurzynski's narrator, Geist, is a thirteen–year–old orphan who works in a bakery and is despondent because of the baker's harshness toward him and the drudgery of his medieval life. He becomes excited, though, when the Piper comes to town and promises to rid it of the rats that trouble the inhabitants. When he successfully does so (manipulating the children to do his work for him) and is then cheated out of his payment, he stays in Hamelin as a musician, loved by the children both for his music and the sweets he gives them. What no one suspects is that the sweets contain a drug

which gives the children hallucinations, enabling the Piper to ensnare them with his piping and lead them away from their home into slavery. A *Horn Book* reviewer wrote that "the pompous councilman, the simple–minded priest, and the children are realistically and convincingly depicted," and a contributor to the *Bulletin of the Center for Children's Books* stated that the story "builds nicely toward the tense final tragedy." In the *New York Times Book Review*, Natalie Babbitt noted that "the reader is left with a strong, lingering awareness of mankind's ever–present corruptibility."

History more recent than that of thirteenth–century Europe fills Skurzynski's 1983 novel *The Tempering*, which is concerned with her father's past. As Skurzynski once wrote, "For a long while I'd wanted to write about my father's boyhood, about his decision to drop out of school to be a steelworker, his first job in the steel mill when he was only fourteen, his love of music and stage shows." Luckily, Skurzynski was able to read sections of the book to her father just before he passed away in 1982. Canaan, a fictionalized Duquesne, serves as the setting for *The Tempering*, the story of a fifteen–year–old boy living in 1912 Pennsylvania. Karl Kerner is eager to quit school so he can work in the steel mill, even though his teacher, Yulyona, encourages him to continue attending class. Because Karl is in love with Yulyona he considers taking her advice, but ultimately goes to work in the mill only to lose his job on his first day when another man pulls a stunt and gets both himself and Karl fired. The metaphor that gives the novel its title compares the process of tempering steel, during which it is melted and formed into shape, with Karl's development into a man throughout the pages of the book. Outside of Karl's struggles, Skurzynski evokes the atmosphere of an early twentieth–century mill town. According to a *Bulletin for the Center for Children's Books* contributor, Skurzynski paints "a vivid picture of the way in which poverty and life–style are shaped by the environment." In the *New York Times Book Review*, Martha Bennett Stiles praised *The Tempering* for its "satisfying portrayals of love, friendship and neighborly decency."

Back to Duquesne

Skurzynski's multiethnic hometown also served as an inspiration for the setting of her novel *Good–bye, Billy Radish*, which tells the story of Hank Kerner and Bazyli Radichevych, a Ukrainian boy whom Hank calls "Billy Radish." Billy, much like Karl in *The Tempering*, looks forward to his fourteenth birthday when he can go to work in the steel mill. The coming–of–age story shows how the two boys, despite their different backgrounds and languages, create a friendship that overcomes those superficial boundaries. "To me," Skurzynski once wrote, "humankind's most pervasive and deadly failing is to see the otherness of people rather than the sameness. Wistfully, I hope that in some future century, goodwill and tolerance for everyone's differences will become a universal virtue." A *School Library Journal* contributor called *Good–bye, Billy Radish* a "richly textured, lovingly crafted historical novel."

Aside from crafting successful and acclaimed fiction, Skurzynski has also written several nonfiction books. *Bionic Parts for People: The Real Story of Artificial Organs and Replacement Parts*, which received a Golden Kite Honor Book Award, was inspired by family members in the same way some of her fiction has been. This time, two of Skurzynski's daughters served as her motivation: one had worked for the Division of Artificial Organs at the University of Utah, and another had studied in a building in which organ research was conducted. *Bionic Parts* examines the medical field's attempts to create machinery based on the functioning of normal, healthy body organs that can replace dysfunctional or injured organs. A reviewer for the *Bulletin of the Center for Children's Books* called *Bionic Parts* "an excellent survey of the subject."

Fascinated by Emerging Technologies

Another of Skurzynski's nonfiction books, *Almost the Real Thing: Simulation in Your High–Tech World*, the second in a series, details some of the techniques scientists use to simulate real–world situations in order to test ideas or products and improve upon them in the early stages of development. A *School Library Journal* reviewer called *Almost the Real Thing* "an excellent and lively book on an offbeat topic," and the American Institute of Physics awarded the book its Science Writing Award in 1992.

Skurzynski's interest in the high–tech world expanded alongside developments in personal computing, virtual gaming, and the Internet. Her 1995 title, *Cyberstorm*, is set in the year 2015, when the friendship between teens Darcy and Erik comes to an abrupt halt after a betrayal. Darcy's family then moves into a restriction–filled community of new homes, and she is miserable. Only her beloved dog provides companionship, but the local authorities threaten this as well after a neighbor complains about barking. As the Animal Control workers near, Darcy takes refuge in a virtual reality machine belonging to her neighbor, Mrs. Galloway. A series of time–warp moments follow, while an actual tornado outside poses a bigger threat. Marsha Valance, writing in *Voice of Youth Advocates*, commended

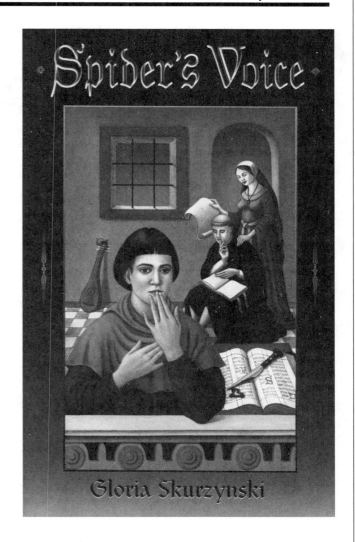

Woven around the twelfth–century romance between Heloise and Abelard, Skurzynski's acclaimed 1999 novel adds a new thread to the classic tale in Aran, a mute boy trained as a spinner who becomes a loyal servant to the love–struck Abelard.

Skurzynski for creating "well–developed characters, breakneck pace, and believable computer world [that] combine to make this novel a real winner." Valance compared the writer to acclaimed cyber-science fiction writer William Gibson, while *Publishers Weekly* likened *Cyberstorm* to a 1950 short story from a master in the genre, Ray Bradbury. The review called it an "imaginative science fiction tale [that] never lets up its thrilling pace."

A True "Game Boy"

In her 1997 book, *Virtual War*, Skurzynski delves into the world of three–dimensional gaming for her premise—a storyline that many reviewers predicted would resonate well with adolescent readers. Set in the year 2080, *Virtual War* presents the planet as a place with just two million inhabitants, due to years of environmental and biological disaster. The survivors live in domed cities awaiting news of improved ecological prospects outside. The plot focuses upon 14–year–old Corgan, a wholly bioengineered teen designed with reflexes that enable him to win at any electronic game. He is the creation of the Council of the Western Hemisphere Foundation, one of the forces that has agreed to fight a virtual war whose victor will receive a coveted archipelago that is fit for human habitation. Corgan will be the primary warrior, but in the days before the onset, he meets the surprise other members of his team: a teen code–breaker named Sharla and a contemptuous ten–year–old strategist, Brig. For Corgan, this is first contact with actual humans, and soon he begins to question the value system with which he has been indoctrinated, one that teaches to win at all costs. "However bleak, Corgan eventually begins to realize that 'real' life is still desirable over the 'perfect' virtual world," noted *Voice of Youth Advocates* reviewer Linda Roberts, who also found *Virtual War* "a quick read" and one that "holds the reader's interest to the very last page."

Skurzynski returned to historical topics with her 1999 book, *Spider's Voice*. The work is a retelling of a classic doomed romance tale from twelfth–century Paris, the story of Heloise and Abelard. Skurzynski's heroine is renamed Eloise, and she recounts her story through the narrative voice of a mute shepherd boy. Eloise is a brilliant and spirited girl raised by her ambitious but untrustworthy uncle, while Abelard is a respected theologian and Roman Catholic priest. The two fall in love, and after Abelard rescues the boy Aran from a brutish circus master, he realizes that the mute Aran is the ideal servant, because the affair with Eloise must be kept secret at all costs. They begin to call him Spider, and he becomes devoted to the pair. Then Eloise becomes pregnant, and her uncle forces them into a marriage, which they then agree to keep secret in order to protect Abelard's career; the uncle becomes enraged and viciously maims Abelard in front of Spider—"but that trauma leads him to find, eventually, a voice of his own," noted a *Kirkus Reviews* assessment, which described it as a "spirited retelling." *Booklist*'s Ilene Cooper also praised the tale: "Throughout, Skurzynski's writing is vivid and intriguing," while Barbara Scotto, writing in *School Library Journal,* described Skurzynski as "masterful in her characterizations, showing the subtleties of each person's nature and the ways in which they are changed from the circumstances of their lives."

"National Parks" Series

In the late 1990s, Skurzynski began to write a series of whodunits for teens with her daughter, Alane Ferguson. Published by the National Geographic Society, these "National Parks" mysteries are set inside various scenic nature and forest preserves belonging the U. S. National Park Service. They feature the Landon family, whose veterinarian mother and photographer father often take work assignments that bring them to one of the National Parks; twelve–year–old Jack and his younger sister, Ashley, come along, often accompanied by one of the foster children that the Landons host from time to time. The first in the series is *Wolf Stalker,* published in 1997, which introduces the Landons on their trip to the first National Park ever created, Yellowstone, whose boundaries date back to an 1872 law. Park officials have asked Dr. Landon to investigate a report that a hunting dog was killed by a pack of wolves. With the family is Troy, a troubled youth with a difficult past. The youngsters spend an unplanned night outside in the park, and a power struggle erupts between the trio. They witness the shooting of a wolf and nurse it through the night. In the end, all are rescued, and the poacher is caught. "This exciting book emphasizes the natural beauty and dangers of the wild," noted Marlene Gawron in a *School Library Journal* review.

In the third National Parks mystery, *Cliff Hanger,* the Landons arrive at Colorado's Mesa Verde preserve. Dr. Landon has been contacted by rangers to look into reports that a cougar in the park is attacking humans. This time, Jack and Ashley are joined by foster sibling Lucky, whose sneaky behavior makes almost all the Landons apprehensive—except for Jack, who has developed a crush on the girl. "The authors do a fine job of integrating lots of material into an exciting story," opined Cooper in a *Booklist* review. In the next book, *Deadly Water,* Skurzynski and Ferguson send the Landons to the Florida Everglades, where several manatees have inexplicably died. Jack and Ashley's foster sibling Bridger comes along as well, and learns as much about himself as he does water mammals. "An engaging read, the story features likable protagonists and plenty of action and suspense," wrote Shelle Rosenfeld in *Booklist.* The authors' 2000 book, *The Hunted,* finds the family at Montana's Glacier National Park to solve the mystery of disappearing grizzly cubs.

Passionate about Work

Skurzynski once declared: "When I work on a book like *Good–bye, Billy Radish,* I find my way back home to the smoky, sooty, western Pennsylvania town where flames from smokestacks set fire to the night. Today the smoke is gone, and so are the steel mills, but in my own memory, and through the stories my parents told me, I can recreate that time and place. It's important that I do that, because if I don't, no one will remember the rumbles and shrieks of the mills, the smell of the smoke, the blaze of the furnaces, and the enormous power of the steel mills over the townspeople.

"Then, after I've relived that past, I can flash forward. On computer screens, I can enter virtual worlds where I touch things that aren't real, and move around in them, and move them around to wherever I please. In laboratories, designers have shared with me the secrets of their work, giving me breath–stopping previews of the twenty–first century for my books *Robots, Almost the Real Thing, Get the Message,* and *Know the Score.*

If you enjoy the works of Gloria Skurzynski, you might want to check out the following books:

Jean Craighead George, *Julie of the Wolves,* 1971.
Russell Hoban, *Riddley Walker,* 1980.
Jan Slepian, *The Broccoli Tapes,* 1989.

"Caught up in the wonderment of the world to come, and infused with equal wonderment over the world long past, I think how lucky I am to be a writer, to be the channel through which this knowledge flows. As much as I admire the work of scientists and engineers and historians and archaeologists, I think my job is the best. I get to have it all. I only wish I could live forever, so I could see how the future turns out."

■ Biographical and Critical Sources

BOOKS

Fifth Book of Junior Authors and Illustrators, H. W. Wilson, 1983, pp. 294–95.

PERIODICALS

Booklist, August, 1997, Susan Dove Lempke, review of *Virtual War,* p. 1891; February 15, 1999, Ilene Cooper, review of *Spider's Voice,* p. 1060; April 15, 1999, Ilene Cooper, review of *Cliff Hanger,* p. 1532; August, 1999, Sally Estes, review of *Tomorrowland,* p. 2045; October 15, 1999, Shelle Rosenfeld, review of *Deadly Water,* p. 446.

Bulletin of the Center for Children's Books, October, 1975; April, 1979, review of *Bionic Parts for People: The Real Story of Artificial Organs and Replacement Parts;* February, 1980, review of *What Happened in Hamelin;* April, 1982; June, 1983, review of *The Tempering;* June, 1984; December, 1984; March, 1986.

Horn Book, December, 1971; October, 1978; February, 1980, review of *What Happened in Hamelin;* August, 1981; January/February, 1997, Margaret A. Bush, review of *The Electromagnetic Universe,* p. 80.

Junior Literary Guild, September, 1978; March, 1984.

Kirkus Reviews, January 15, 1999, review of *Spider's Voice,* p. 152.

New York Times Book Review, March 30, 1980, Natalie Babbitt, review of *What Happened in Hamelin,* p. 16; May 22, 1983, Martha Bennett Stiles, review of *The Tempering,* p. 40.

Publishers Weekly, April 1, 1983; June 26, 1995, review of *Cyberstorm,* p. 107; May 19, 1997, review of *Virtual War,* p. 76; January 18, 1999, review of *Spider's Voice,* p. 340.

School Library Journal, October, 1991, Alan Newman, review of *Almost the Real Thing: Simulation in Your High–Tech World,* p. 141; October, 1992, pp. 46–47; December, 1992, Marcia Hupp, review of *Good–bye, Billy Radish,* p. 114; January, 1998, Marlene Gawron, review of *Wolf Stalker,* p. 114; May, 1998, Bonnie Kunzel, review of *Cyberstorm,* p. 51; November, 1998, John Peters, review of *Discover Mars,* p. 143; March, 1999, Barbara Scotto, review of *Spider's Voice,* p. 215; May, 1999, Eldon Younce, review of *Cliff Hanger,* p. 130; November, 2000, Ann Cook, review of *Ghost Horses.*

Voice of Youth Advocates, August, 1995, Marsha Valance, review of *Cyberstorm,* p. 174; August, 1997, Linda Roberts, review of *Virtual War,* p. 196; April, 1999, Vicky Burkholder, review of *Spider's Voice,* p. 42.

ON–LINE

Gloria Skurzynski's Web site, located at http://www.gloriabooks.com (October 7, 2000).

Jeff Smith

Personal

Born February 27, 1960, in McKees Rock, PA; son of William Earl (a manager at an ice cream factory) and Barbara Smith; married Vijaya Iyer (a publisher), June 3, 1989. *Education:* Attended Ohio State University, 1982–86.

Addresses

Office—Cartoon Books, P.O. Box 16973, Columbus, OH 43216. *E–mail*—vijaya@boneville.com.

Career

Cartoon Books, Columbus, OH, cartoonist and publisher of *Bone* comic books. Character Builders (animation studio), cofounder, producer, and director.

Awards, Honors

Nine Eisner Awards for best humor publication, best continuing series, best writer/artist or cartoonist, and best serialized story, 1993–99; Genie Award, 1994, for best continuing series; eight Harvey Awards for best cartoonist, best graphic album, and special award for humor, 1994–99; Prix Vienne Award (Germany) for best book, 1995; two *Comic Speedline* Awards (Germany), 1995, for best newcomer and best graphic novel; Alph–Art Award (France), 1996, for best comic originally written in a foreign language; award for best comic book artist, National Cartoonist Society, 1996 and 1997.

Writings

The Complete BONE Adventures, Cartoon Books (Columbus, OH), 1993.
BONE, Volume One: Out from Boneville, Cartoon Books, 1995.
BONE, Volume Two: The Great Cow Race, Cartoon Books, 1996.
BONE, Volume Three: Eyes of the Storm, Cartoon Books, 1996.
BONE Reader, Cartoon Books, 1996.
BONE, Volume Four: The Dragonslayer, Cartoon Books, 1997.
BONE, Volume Five: Rock Jaw: Master of the Eastern Border, Cartoon Books, 1998.
BONE: Volume Six: Old Man's Cave, Cartoon Books, 1999.

Adaptations

Nickelodeon Movies has purchased the film rights to *BONE.*

■ Sidelights

Cartoonist Jeff Smith, the creator of the award–winning *BONE* comic book series, often says that he has his ideal job: he is living his childhood dream of being a cartoonist while indulging his own fantasies for adventure through the characters he has created. As a boy, Smith was inspired by reading *Peanuts*, *Uncle Scrooge*, and the now–defunct comic strip *Pogo* by the late Walt Kelly. In his teenage years, he admired the politically savvy *Doonesbury*. Smith once said that he "always wished that my childhood cartoon heroes would go out on an adventure that had actual danger in it . . . or an adventure that would have consequences that might actually alter their existence."

Now that he is an adult and is creating his own comics, Smith has his characters doing exactly that. Smith once irreverently said that *BONE,* his signature creation, is a "postmodern, neo–retro, deconstructed docu–dramedy . . . fat packed with info-tainment." On a more factual level, *BONE* is a comic book fantasy adventure that tells the story of Fone Bone, Phoney Bone, and Smiley Bone, three Pogo–like cousins from a town called Boneville. After being chased out of their hometown, the intrepid trio are separated by a swarm of locusts and get lost in a desert. One by one, they each find their way into an uncharted forest valley that is filled with all kinds of weird, wonderful, and dangerous creatures. There are dragons, a shadowy villain known as The Hooded One, and hordes of fearsome rat creatures who do his bidding. Fone Bone finds a strange map and is befriended by a beautiful young woman named Thorn, who promises to help him find his cousins and get back to Boneville.

As the story unfolds in successive installments, Fone Bone falls in love with Thorn, and he realizes that the map that he has found was drawn by her many years earlier, when she was a princess in the land of Atheia. The rat creatures have murdered Thorn's parents, and she survived only because her Gran'ma Ben spirited her away to safety, living under the protection of the dragons. Thorn, the only true heir to the throne of Atheia, has long dreamed of being a princess. Now that she knows her dreams reflect what was once real, she sets out with Gran'ma Ben and Fone Bone to recover her throne and avenge the murder of her parents. The fantastic adventures that follow have elements of J. R. R. Tolkien's classic *Lord of the Rings* trilogy of fantasy novels and George Lucas' *Star Wars* movies. Smith told Jeff Mason, the editor of *indy magazine* (the bi–monthly trade publication of the independent comic industry) in a 1994 interview, "I usually describe [*BONE*] as Bugs Bunny meets *The Lord of the Rings*."

He also once commented, "*BONE* is about growing up and leaving home for the first time. The story is about what happens when the Bone cousins leave Boneville . . . this sheltered little world they grew up in and then go out into this wilder, outside world."

Jeff Smith himself grew up in the safe, insular world of small–town America. He was born in McKees Rocks, Pennsylvania, a town of about nine thousand people on the western outskirts of Pittsburgh. Smith was the eldest of two brothers. "My father was a production manager at a local ice cream novelty company," Smith quipped in a June 2000 interview with *Authors and Artists for Young Adults* (*AAYA*). "He made Drumsticks, Push–ups, and Popsicles. Kinda makes sense that his son would go into funny books, doesn't it?"

Earliest Memories Are of Drawing with Crayons

The Smith family moved to Columbus, Ohio, in the early 1960s, and it was there that young Jeff received his early schooling. In his spare time, he loved watching movies (and still does), and reading. However, his favorite pastime was sketching and cartooning; Smith drew his inspiration—both literally and figuratively—from the comic strips and comic books that he read, and from the animated cartoons that he watched on television. "My earliest memories are of drawing pictures in crayon, so I must have been pretty young," Smith told *AAYA*. "I know I had made up a number of cartoon characters by the time I started drawing the *BONE* characters. I made up the *BONE* characters by the time I was in kindergarten."

Smith continued to hone his artistic talents throughout his early years. Following his 1982 graduation from high school, Smith enrolled at Ohio State University. There he began drawing a cartoon strip called *Thorn*, which appeared in the fifty–thousand circulation daily campus student newspaper *The Lantern* for more than two years, from September 20, 1982, to November 30, 1984. That strip was the testing ground for the work that Smith would do later, since it featured most of the characters who have become regulars in the *BONE* comics, and the seeds of the basic storyline were also there in nascent form.

When *Thorn* became popular, it attracted the attention of national comic syndicates. Smith was interested in their offers, at first. "Originally, I wanted to do a comic strip in newspapers. I went to visit the editors in New York. They liked *BONE*; they wanted

In 1995 *BONE, Volume One: Out from Boneville* became the first hardcover collection of Smith's strips featuring cousins Fone Bone, Phoney Bone, and Smiley Bone as they traverse a monster–filled wilderness and engage in hilarious hijinks.

Smith's quirky mix of humor and danger permeates his second "BONE" collection, released in 1996 and featuring his characteristic "postmodern, neo–retro" storylines.

to do it, but they had some suggestions. Basically, it came down to that they didn't want it to be an adventure strip; they wanted it to be a joke–a–day strip, and they wanted to own it. So I knew I wanted to self–publish right away. I never, never even wanted to show it to another company."

However, self–publishing his own comics would have to wait. Since Smith never picked a major at Ohio State—"I floated back and forth between journalism and art," he told *AAYA*—he did not receive his degree. Instead, Smith left school in 1985. The following year, he and partners Jim Kammerud and Martin Fuller co–founded the Character Builders animation studio in Columbus, Ohio. "[We] were all self–taught, learning everything we could from books like *Disney Animation: The Illusion of Life*,"

Smith told Jeff Mason in his *indy magazine* interview. For the next five years, Smith and his two partners were preoccupied with various film projects, and so it was not until 1991 that Smith finally launched the company Cartoon Books to publish *BONE* in comic book format.

The first *BONE* comic book that appeared in 1991 was a no–frills, black–and–white product with a press run of a mere three thousand copies—"about as rare as it gets in the modern age of comics," Smith told Mason. Had it not been for the fact that Smith published *BONE* himself and was determined to make it a success, the comic book probably would have quietly disappeared after a couple of years. Instead, the cartoonist–turned–publisher stubbornly kept the comic book in print. At first, he relied mostly on word–of–mouth to generate new sales. All that changed in a flash when Smith started attending comic book distributor/retail conferences and showed *BONE* to other artists and people in the comic book business.

Smith met Dave Sim, the creator of a successful comic book *Cerebus the Aadrvark*, and the two became good friends. Sim generously printed a "preview" of Smith's third installment of *BONE* in issue #161 of *Cerebus the Aardvark*. Sim also invited Smith to take part in a "jam drawing" session with fellow comic book artists Martin Wagner, Colleen Doran, and James Owen. The five of them began networking and going to retailer shows together. About this same time, and because of the other industry connections that he had made, Smith met Don and Maggie Thompson, the publishers of an influential comic book industry publication called the *Comic Buyer's Guide*. The Thompsons liked *BONE,* and they gave it a favorable review. The *Cerebus the Aardvark* preview and the *Comic Buyers' Guide* notice appeared at the same time, and the combined impact forever changed Jeff Smith's fortunes. "I'd have to say that once the [*Comic Buyers' Guide*] review hit, I went from getting something like ten pieces of mail a week to ten pieces of mail a day, and all saying that they read it in *Comic Buyers' Guide*," Smith told Jeff Mason in another January 1994 interview that is posted on the *BONE Network* web site.

Smith Wins Numerous Cartooning Awards

With his work now reaching an ever–increasing readership, Smith was able to continue publishing new installments of *BONE*. Then in 1993, Cartoon Books released *The Complete BONE Adventures,* a softcover anthology of the first six installments of

In his third "BONE" collection, award–winning cartoonist Smith turns up the dial on adventure as Fone, Phoney, and Smiley begin to understand the secrets of the valley outside the safe haven of Boneville.

the *BONE* adventures. As word of mouth spread, demand for the collection grew, and Cartoon Books began reprinting the volume. Eventually, about ninety thousand copies were sold in English–language editions alone. Then the book was released in Europe, where it continued to sell in Italy, Spain, Germany, and Finland. Readers and critics far and wide were becoming fans of Smith's work. In 1993 alone, Smith won five cartooning awards—an Eisner Award (Best Humor Publication), Russ Manning Award (Most Promising Newcomer), three Harvey Awards (Best Graphic Album, Special Award for Humor, Best Cartoonist), and a Gem Award (Product Vanguard of the Year). The success continued the following year, when Smith added seven more awards to his office wall. That trend has continued each year since. In 1996, Smith won the Best Comic Book from the National Cartoonist Society (sharing the platform that day with *Doonesbury* creator Garry Trudeau, one of his idols).

Some critics have favorably compared Smith's work to that of such celebrated cartoonists as Walt Disney, Al Capp (*L'il Abner*), and Walt Kelly (*Pogo*). "Smith is our generation's Walt Kelly, and he's unrestrained by the four–panel barrier of daily strips that must've frustrated Kelly," observed writer Frank Miller of *Village Voice*. Commenting on this, Smith told *AAYA,* "Yes, I think [the comparisons] are valid. On the surface level, my technique is very similar to Kelly's. I learned to ink by copying his style, and I try to write distinct dialogue for each character's personality. If we go down another layer, Pogo and *BONE* have less in common, because Walt Kelly was interested in allegory and politics, whereas I am more interested in metaphor and myth. But, if we delved down to yet a deeper level, then you can see what I really learned from Walt Kelly: Truth."

The Complete BONE Adventures was re–released in 1995 as *Volume One: Out from Boneville,* and was quickly followed by *Volume Two: The Great Cow Race.* By now awareness of Smith's work was spreading, and even trade publications in the publishing and teaching worlds were beginning to take note. Reviewer Stephanie Zvirin of *Booklist* praised the book's "suspense and humor," terming it "a graphic novel" that would likely appeal to young readers who enjoy the comic section of the Sunday newspaper. Another *Booklist* reviewer, Gordon Flagg, echoed that praise when assessing *The Great Cow Race.* Flagg pointed out the "Tolkienesque aspects" of *BONE* and added, "Smith's animation–inspired story–telling, with its traces of Walt Kelly and Carl Barks and its impressive balancing of humor and adventure, continues to astound." Smith's work, Flagg added, "is the '*BONE*' to pick."

An uglier–than–ugly rodent chieftain, Phoney Bone's skills at playing Pied Piper, and other unexpected events dot Smith's fourth "BONE" compendium, published in 1997.

A *Publishers Weekly* reviewer commented that the book "will appeal to both children and adults." *Voice of Youth Advocates* reviewer Katharine L. Kan also praised *The Great Cow Race.* "This is one for the whole family to enjoy," she wrote, "full of raucous humor, great dialogue and marvelously twisted plotting." She was no less complementary of Smith's work generally: "He's a great independent success in a field jammed full of mass–market glitzy 'product.'"

Asked by *AAYA* to explain the success of *BONE,* Smith was uncertain. "It's difficult to say," he noted. "The humor probably helps, and I think the story is something that everyone can relate to." What Smith is more definite about is that he has some carefully devised plans for *BONE,* for Cartoon Books, and for himself. The early editions of the comic book have now become collector items, with originals of the very first issue of *BONE* selling for as much as two hundred dollars. Excerpts from *BONE* have also been reprinted in the mass–market magazine *Disney Adventures.* There are *BONE* trading cards and figurines, and in 1998 Nickelodeon Movies purchased the film rights to *BONE.* A feature film to be directed by Smith is in the works, although the cartoonist told *AAYA,* "The project is not on hold, but it is taking longer than I thought it would. We're still working on it."

If you enjoy the works of Jeff Smith, you might want to check out the following:

George Herriman, *Krazy Kat: The Comic Art of George Herriman,* 1999.
Charles M. Schulz, *Peanuts: A Golden Celebration,* 1999.
The works of *Pogo* creator Walt Kelly.

Despite all of this success, Smith has made it clear that *BONE* will not go on indefinitely. "The comic has a definite story to tell that could take as much as five or ten years to complete," he told Jeff Mason in the 1994 *indy magazine* interview. "The ending is written and I have four or five major subplots I have to tell in order to move the story toward its conclusion." Echoing those comments, he told *AAYA,* "I do have an end for the story planned, and it should take me between fifteen to twenty more issues to tell." For now, at least, Smith continues to produce a new *BONE* comic book every ten weeks or so. Issue number thirty–eight, which begins "the

third and final Act of *BONE*" appeared in comic book stores in July 2000. "I could probably write . . . and draw . . . on a monthly basis, but that doesn't give you time to think about it," Smith told Jeff Mason.

■ Biographical and Critical Sources

PERIODICALS

Booklist, August, 1995, Stephanie Zvirin, review of *Out of Boneville,* pp. 1935–36; July, 1996, Gordon Flagg, review of *The Great Cow Race,* p. 1794.
indy magazine, January 21, 1994, Jeff Mason, "Interview with Jeff Smith."
Publishers Weekly, August 19, 1996, review of *The Great Cow Race,* p. 57.
Village Voice, January 7, 1997, Frank Miller, review of *The Great Cow Race,* p. 43.
Voice of Youth Advocates, December, 1994, Katharine L. Kan, review of *The Great Cow Race,* p. 260.

OTHER

The Bone Network, located at http://members.tripod/BoneNET/.
Cartoon Books, located at http://www.boneville.com/.
Nickelodeon Movies Has Picked Its Own Bone, located at http://web4.iac–insite.com/ (March 29, 2000).
Smith, Jeff, in an interview conducted by *Authors and Artists for Young Adults,* June 8, 2000.
Smith, Jeff, "Jeff Smith Has a Bone to Pick: The Creation of a Fantasy Epic," located at http://www.amazon.com/ (September 4, 2000).

—Sketch by Ken Cuthbertson

Neal Stephenson

■ Personal

Born October 31, 1959, in Fort Meade, MD; son of David Town (a professor) and Janet (a laboratory technician; maiden name, Jewsbury) Stephenson; married Ellen Marie Lackermann (a physician), June 28, 1985; children: two. *Education:* Boston University, B.A., 1981.

■ Addresses

Agent—Liz Darhansoff, 1220 Park Ave., New York, NY 10128.

■ Career

Ames Laboratory, U.S. Department of Energy, Ames, Iowa, research assistant, 1978–79; Boston University, Boston, MA, teaching assistant in physics department, 1979; Corporation for a Cleaner Commonwealth (environmental group), Boston, researcher, 1980; University of Iowa, Iowa City, clerk in library, 1981–83; writer, 1984—; Ernst & Young Center for Business Innovation, visiting fellow.

■ Awards, Honors

Prix Ars Electronica, Internet category, for depiction of virtual universes in *Snow Crash* and *Cryptonomicon*; Hugo Award, 1996, for *The Diamond Age*.

■ Writings

NOVELS

The Big U, Vintage Trade (New York City), 1984.
Zodiac: The Eco–Thriller, Atlantic Monthly Press (New York City), 1988.
Snow Crash, Bantam (New York City), 1992.
The Diamond Age: Or, A Young Lady's Illustrated Primer, Bantam, 1995.
Cryptonomicon, Avon (New York City), 1999.
In the Beginning . . . Was the Command Line (nonfiction), Avon Books, 1999.

OTHER

Contributor to the *Akron Beacon Journal, Wired,* and *Time.*

■ Work in Progress

A series of novels about cryptography.

■ Sidelights

Though Neal Stephenson has authored just a handful of books, his science–fiction thrillers that blend high–tech intrigue with sly humor have made him one of the most successful new authors in the genre. Called "the hacker Hemingway" and compared even to renegade indie filmmaker Quentin Tarantino, Stephenson enjoyed a significant career breakthrough when his 1999 title, *Cryptonomicon,* made it to the *New York Times* bestseller list.

Born in 1959, Stephenson grew up in the college–campus towns of Champaign–Urbana, Illinois, and Ames, Iowa. A career in the sciences seemed pre-ordained—his father was a professor of electrical engineering, his mother worked in a biochemistry laboratory, and even his grandfather had been a physics professor. This last field was Stephenson's original major when he began at Boston University in the late 1970s, but he discovered that the geography department at the college had far more advanced computers. Already fascinated by emerging information technology, Stephenson eschewed the idea of pursuing it as an academic course, believing it changed too quickly to keep pace.

Cult Status with *Snow Crash*

Stephenson began writing in college and moved to the Pacific Northwest area in 1984, the same year his first novel was published. That work, *The Big U,* revolves around American Megaversity, a huge, modern university which is funded by a radioactive waste dump and whose students arm themselves with machine guns. The satirical book is loaded with student pranks reminiscent of those in the 1978 film *National Lampoon's Animal House* and was deemed "a lot of fun" by Alan Cheuse in the *New York Times Book Review.* Cheuse added that *The Big U* would appeal greatly to "alert and inquisitive students with a taste for campus comedy." Despite positive reviews, *The Big U* did not find a readership. Stephenson's second outing, *Zodiac: The Eco–Thriller,* was described by Steven Levy of *Newsweek* as "a tale of ecoactivism that won the hearts of tree huggers but didn't sell, either."

Stephenson's third novel, the widely acclaimed *Snow Crash,* was his breakthrough book, granting him cult status as one of the major cyberpunk novelists. According to *Entertainment Weekly* writer Chris Nashawaty, "The young and wired have turned . . . *Snow Crash* . . . into their dog–eared bible." Nadine Kolowrat, also of *Entertainment Weekly,* observed that "*Snow Crash* proved to be the pass–along favorite of sci–fi heads, hackers, and regular joes alike. . . ." *Snow Crash* takes place partly in the Metaverse, a complex virtual–reality creation, and partly in the world that spawned it, a high–tech future dominated by corporations that are, in turn, opposed by

AUTHOR OF *THE DIAMOND AGE* AND *SNOW CRASH*
NEAL STEPHENSON
ZODIAC
AN ECO-THRILLER

Stephenson's 1988 novel finds eco–evangelist Sangamon Taylor attracting the unwanted attention of the Mafia, the FBI, and several drug dealers while waging his high–profile battle against Boston–based corporations dumping toxic waste into the city's waterways.

renegade computer hackers. A similar setting was first made popular in William Gibson's seminal cyberpunk novel *Neuromancer* (1984) and has become the *sine qua non* of the genre.

Sharp Take on Hacker Culture

However, many reviewers agree that Stephenson manages his own original and compelling take on what has become a cliche in the science fiction field.

John Leonard of *The Nation* felt that no other cyberpunk writer has depicted virtual reality "so lyrically" as Stephenson, while Levy believed that "[w]hen it comes to depicting the nerd mind–set, no one tops Stephenson." The hacker heroes in his books, Levy noted, seem to be "awkward, chatty mensches whose insistence on logic makes them borderline nut cases." The snow crash of the book's title refers to a street drug/computer virus that has invaded the Metaverse, causing not only computer crashes in the virtual world but the physical collapse in the real world of those who encounter it. The central character of the novel, Hiro Protagonist (who has chosen his own name), employs information both from the Bible and ancient Summerian culture to track down the origins of snow crash. In the process he discovers a plot to take over and transform civilization. A writer for the *New York Times Book Review* noted that "Hiro's adventures . . . are brilliantly realized," and praised Stephenson as "an engaging guide to an onrushing tomorrow that is as farcical as it is horrific."

An *Entertainment Weekly* reviewer described Stephenson's follow–up to *Snow Crash, The Diamond Age: Or, A Young Lady's Illustrated Primer,* as "equal parts Victorian novel, fairy tale, and science fiction." Whereas virtual reality serves as the technological background for *Snow Crash, The Diamond Age* explores nanotechnology, the manipulation of atomic particles both to transform matter and to create submicroscopic machines. Though traversing several continents in the course of its action, the novel is set for the most part in a future Shanghai at a time when the nations of the world have been replaced by enclaves of individuals that share common cultural identities and beliefs. Computer engineer John Hackworth is hired by a rich and powerful neo–Victorian to write a primer to help educate his granddaughter. The plot of the book turns on the complications that arise when a stolen copy of the primer falls into the hands of a working–class girl who uses it for her own education. "Building steadily to a wholly earned and intriguing climax," stated a reviewer for *Publishers Weekly*, "this long novel, which presents its sometimes difficult technical concepts in accessible ways, should appeal to readers other than habitual SF users." In *Entertainment Weekly*, Kolowrat took a more critical stance, commenting that "reading about someone reading a book is about as riveting as watching an actor think"; she also found Stephenson's use of a Victorian vocabulary in a science fictional environment to be jarring. However, Kolowrat granted that *"The Diamond Age* does have great riffs on a futuristic world and some mindbending settings."

The Business Plan as New Literary Genre?

Stephenson has been involved in some start–up technology ventures, primarily in the field of interactive media, which forced him to learn to how to write a business plan. He became so adept at scripting them—the formulaic document that presents an idea for a new business in order to lure potential investors, describing what the market will be for a product or service, and how the entrepreneurs plan to make it prosper—that he was hired to teach the art to others. Ernst & Young's Center for Business Innovation in Cambridge, Massachusetts, has even made him one of a handful of teaching fellows at their prestigious institute. "In a weird way, high–tech business plans are a literary form unto them-

In a futuristic world, virtual reality allows a pizza delivery man to lead a double life as a warrior hunting down the source of a computer virus laying waste to hackers everywhere in Stephenson's 1992 thriller.

selves, and so it was fun to approach them as a writer, in the same way that I might try my hand at writing a sonnet or haiku," Stephenson told Michael Warshaw in an interview for *Inc.*

Stephenson became so intrigued by the form that he decided to include it in his next novel, *Cryptonomicon.* Its characters author one to launch their start–up technology venture. As Stephenson declared in *Inc.,* he believes this new breed of entrepreneurs—especially those in the very risky but potentially profitable high–tech sector—are the contemporary version of the explorers and gold miners of nineteenth–century American history. "The people who, 100 years ago, would have been carrying their crates over the Chilkoot Pass to join the Klondike Gold Rush now start companies," he told Warshaw. "Starting your own company has become a standard rite of passage."

Code–Cracking and the New Technology

Regarding *Cryptonomicon,* his fifth novel, Stephenson told Amazon.com, "This novel . . . is eventually going to be part of a series of novels about crypto[graphy] that cover a long span of historical time." The most mainstream of Stephenson's works, the 928–page *Cryptonomicon* centers on two major characters, mathematician Lawrence Waterhouse and his programmer grandson, Randy. The book moves back and forth in time between World War II, when Lawrence is employed deciphering German and Japanese military codes, and the present, when Randy is involved in the technological development of Southeast Asia. A hidden treasure in Japanese gold ties the two story lines together, as does their examination of the birth and development of information technology. Lev Grossman of *Entertainment Weekly* noted, "[D]on't write off Stephenson's novel as just another fast–paced, find–the–MacGuffin techno–thriller. It's an engrossing look at the way the flow of information shapes history—as well as a rare glimpse into the soul of the hardcore geek." Jackie Cassada of *Library Journal* called *Cryptonomicon* "a story of epic proportions," and concluded: "Stephenson's freewheeling prose and ironic voice lend a sense of familiarity to a story that transcends the genre and demands a wide readership among fans of techno thrillers as well as a general audience." Reviewing *Cryptonomicon* for the *New York Times Book Review,* Dwight Gardner made a general observation about Stephenson's novels, "Despite all the high–tech frippery, there's something old–fashioned about Stephenson's work. He cares as much about telling good stories as he does about farming out cool ideas. There's a strong whiff of

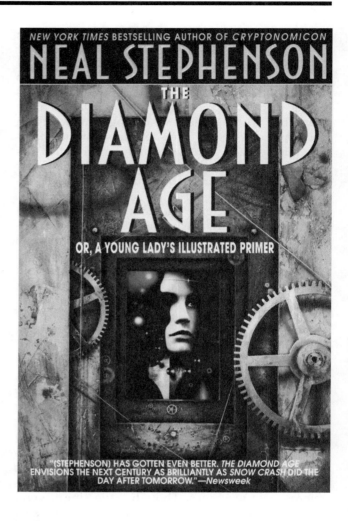

NEW YORK TIMES BESTSELLING AUTHOR OF *CRYPTONOMICON*
NEAL STEPHENSON
THE **DIAMOND AGE**
OR, A YOUNG LADY'S ILLUSTRATED PRIMER

"(STEPHENSON) HAS GOTTEN EVEN BETTER. *THE DIAMOND AGE* ENVISIONS THE NEXT CENTURY AS BRILLIANTLY AS *SNOW CRASH* DID THE DAY AFTER TOMORROW." —*Newsweek*

Dubbed the king of post–cyberpunk fiction, Stephenson dished up another dose of futuristic sci–fi in his 1995 novel about a homeless girl named Nell after she discovers a device that can radically alter all life in twenty–first–century Shanghai.

moralism in his books, too. The bad guys in his fiction—that is, anyone who stands in a well–intentioned hacker's way—meet bad ends."

Cryptonomicon was a surprising success for Stephenson and Avon Books, its publisher, in 1999. A number of other titles and, in Britain, television programs, focused on cryptography and the British intelligence service's breakthrough in deciphering the codes used by German and Japanese military communications during World War II; the novel's fictional mathematician, Lawrence Waterhouse, is part of that historic team. Yet cryptography also has a modern relevance; some concerns about Internet privacy are alleviated by emerging new encryption technology. Avon's advance marketing team for *Cryptonomicon* sent out a special "code key" card which contained a password to their Web site, where certain industry professionals and reviewers could read a humorous, easily digested essay on the history of computer–operating systems. Stephenson had originally written the piece, which clocked in at 37,000 words, for *Wired* magazine, which passed on it. But a buzz about "In the Beginning . . . Was the Command Line" spread, and then links on other sites were posted. So many visitors arrived at the Avon site to read it that the server at the publishing house crashed.

What the Future Holds

Avon and Stephenson decided to issue the essay as a book. *In the Beginning . . . Was the Command Line* appeared in late 1999. The work explains the history of computer operating systems, but tracks the modern era with a sly humor and forthright opinion, which prompted some to describe it as a manifesto. Stephenson discusses the U.S. Justice Department's anti–trust suit against Microsoft, for instance, but also reveals the onetime strategy of its competitor, Apple, to create a monopoly in the industry as well. He also writes about the rise of Linux, a free operating system, and its creators, both of which receive "a thorough—but fair—skewering," according to Jennifer Buckendorff, who reviewed it for Amazon.com. Buckendorff commended the author for writing in a style that made complex issues accessible to the lay reader, and for a book that "convincingly encourages us as a society to examine the metaphors of technology—simplifications that aren't really much simpler—that we greedily accept."

If you enjoy the works of Neal Stephenson, you might want to check out the following books:

Pat Cadigan, *Synners*, 1991.
William Gibson, *Neuromancer*, 1984.
Maureen F. McHugh, *China Mountain Zhang*, 1992.
Bruce Sterling, *Islands in the Net*, 1988.

Stephenson is working on the successor to *Cryptonomicon* from his home in Seattle, where he lives with his physician wife and their two children. To give himself a break from writing, Stephenson likes to tinker and build his own toys, such as kayaks and rockets. Programming and computer technology are still vital to his world. He predicted in a 1995 interview with *Entertainment Weekly*'s Nashawaty that Internet technology and its growing ubiquity will actually impact book publishing in a positive way. "I have the feeling that in the future we're going to see a smaller market for formulaic junk fiction because it will be possible to act out your own junk fiction on–line," Stephenson remarked. "But I'm still optimistic about reading in general. There's something about reading that makes you smarter, even if it's a crappy novel."

■ Biographical and Critical Sources

PERIODICALS

Analog Science Fiction and Fact, August, 1995, Tom Easton, review of *The Diamond Age,* pp. 165–167.

Booklist, April 1, 1999, Roland Green, review of *Cryptonomicon,* p. 1366.

Economist, April 15, 2000, "Why Codes Are Cool," p. 90.

Entertainment Weekly, January 27, 1995, Nadine Kolowrat, review of *The Diamond Age,* p. 43; June 23, 1995, Chris Nashawaty, "Foreseeable Future," p. 60; March 15, 1996, p. 59; May 21, 1999, p. 24.

Extrapolation, summer, 1999, Peter Brigg, "The Future as the Past Viewed from the Present," p. 116.

Inc., October, 1999, Michael Warshaw, "Field Notes," p. 21.

Kirkus Reviews, March 15, 1992, review of *Snow Crash.*

Library Journal, May 15, 1999, Jackie Cassada, review of *Cryptonomicon,* p. 130.

Locus, January, 1995, Gary K. Wolfe, review of *The Diamond Age,* p. 19.

Los Angeles Times, September 7, 1984.

Nation, November 15, 1993, John Leonard, "Gravity's Rainbow," p. 580.

Newsweek, May 10, 1999, p. 90.

New York Times Book Review, September 30, 1984; December 14, 1992; March 12, 1995, Gerald Jonas, review of *The Diamond Age,* p. 25; May 23, 1999.

Publishers Weekly, March 16, 1992, p. 74; December 19, 1994, p. 49; March 22, 1999, review of *Cryptonomicon,* p. 67; May 12, 1999, p. 24; May 24, 1999, Daisy Maryles, "'Cryptonomicon' Cracks the Charts," p. 24; August 16, 1999, Judy Quinn, "'Cryptonomicon' Spinoff Is Out of Site," p. 31.

Reason, August/September, 1999, Mike Godwin, review of *Cryptonomicon,* p. 65.

Village Voice, January 31, 1995, Richard Gehr, "Victorians' Secret," pp. 73–74.

Voice of Youth Advocates, August, 1995, Rachelle M. Bilz, review of *The Diamond Age,* p. 175.

Wilson Library Bulletin, December, 1992, Gene La-Faille, review of *Snow Crash,* pp. 94–95.

ON—LINE

Buckendorff, Jennifer, review of *In the Beginning . . . Was the Command Line* located at http://amazon.com/ (May 9, 2000).

Cryptonomicon Web site, located at http://www.cryptonomicon.com/main.html (May 16, 2000).

SF Site, located at http://www.sfsite.com (May 16, 2000).*

Richard Wormser

■ Personal

Born in 1933. *Education:* Bucknell University, graduated 1955.

■ Addresses

Office—Videoline Productions, 1697 Broadway, Room 901, New York, NY 10019.

■ Career

Documentary filmmaker and writer of nonfiction for young adults. Also worked as a logger in the Pacific Northwest, a translator of French film treatments, a newspaper salesman in Paris, a longshoreman in London, and as a journalist for the *Shamokin Citizen*, Shamokin, PA.

■ Member

PEN.

■ Writings

NONFICTION; FOR YOUNG ADULTS

Pinkerton: America's First Private Eye, Walker, 1990.

Lifers: Learn the Truth at the Expense of Our Sorrow, Simon & Schuster, 1991.

Countdown to Crisis: A Look at the Middle East, Simon & Schuster, 1992.

Three Faces of Vietnam, Franklin Watts, 1993.

The Iron Horse: How Railroads Changed America, Walker, 1993.

Growing Up in the Great Depression, Atheneum, 1994.

Hoboes: Wandering in America, 1870–1940, Walker, 1994.

Juveniles in Trouble, Simon & Schuster, 1994.

American Islam: Growing Up Muslim in America, Walker, 1994.

The Titanic, Explorer Books, 1994.

American Childhoods: Three Centuries of Youth at Risk, Walker, 1996.

The Rise and Fall of Jim Crow: The African–American Struggle against Discrimination, 1865–1954, Franklin Watts, 1999.

The Dictionary of the Civil War and Reconstruction, Franklin Watts, 2000.

Defending the Accused: Stories from the Courtroom, Franklin Watts, 2001.

Wormser has also written and produced over forty documentary films.

Richard Wormser, about 1983.

■ Work in Progress

Whistle–Blowers (working title), for Franklin Watts.

■ Sidelights

Richard Wormser is a filmmaker turned writer who has published several works of nonfiction for young adult readers on such varied topics as teens at risk, Vietnam, hoboes, railways, American Islam, and even a biography of Allan Pinkerton, the first private investigator in America. Wormser's writings generally have a social slant, and he often chooses to feature those who, "having experienced the worst that life has to offer, are able to pick themselves up, tumble forward, and move out of the darkness of their lives into some light," as Wormser wrote in an essay for *Something about the Author Autobiography Series* (*SAAS*).

Born in 1933, Wormser was a child of the Great Depression and a great fan of baseball, partly because Babe Ruth lived only two blocks away from his home. Playing hooky to go to a Yankees game, he was later caught by his father and spent a "long period of confinement to my room without allowance," the author noted in *SAAS*. Reading came easily to the young Wormser, who devoured "comic books, boy's adventure stories of super–macho idiotic heroes who speak in near–grunts or single–syllable words," and of course baseball stories. Writing, however, was another matter; penmanship was a perennial problem for Wormser, and he spent tortured hours in the second grade trying to master cursive handwriting. But it was not simply the me-

chanical aspect that bothered him; content proved difficult as well. "Writing remains hard for me," Wormser admitted in *SAAS*. "I never seem to say exactly what I want to say in the way I want to say it. The nuances of feelings I want to express elude me. Trying to capture the right word is like trying to catch butterflies."

Exploring America

Prep school was a trial for Wormser, who was smaller and less mature than the other boys. He turned to books during these years and soon graduated from "junk" reading to novels and history. His first years in college, however, almost extinguished this light, until a sociology course awoke intellectual passion in him. He also began reading the works of the Beat generation, including Jack Kerouac's novel *On the Road,* which became Wormser's "Bible." Wormser explored America between his junior and senior years, riding Greyhound buses and talking to everyone he met. In California he stayed with friends for a time, taking odd jobs, then travelled on to the Southwest and Denver, where he drove a dealer's car to Seattle. During these travels he first came into contact with that mobile class of itinerant workers, the hoboes who hitchhiked and rode the rails from one job to the next. The experience of meeting these men would later come to fruition in a book on hoboes.

In Washington state, Wormser worked for a time as a choker setter on a logging crew, one of the most dangerous jobs in the woods. Back at school, Wormser graduated in 1955, then went on to law school, which he ultimately quit, and then to graduate school. In 1959 he left for Paris, where he intended to pursue his doctorate at the Sorbonne; in any event, he attended the school of life in that city, staying on for two years during the turbulent era of the Algerian–French conflict. In Paris he met some of the Beat poets and writers such as Allen Ginsberg and William Burroughs and began his own attempts at writing.

The Documentarian

Returning to the United States in 1961, Wormser took a job for a time at a small weekly newspaper in Pennsylvania, where he covered everything from city politics to the coal mines which employed most of the local population. This work provided him with valuable experience in journalism and photography, and as the 1960s got into full swing, he began to discover his own creative voice. Visiting an

Wormser gathering the footage in 1963 at Pennsylvania's Selingsgrove State School and Hospital for the mentally disabled that would become his first documentary film.

institution for retarded children in Pennsylvania, he decided that the only way he could do justice to the story of such children was by making a documentary film about them. He had never made a film nor shot footage, but managed to find funding and learned as he went along. Once finished, his first film won a number of awards. He also helped to make a film about the 1968 Democratic Convention in Chicago when the police force literally ran riot against demonstrators. Suddenly, Wormser saw what he wanted to do with film: to make movies about "the past and present struggles of people to win the political, civil, and human rights denied them by their fellow Americans, politicians, police, and courts," as the author put it in *SAAS*.

In the 1970s and 1980s, Wormser travelled far and wide, documenting lives throughout the Middle East and Egypt as well as in the United States. As the 1990s approached, and Yippie—"those opposed to the killing in Vietnam"—was replaced by Yuppie—"those in favor of making a killing on Wall Street"—Wormser found it increasingly difficult to produce his social and political documentaries and

turned to writing instead. His first title resulted from a failed film project about the life of Allan Pinkerton, the founder of the Pinkerton Agency, whose name is often associated with strike breaking. Wormser discovered, however, that far from being a social conservative and tool of the ruling class, Pinkerton was a labor radical in his native Scotland and had to emigrate to the United States to avoid arrest. A staunch abolitionist, Pinkerton helped slaves escape from the South and put his new agency at the service of the Union during the Civil War.

In a review for *School Library Journal,* Jacqueline Elsner described Wormser's debut book, *Pinkerton: America's First Private Eye,* as an account "told with exciting pacing and engrossing anecdotes." Elsner concluded that "readers are treated to a fast–paced, absorbing look at this complex, unique man and to a vivid view of U.S. history during his lifetime." Leone McDermott, writing in *Booklist,* noted that an "intriguing subject, lively prose, and in–depth analysis combine to make this a first–rate biography." Concluding a review for *Voice of Youth Advocates,* Pat Costello wrote that "history comes

A trip made throughout the West and Southwest during the 1950s introduced Wormser to the culture of America's itinerant workers, and became the inspiration for his 1994 work realistically profiling what was often viewed romantically as the "hobo life."

alive through the author's efforts and it is just this effect which should encourage more young people to sample the nonfiction genre."

Such a warm critical reception encouraged Wormser to continue with YA nonfiction. In *SAAS* Wormser wrote that he realized that "writing for the young adult market allows me to write about subjects I care about, and for which there is no longer a strong support for [in] documentary films.... Perhaps through my books I can reach an audience that is not yet indifferent to the plight of America's dispossessed—those for whom society seems to have no place."

Examines Lives Affected by Crime

Wormser's next book deals with crime and young people at risk. After a year's research at the East Jer-

sey State Prison in New Jersey, and interviewing four men sentenced to life imprisonment, Wormser penned *Lifers: Learn the Truth at the Expense of Our Sorrow.* The book, rather than trying to scare adolescents away from a life of crime, simply presents the facts about life inside prisons. Wormser documents how these "lifers" got into trouble on the outside and why, and he also looks at what impact prison has on their lives. "This includes graphic language and a tough, no–nonsense treatment ... to demonstrate the realities and brutalities of life in a maximum security facility," remarked Celia A. Huffman in a *School Library Journal* review. *Booklist* commentator Candace Smith called the book a "grim but perceptive look at the real horrors of prison—monotony, boredom, despair, and wasted lives."

In a similar vein are Wormser's *Juveniles in Trouble* and *American Childhoods: Three Centuries of Youth at Risk,* both dedicated to investigations of troubled and difficult adolescence, historical and contemporary. In *Juveniles in Trouble,* Wormser "describes the lives of young people who run away from home and live on the streets, who are addicted to drugs, who are in gangs, and who commit crimes," observed *School Library Journal* contributor Jacqueline Rose. Jeanne Triner commented in *Booklist* that "teens need more hard–hitting, factual information like this to help them understand how important the choices they make today are going to be for the rest of their lives."

In *American Childhoods,* Wormser does much the same for the historical view of adolescence, showing the grim realities of child labor and enforced military servitude, among other injustices. Deborah Stevenson, reviewing the book in *Bulletin of the Center for Children's Books,* commented that Wormser "pays particularly close attention to those groups that fared least well—immigrants, minorities, and the poor—and finishes each chapter with an extensive discussion of the contemporary situation."

The Importance of History

Wormser has also turned his hand to historical issues such as the Vietnam conflict in *Three Faces of Vietnam,* the effect of railroads on America in *The Iron Horse,* the Great Depression in *Growing Up in the Great Depression,* and religion in America in *American Islam: Growing Up Muslim in America.* It is Wormser's gift to approach his subjects with an editorial slant as well as to come at them from a new and different angle. In *Three Faces of Vietnam,* for example, he presents the war "through the eyes of antiwar protestors, American GIs, and the Vietnamese

American Childhoods

Three Centuries of Youth at Risk

RICHARD WORMSER

In this 1996 work Wormser outlines the tragic lives of orphaned, migrant, and other children forced to give up their education and their hopes for a better future.

people," according to Mary Mueller in *School Library Journal*, "attempting to capture the feelings and attitudes of that era." *Booklist* critic Sheilamae O'Hara concluded that Wormser's book "does effectively show the tragic marks the war left on both the Vietnamese and Americans." Of Wormser's book *The Iron Horse*, a *Publishers Weekly* critic noted that it "provides an evenhanded history of the growth and impact of the railroads in 19th–century America," while Allison Rogers Hutchison declared in *Voice of Youth Advocates* that "this is such a good read for a nonfiction YA title that it comes highly recommended for any YA collection."

Wormser did not forget the effect that meeting hoboes and tramps had on him when he was a young man: in 1994 he wrote a book documenting their lives that spans seventy years of American history. His *Hoboes: Wandering in America, 1870–1940* focuses on the rules, literature, jokes, modes of life, customs, and politics of this class of wandering workers, similar to today's itinerant laborers. Hazel Rochman noted in a *Booklist* review that while "Wormser evokes the adventure of the hobo journey, the romance of the rugged individual ... he's frank about the brutal reality of living on the edge in hard times—the hunger, the viciousness, the 'jungle' warfare." A *Kirkus Reviews* contributor called that same book an "engaging account of the penurious workers who crisscrossed America as 'internal refugees' from the Industrial Revolution" and concluded by calling Wormser's work "informative and fascinating."

If you enjoy the works of Richard Wormser, you might want to check out the following:

The works of Brent Ashabranner, including *Always to Remember: The Story of the Vietnam Veterans Memorial*, 1988.
The nonfiction works of Nat Hentoff, including *The First Freedom: The Tumultuous History of Free Speech in America*, 1980.
The works of Russell Freedman, including *Lincoln: A Photobiography*, 1989.

Wormser is aware of the impression he wants to create; as with his films, he is seeking in his books to give voice to the silent in society, to illuminate today's concerns by examining yesterday's failures and successes. "I still write for young people," Wormser concluded in *SAAS*, "finding that the ideas and opinions of most adults are hopelessly set in concrete and are all but impossible to break through. In many young people, the concrete, though hardening, has not yet solidified in their brains. Some are still open to new experiences, willing to suspend judgment until they have more understanding of issues, and listen to different sides. So I write for those who can make a difference in the world, can change it, and help make it a place where all people can have a chance to live decent and productive lives."

■ Biographical and Critical Sources

BOOKS

Something about the Author Autobiography Series, Volume 26, Gale, 1998, pp. 271–85.

PERIODICALS

Booklist, January 1, 1991, Leone McDermott, review of *Pinkerton: America's First Private Eye,* p. 920; September 15, 1991, Candace Smith, review of *Lifers: Learn the Truth at the Expense of Our Sorrow,* p. 140; February 15, 1994, Sheilamae O'Hara, review of *Three Faces of Vietnam,* p. 1070; May 15, 1994, Jeanne Triner, review of *Juveniles in Trouble,* p. 1673; June 1 & 15, 1994, Hazel Rochman, review of *Hoboes: Wandering in America, 1870–1940,* p. 1794; October 15, 1994, p. 417; December 15, 1994, pp. 746–47.

Bulletin of the Center for Children's Books, December, 1991, p. 110; January, 1994, pp. 171–72; September, 1994, p. 29; October, 1996, Deborah Stevenson, review of *American Childhoods: Three Centuries of Youth at Risk,* p. 81.

Kirkus Reviews, June 15, 1991, pp. 794–95; May 15, 1994, review of *Hoboes: Wandering in America, 1870–1940,* p. 710; July 15, 1996, p. 1058.

Publishers Weekly, November 22, 1993, review of *The Iron Horse: How Railroads Changed America,* p. 65; December 5, 1994, p. 78.

School Library Journal, December, 1990, Jacqueline Elsner, review of *Pinkerton: America's First Private Eye,* p. 120; December, 1991, Celia A. Huffman, review of *Lifers: Learn the Truth at the Expense of Our Sorrow,* p. 147; January, 1994, Mary Mueller, review of *Three Faces of Vietnam,* p. 143; June, 1994, Jacqueline Rose, review of *Juveniles in Trouble,* p. 158; July, 1994, p. 127; December, 1994, p. 129.

Voice of Youth Advocates, December, 1990, Pat Costello, review of *Pinkerton: America's First Private Eye,* pp. 323–24; December, 1991, pp. 343–44; April, 1994, Allison Rogers Hutchinson, review of *The Iron Horse: How Railroads Changed America,* p. 55; February, 1995, p. 366; December, 1996, p. 294.

Wilson Library Bulletin, March, 1992, p. 122.

Thrust, summer, 1979.

Times Literary Supplement, July 8, 1977.

Washington Post Book World, April 26, 1981; May 13, 1990, p. 8; May 31, 1992, p. 6; July 2, 1995, p. 4.

Author/Artist Index

The following index gives the number of the volume in
which an author/artist's biographical sketch appears: